Y0-CAZ-498

GIANTS
In Their Own Words

RICHARD WHITTINGHAM

CB
CONTEMPORARY
BOOKS
CHICAGO

Library of Congress Cataloging-in-Publication Data

Whittingham, Richard, 1939–
    Giants, in their own words : New York Giants greats talk
about the team, the game, the coaches, and the times of their
lives / Richard Whittingham.
        p.   cm.
    ISBN 0-8092-3921-3 (cloth)
    ISBN 0-8092-3717-2 (paper)
    1. New York Giants (Football team)—History.
2. Football players—United States—Biography.   I. Title.
GV956.N4W475   1992
796.332′64′097471—dc20

92-18462
CIP

This book is dedicated to the Mara family—Tim, who
founded the team, and his two sons, Jack and Wellington,
who developed it into one of the finest organizations in
professional sports—and to all those Giants who played for
them and brought so much excitement and entertainment
to pro football fans during the past seven decades.

Excerpt on pages 169–170 from *Gifford on Courage*, by Frank
Gifford with Charles Mangel. Copyright © 1976 by Frank Gifford.
Reprinted with permission of the publisher, M. Evans and
Company, Inc.

Copyright © 1992 by Richard Whittingham
All rights reserved
Published by Contemporary Books, Inc.
Two Prudential Plaza, Chicago, Illinois 60601-6790
Manufactured in the United States of America
International Standard Book Number: 0-8092-3921-3 (cloth)
                                    0-8092-3717-2 (paper)

10   9   8   7   6   5   4   3   2   1

Contents

Introduction

When the New York Giants joined the National Football League in 1925, only three teams that are members of the NFL today were already in the football business: the Chicago Bears, Green Bay Packers, and Chicago (later St. Louis and still later Phoenix) Cardinals. Making up the rest of the membership in the twenty-team league that year were teams from cities such as Rochester, Buffalo, Dayton, Duluth, Providence, Milwaukee, Akron, Kansas City, Pottsville (Pa.), and Canton (Ohio), long since lost in the lore of professional football.

Wellington Mara, co-owner and co–chief executive officer of the Giants, was a nine-year-old boy on October 18, 1925, when he heard his father, Tim, say, "I'm gonna try to put pro football over in New York today."

That afternoon, with an aged Jim Thorpe in the lineup, the Giants played their first game in New York City, taking on and losing to the Frankford Yellow Jackets 14–0 at the Polo Grounds.

Tim Mara, a bookmaker in New York when that was a legal occupation there and a close friend of Mayor Jimmy

Walker and New York Governor Al Smith, bought the franchise for either $500 or $2,500, depending on who is telling the story. Then, with a sense of impending doom, he bore witness to the sparse crowds that speckled the Polo Grounds on Giants Sundays and watched the money regularly flow out at a faster rate than it trickled in.

Until December, that is. With the franchise about $40,000 in the red and the rumor that Mara might abandon the sinking ship, the Chicago Bears came to town with their most recent acquisition, the already legendary halfback Red Grange. Instead of the usual five thousand to ten thousand spectators that attended a Giants game in 1925, a crowd estimated at seventy-two thousand jammed the Polo Grounds, and several thousand more clustered above on Coogan's Bluff to gaze down into the stadium where the fabled Galloping Ghost was to carry. the football that afternoon.

With the franchise saved that day, the Giants moved on through the Depression and World War II, through lean years financially and losing years on the field of play but also through the glory of abundant championships and spectacular performances.

Steve Owen, onetime Giants tackle, guided the team as head coach from 1931 through 1953. Ken Strong ran the ball, passed it, and kicked it; Mel Hein won All-Pro honors eight consecutive times; Ray Flaherty and Red Badgro gathered in passes; Tuffy Leemans burst through myriad defenses designed solely to stop him—all of them on one-way tickets to the Pro Football Hall of Fame.

From those early years through World War II, the Giants managed to win nine division or league championships and held the honor of having played in more NFL championship games up to that time than any other team in the history of the league.

In the 1950s and early 1960s came another dynasty, when Charlie Conerly and Y. A. Tittle threw the ball to the likes of Frank Gifford, Kyle Rote, Joe Morrison, and Del

Shofner; when Gifford and Morrison and Alex Webster and Mel Triplett ran behind the blocks of Rosey Brown, Jack Stroud, and Ray Wietecha; when the Fearsome Foursome—Andy Robustelli, Rosie Grier, Dick Modzelewski, and Jim Katcavage—augmented by such stellars playing behind them as Sam Huff, Emlen Tunnell, Tom Landry, Jimmy Patton, and Dick Lynch, formed the league's most impregnable defense. From 1956 through 1963, those Giants of their time played in six NFL title games in eight years.

It was during those eras that the team and its raft of extraordinarily talented players built the following of fans that is today perhaps the largest and most devoted in all of professional football. They were the building blocks around which the substance and color of New York Giants history was constructed.

In the pages that follow, many of the greatest and most entertaining Giants players of those eras tell their stories about what life was like on and off the field. Pro Football Hall of Famers Mel Hein, Frank Gifford, Andy Robustelli, Y. A. Tittle, Tom Landry, Arnie Weinmeister, Rosey Brown, Sam Huff, and Red Badgro as well as many other Giants household names reminisce about their times, their teammates, and those teams and players they battled against.

Mel Hein talks of going up against Bronko Nagurski. Harry Newman tells of the trick play that turned center Mel Hein into a running back. There is the story of how Abe Cohen saved the day by delivering the sneakers so the Giants could score 27 unanswered points and win the "Sneakers" championship game of 1934. There are Giants anecdotes from the pens of Damon Runyon, Grantland Rice, and Westbrook Pegler.

Those who were there provide insights into the runaway victory in the 1956 championship game against the Bears; the sudden-death overtime championship of 1958 against the Colts, perhaps pro football's greatest game; Pat Summerall's fabulous field goal in a snowstorm to save the day in 1958; Y. A. Tittle's 7 touchdown passes in a single game to tie the NFL record; Emlen Tunnell's gaining more yards on kick returns and interceptions than any back gained rushing in 1952.

There are good memories as well as bad: the day the Giants scored a record 62 points against the Philadelphia Eagles in 1972, and the day they gave up 72 to the Washington Redskins in 1966.

Rosey Brown talks about what it was like being a black player in the NFL of the 1950s. Shipwreck Kelly gives his ribald and uncensored observances of pro football in the 1930s. Sam Huff tells how Vince Lombardi kept him and fellow rookie Don Chandler in training camp when they were set to end Giants careers before they ever got started.

From the Polo Grounds to Yankee Stadium to Giants Stadium, the Giants have been around more than sixty-five years. From the time players wore leather helmets and earned maybe $150 a game to the age of flak jackets and multimillion dollar contracts, the Giants have provided a vast array of excitement and entertainment and have proven themselves to be one of the most interesting and successful teams in NFL history.

These men, who tell their stories here, were truly Giants in their time.

Frank Gifford

Frank Gifford was one of the most versatile backs to play in the modern era of NFL football. A runner, receiver, passer, and kicker, he was a throwback to the multitalented tailbacks who were expected to do so much in the earlier days of the game—greats such as Ken Strong, Ace Parker, and Charley Trippi. In the words of Wellington Mara, his presenter when Gifford was inducted into the Pro Football Hall of Fame in 1977, "Frank brought so many refined talents to the game. You could depend on him in so many different ways, and we at the Giants did depend on him so often."

Born in Santa Monica, California, Gifford had a rather peripatetic childhood. His father was an oil worker, and, according to Frank, "we moved to wherever they were drilling an oil well." They stopped long enough for Gifford to prove himself a fine football player in high school at Bakersfield, good enough to get a scholarship to the University of Southern California.

At USC, it was not until his senior year that Gifford's diverse talents as a back were fully exploited. The new coach that year, Jess Hill, shaped his offense around Gifford, just as Vince Lombardi would do when he became the Giants' offensive coordinator in the mid-1950s. As a halfback, Frank earned All-

America honors at USC in 1951 and was named the Most Valuable Player in both the East-West Shrine Game and the Senior Bowl after that season.

Gifford was the first-round selection of the Giants in 1952. He started out as a defensive back under old-line coach Steve Owen but was switched by Lombardi to left halfback in 1954 and finally to flanker in 1962. He is perhaps the only player in NFL history to go to the Pro Bowl at three different positions.

During Gifford's twelve-year career with the Giants, he was named All-Pro four times, went to seven Pro Bowls, and played in five NFL championship games. After the Giants won the title in 1956, a year in which he led the team in scoring (65 points), rushing (819 yards, an average of 5.2 per carry), and receiving (51 catches for 603 yards), he was named NFL Player of the Year.

In the years between 1952 and 1964 (he missed the 1961 season because of an injury), Gifford racked up a total of 9,753 combined yards for the Giants, an all-time club record, and scored 484 points, second only to kicker Pete Gogolak in Giants' history.

Gifford ranks second in career pass receptions with 367 (including 43 touchdowns), behind Joe Morrison, and fourth in rushing with 3,609 yards (and 34 touchdowns), behind Joe Morris, Alex Webster, and Ron Johnson. He also led the club in both rushing and receiving four consecutive years (1956–59).

Other individual Giants records held by Gifford are most touchdowns (78), most consecutive games scoring a touchdown (10), highest average gain rushing (4.3), and most yards gained on pass receptions (5,434).

After football he continued his other extraordinarily successful career—in broadcasting, on both radio and television. And, of course, he became a member of the Monday Night Football team with Howard Cosell and Dandy Don Meredith in 1971, where with new partners he still holds court on Monday nights during the football season.

Frank Gifford authored the book *Gifford on Courage* (New York: M. Evans and Company, 1976), in which he chronicled the courageous comebacks from adversity by a variety of different people. He has written several children's books and is currently at work on his autobiography, which is due to be published in 1993.

I was, I have to admit, surprised when I ended up with the Giants in the 1952 draft. Before it, I had been contacted by the Los Angeles Rams and was under the impression they were going to take me. At the time I knew one of the minority owners, and he had told me the Rams were seriously considering taking me in the first round.

The Rams drew the bonus pick that year, which gave them the very first choice in the draft, but they didn't take me. Instead they selected Bill Wade, a quarterback from Vanderbilt. The Giants took me somewhere farther down the line in the first round.

I was a little teed off about the whole situation and even considered not playing, and that thought got even stronger when the Giants offered me my first contract. I was making more money working part-time in the studios in Hollywood in bit parts as an extra and a stuntman. I'd been offered several thousand more dollars for a full-time job with a studio than the Giants were putting up for me to play professional football. I was also offered more money to play for Edmonton in the Canadian Football League.

I guess I was just miffed at being misled by the Rams. At the same time I'd gotten married in college and we had a baby, and so naturally I was concerned about what I'd be earning and also the security. The first contract the Giants offered me was, I believe, for $7,500. Edmonton had offered me $10,000.

At any rate, Mel Hein, the Giants' great center of the 1930s and early '40s, was one of our assistant coaches at USC—the line coach—and he told me about what a fine organization the Giants were and how much he liked and respected the Maras. Then I got a call from Wellington Mara, congratulating me and saying they would shortly be sending me a contract. I didn't even ask about the money at that time.

When I got the contract, I called Wellington Mara and told him I couldn't do it for $7,500. We talked a couple of times and I wound up finally signing for—I think it was—$8,000 and a $250 signing bonus.

It wasn't easy around that time because I had a family and now, after the football season, I was trying to catch up on some courses at USC that I needed, and so I couldn't cut classes to work at the studios.

I did, however, want to play football. It had been a great experience at USC. My coach at Bakersfield High School, a man by the name of Homer Beattie, had played for USC and at that time he was certainly one of the most important persons in my life. He got me going in the right direction academically as well as on the football field. I hadn't been the greatest of students. He felt I could possibly play for USC, and he knew I would have to qualify on both levels if I were to be accepted at that school.

After my fourth year at Bakersfield, USC did indeed offer me a football scholarship, but I was deficient in a few academic units and I had to make them up. So I went for a year to Bakersfield Junior College, and then moved on to USC.

At USC, they never really could find just what to do with me. I had played offense and defense in high school and ended up a T formation quarterback my junior year. I played safety on defense. And in my senior year they switched to a wing T and I became a running back. Then in junior college we had an offense where I both ran and passed the ball.

So, at USC I didn't exactly fit anywhere in particular. For two years I played defense. Then in my senior year they brought in a new coach, Jess Hill, and he designed an offense that was pretty much suited to me, a single wing and a wing T, and I was sort of the focus of it, running and passing and receiving. He also had a fine staff with Mel Hein and Don Clark, who would later become head coach at Southern Cal. And it made a big difference. We were 3-7-0 in 1950, my junior year, and won our first seven games in 1951. The fifth game that we won that year was over the University of California, and at the time they were ranked number one in the nation and had a 39-game winning streak. Well, after that all the bells went off and we jumped from nothing to something like fourth or fifth in the nation. Suddenly the press and the media were all over the campus, and a week later I was being photographed for All-American. It was the weirdest thing—we all kept wondering how it happened so fast.

We didn't go to the Rose Bowl because we lost our last three games that year, but I did play in the East-West Game and the Senior Bowl. As I learned later, Wellington Mara had scouted both those games. Mel Hein had told him to take a close look at me. That's really how they scouted in those days. There weren't any combines or things like that, or even scouting departments for the individual teams. People like Wellington Mara relied on coaches they knew, former players, and they listened to their recommendations.

When I think of it now, I really should have been flattered that the Giants drafted me because Well Mara drafted you on a pair of criteria: your playing ability and what he thought of your character.

I had been to New York my senior year, so the city wasn't totally new to me. We had played Army at Yankee Stadium that year—in fact, that was the seventh win of our streak. It was snowing and sleeting, a really dismal day, and Army wasn't much, nothing like the old Blanchard and Davis days, and they were involved in a recruiting scandal around that time, too. We beat them 28–6. I had a good day—I think I scored two or three touchdowns, and I believe that helped bring me to the attention of the Maras.

When I came to the Giants, it was like being back at USC again—they really didn't seem to know what to do with me once they had me. Kyle Rote was there at halfback but he had a bad knee, and they kind of penciled me in behind him. Tom Landry was playing but he was also, for all practical purposes, coaching the defense, and he made it known he wanted me in the defensive secondary. So I wound up my first year as a defensive back and a backup to Rote on offense.

In 1953 I started out as a defensive back, and then Kyle

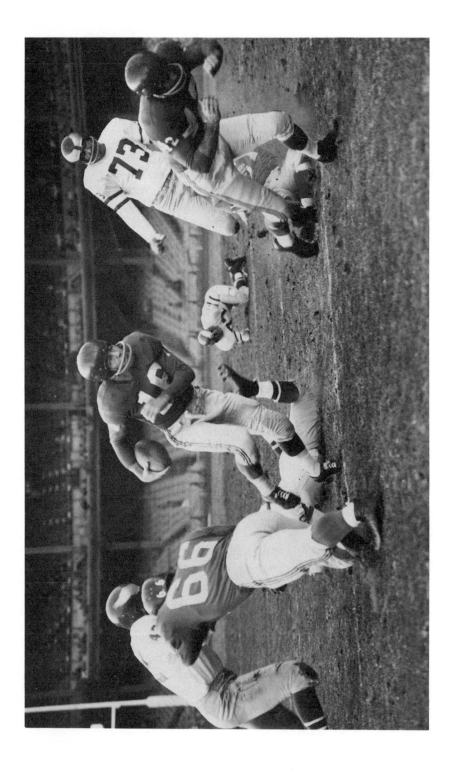

got hurt again. So the last five games of the season I ended up playing both ways. I never came out of one of those games. And I made the Pro Bowl as a defensive back.

At that point, I'd about had it. I didn't know where I was going to play the next year. I wasn't making much money, and '53 had been a miserable season for us. We were 3–9–0 that year, and Steve Owen was sacked as head coach.

Jim Lee Howell was brought in as the new head coach; but, more important, Vince Lombardi was hired as the offensive coordinator. I got along with Vince fine, but a lot of the guys didn't. He was very gregarious, loud, fearless. He was also one of the kindest persons I ever met. He could be abrasive, but at the right moment, when it was needed. There was always the rap against him about being a dictator, but that wasn't really so. I remember we used to go over to his house in New Jersey all the time and spend evenings looking at films, talking about upcoming games, and eating spaghetti. I got to know him as a dear friend, and later we spent a lot of time together. I was with him, in fact, just a couple of days before he died.

When Vince came to the Giants, the first thing he said to me at training camp up in Salem, Oregon, was—he didn't equivocate—"Look, I've looked at a lot of films and I just want you to know, you're my halfback." He intended to build an offense around a halfback, the same kind of offense he later refined at Green Bay after converting Paul Hornung to a halfback. He wanted a versatile left half-back—one who could run, catch passes, and occasionally throw them. His left halfback was always the core of his offense.

◀ Frank Gifford (16) finds a big hole here in a game against the Philadelphia Eagles. A first-round draft pick of the Giants in 1952, Gifford was the all-purpose back: he could run, pass, catch passes, and even play defensive back when he was asked. As a result of his accomplishments in twelve years with the Giants (1952–60, 62–64), he earned a berth in the Pro Football Hall of Fame. Leading interference for him here is quarterback Charlie Conerly; number 66 is guard Jack Stroud.

What worked for me was that I could do all of it pretty well. I wasn't a great runner, I wasn't a great passer, I wasn't a great receiver. But I could do each thing well enough. Once Lombardi finally got that formation installed the way he wanted it, I ended up leading the team in both rushing and receiving for a couple of years [1956 through 1959].

Vince saw the same kind of things in Hornung, who was a strong, powerful runner—and Paul was big. That's why he moved him from quarterback, which Paul had played at Notre Dame—well enough to win the Heisman Trophy—to halfback. Ray Nitschke [Green Bay's Hall of Fame middle linebacker] once said at a roast, "Hornung's just a big Frank Gifford."

Lombardi, needless to say, made a big difference in my football life. He stuck around New York for five years, and those were great years for me.

In those days, we did a lot in the huddle, too. Charlie Conerly would call the plays in there. A lot of times he'd come into the huddle—it might be a third and eight or something like that—and he'd say, "What've you got, Giff?" And I might say something like, "Brown right and split the left end." And he might not even call the play—just say, "On three," and we'd break. We had all kinds of guys who had ideas in the huddle. It worked because we all knew each other so well. There were no egos in the huddle.

I kept pretty busy in the off-season during those years, too. I studied radio broadcasting and acting. I had a lot of time on my hands, and I really liked to do a lot of things. I actually went back and forth between New York and Los Angeles in those days. In about 1957, however, I started spending most of my time in New York, and I began filling in for Phil Rizzuto [the former Yankees shortstop turned broadcaster] on radio—he had a network show—and then I got my own local television show.

I sat out the 1961 season after I got a concussion near

the end of the 1960 season [in a game against the Philadelphia Eagles]. I did quite a bit of radio that year and my local television show. When I came back in 1962, I kept working on television at the same time.

The thing about the concussion comes up all the time—about the hit I took from Chuck Bednarik. Was it a cheap shot? What do *I* think about it? Well, it's all a lot of bull made up by a lot of people who don't understand what this game is about. I get real tired hearing about it.

I remember Kathie came home one day not long after we were married and said, "Who's Bednarik?" I said, "It's not somebody, it's a pasta." I told her, "You're going to hear that name a whole helluva lot." Nobody seems to be able to forget about the incident. Bednarik has perpetuated it more than anybody. But he's a good guy, and I have no animosity. I was simply looking back to catch a football and he hit me just right and knocked me over. I ended up with a concussion—that's all.

On a better note, I remember in a game in 1959 against the Redskins I had my longest run from scrimmage, 70-some yards [79 yards]. When you run that far, it's pretty much luck—somebody on the defense makes a pretty big mistake. The play was a 48 pitchout, an option—I could either run with the ball or pass it. Actually, on that particular play I got a helluva block from Rosey Brown; in fact, I got two blocks from him on that play. One was at the line of scrimmage, and after I cut back a couple of times, he made another great block about 20 yards downfield. Rosey was so big and fast—as fast as a lot of backs. He was really a great one.

The end of the 1958 season was another exciting time—we had to win our last four games of the regular season and then the playoff with the Browns to get to the championship game. Every one of those five games we played was on a frozen field. We beat Washington [30–0] and Philadelphia [24–10] at home and then the Lions at Detroit [19–17]. Both of the Cleveland games were at Yankee Stadium—the snowstorm game where Pat [Summerall]

kicked the seemingly impossible field goal [13-10], and then the playoff, which was on another bitterly cold day [10-0].

We were really beat up by the time we got to the championship game against the Colts. We had guys who didn't even practice the week before. Charlie Conerly didn't—he was hurting so much he would just come out and walk through the offense we were going to use. I was about in the same kind of shape: both knees were sore and I had a huge swelling on my elbow about the size of a volleyball, which I couldn't get to go down. That game, the sudden-death championship [the Giants lost 23-17], wasn't as memorable as what it took to get there. They were actually a better team than we were—better physically—and they had the advantage of a relatively easy walk to their conference title.

After I came back in 1962, we had a couple of good years. A lot of people said I should give it up and concentrate on other things. I'd put in nine years and gone to a number of championship games. Some were saying that maybe I would be pressing my luck by going back. But I wasn't totally out of football in 1961—I scouted for the Giants all that year. But I said to myself after I watched the Giants get beat pretty badly in the title game of '61—they lost 37-0—this is kind of ridiculous that I'm not playing. I still had a few more good years in me, I felt. I was in good shape. I'd been working out. And what the hell—I could always do later what I was doing then; the broadcasting business would be there forever. And the overriding thing was, I genuinely missed the game. So I decided to come back.

◀ Frank Gifford's experience with NFL savagery. Above: the tackle, with Gifford going down under a thunderous hit delivered by Chuck Bednarik of the Philadelphia Eagles in 1960. Below: the aftermath, with Gifford suffering a major concussion. He did not return until the 1962 season.

It was tougher than I thought it would be getting back into shape. You tend to forget how hard the knocks are and how demanding the game of pro football is. But I'm really glad that I did it.

When I came back it wasn't as a halfback, however. It was as a flanker, which suited me fine. I even got invited to the Pro Bowl in '62 as a flanker. It was the third different position I'd gone to the Pro Bowl at: flanker, halfback, and defensive back.

I got to two more championship games as a result of coming back. We played Vince's Packers for the title in 1962, but we lost [16-7]. And we played the Bears the next year for it and lost that, too [14-10]. That year, 1963, was an especially good year for us offensively. We came close to setting an NFL record for points scored in a single season: we scored 448, which was an average of 32 a game [the NFL record at the time was 466, set by the Los Angeles Rams in 1950, an average of 38.8 a game in the then twelve-game regular season; the Houston Oilers had scored 513 points in the AFL in 1961, a 36.6 average per game].

We probably should have beaten the Bears that year. We got off to the lead when Y. A. Tittle threw a touchdown pass to me in the first quarter. But then Y.A. hurt his knee, and he couldn't really get around at all. And our backup quarterback, Glynn Griffing, the only one we had, hadn't even practiced with the team the week before the game because he had gone down to Mississippi to get married; so he wasn't going to be of any help to us. So they just shot up Y.A. and sent him back out there. He tried to hobble through it, but he couldn't really throw the ball. I don't want to take anything away from the Bears. They played a tough game. They had a great defense that year—Bill George, Ed O'Bradovich, Doug Atkins, Richie Petitbon.

After the '63 championship game with the Bears in Chicago, it was pretty much a downhill slide—plummet might be a better word—for the Giants. And I knew it was time to go after the 1964 season.

We had a great group of guys on the teams in those days, and we still keep in touch. I'm fortunate because I get to fly around so much—it's easy to get together with a lot of them. I go to San Diego, and Harland Svare's out there and so is Cliff Livingston. I see Charlie [Conerly], who lives down in Mississippi, all the time. We roomed together for nine years back in our playing days. Alex Webster's down in Florida. I named one of my sons Kyle; I'd never heard the name before I met Kyle Rote, who remains a good friend of mine to this day.

After football, it was the broadcast business. I'd been with WCBS while I was playing. I'd started there doing local news for them back in 1962 while there was a newspaper strike in New York. After that, they decided to expand their news reporting to include sports and weather. And after I finished playing I began broadcasting NFL games.

I stayed with that until Roone Arledge asked me to be part of the NFL Monday Night Football team. Actually, he asked me in 1970, the year it began, but I couldn't take it because of my other contractual obligations. But the following year I was able to. Keith Jackson did it with Howard [Cosell] and Don [Meredith] the first year. Keith's nose was kind of out of joint when I came over the next year, but it all worked out very well. He went over to broadcasting college football, which he does very well, and he has been at it ever since. He and I are still doing the same thing today that we were doing in 1971.

The days with the Giants were terrific. I am still very good friends with Well Mara, and his nephew, Tim Mara, is one of my closest friends. We had a very special team, a unique situation, in the 1950s and early '60s in New York. I really enjoyed being a part of it.

□

Gifford's Visitor

While Frank Gifford was having his injured knee attended to in a New York hospital in 1958, he awoke at about five-thirty one morning to find a large, trembling young man at the foot of his bed. The immobilized Gifford watched as the man shook the bed and ranted, "What's the matter with your Giants? What's the matter with all of you, Gifford?"

The man walked over to the venetian blinds and ran his hand up and down them to make noise. "What you need is someone like me, a killer. I was in Korea."

Gifford grabbed the water pitcher beside his bed. "If he was going to come at me, I was going to gong him," Gifford said later. The man didn't, but he also did not leave. He just stood there, running his hands along the blinds.

Gifford finally said to him, "If you really think you can help the team, get your ass down to Yankee Stadium. Tell them what you can do." The man sort of nodded and left, much to Gifford's relief.

However, the man did take the Giff's advice and went to Yankee Stadium. He managed to get into the locker room, where most of the players by that time were suiting up for practice, and began screaming, first at 260-pound Dick Modzelewski and then at some others. According to New York sportswriter Barry Gottherer, the man then began drop-kicking footballs around the room, castigating the team before several policemen arrived to take him away.

As he was leaving, Gottherer quoted him as shouting back, "All right, so you don't appreciate me. I'll go down to Baltimore and help Johnny Unitas out."

Pat Summerall

It would be hard to find a more visible former professional football player than Pat Summerall: he is seen and heard regularly in the broadcast booth with partner John Madden at Super Bowls and countless other CBS network NFL games, announcing the action at major PGA Tour golf tournaments, and handling spokesman chores for True Value Hardware. He is one of the most familiar faces on American television in the 1990s.

But he was also an excellent football player who forged a ten-year career (1952–1961) in the National Football League, including four memorable years as a member of the New York Giants.

After graduating from the University of Arkansas, Summerall was the fourth-round draft choice of the Detroit Lions in 1952, traded the next year to the doormat Chicago Cardinals, and finally sent in 1958 to the upscale Giants, who participated in three NFL championship games during his four years with them.

Pat Summerall played in the prespecialist era of NFL football, a time when kickers were not merely kickers. When they were not putting their toes to the football, for example, Lou

19

Groza was an All-Pro tackle for the Cleveland Browns; Paul Hornung of the Green Bay Packers was an All-Pro halfback; Bob Waterfield of the Rams and George Blanda of the Bears/Oilers/Raiders were full-time quarterbacks; Doak Walker, a halfback, and Jim Martin, a linebacker, contributed to the offense and defense of the Detroit Lions; and Bobby Walston carried the ball and caught passes for the Philadelphia Eagles.

A peer of all of them, Summerall played defensive and offensive end and was a member of a variety of special teams in addition to his duties as premier field-goal and extra-point kicker for the Cardinals and the Giants. During his nine years of kicking in the NFL (he sat out his rookie season at Detroit after breaking an arm in a preseason game), Summerall connected on 100 of 212 field goals and 257 of 265 points after touchdown. He scored a total of 563 points, which includes one touchdown.

Pat led the Giants in scoring all four years; his most productive years were 1959, with 90 points, and 1961, with 88 points. The 20 field goals he kicked in 1959 were the most in the NFL that year and his 69 percent success ratio was also the league high. In 1961, he led the league with 46 extra points and a 100 percent success ratio.

The 313 points (59 field goals, 136 extra points) he scored for the Giants ranks seventh in club history. He scored in 46 consecutive games between 1958 and 1961, third best in team annals. He is the Giants' third-ranking field-goal kicker, behind only Pete Gogolak and Joe Danelo.

His most famous field goal, of course, was the 49-yarder he booted in a swirling snowstorm to defeat the Cleveland Browns (13–10) in the waning minutes of the last game of the 1958 regular season, which clinched a tie for the NFL East crown and kept alive the Giants' championship hopes. The 49-yarder was also the longest field goal of Summerall's career and the longest kicked in the NFL that year.

I've been closely associated with the game of football almost my entire life. The only time I wasn't, I guess, was my early childhood.

I got into what you might call semiorganized football in junior high school down in Lake City, in northern Florida—the town where I was born and raised. In high school, of course, it was well organized. Down there, it was one of the things you just did if you were one of the bigger guys in the class—you sort of had an obligation to play.

It was in high school that I really got to love playing football. I had had a rather unfortunate childhood. I was born with a clubfoot—the right one. Basically it was turned around backwards. At that time, the way they treated it was by breaking both bones in the bottom of the leg and just turning the foot around. The doctor told my mother afterwards that I would be able to walk but I would probably never be able to run or play with other kids. As time passed, however, through nature's help and the Good Lord's help, it got better and better. And as it turned out, that was the foot I used to kick with—although that was way down the road.

By the time I got to high school, things had pretty well worked out. I was on the track team and ran the 100-yard dash and the 440. I ran the 100 in about 10.1, which at that time was considered pretty good. I also played baseball and, of course, football. And actually, my best sport in high school was basketball.

I went on a lot of college recruiting trips as a high school senior. In those days you could go and put on a uniform and work out with the college teams, a lot of things like that. The NCAA rules have changed considerably since then. The two places that I was invited to and was most serious about were West Point and the University of Florida. West Point, I thought when I went there, looked a little too much like a jail. They were also suggesting that they would be sending me first to Kentucky Military Institute to study to be sure I could pass Army's entrance exams—my high school grades weren't all that good. Adding these things up, I decided I didn't really want to go there.

At the University of Florida, they wanted me to play both basketball and football. At that time it was relatively easy to do that because the seasons were shorter and the quality of both games was not nearly what it is today. Anyway, I didn't want to do that.

At the same time, my high school football coach, a gentleman named Hobart Hooser, had been hired by the University of Arkansas as their line coach. Well, he had been kind of like a father to me. He came back down to Florida and talked to me about going to Arkansas, and I went.

It was at Arkansas where I really got started as a kicker. When I was a sophomore—that must have been 1949—the coaching staff was not happy with the guy who was kicking off, not field goals or extra points. They said anyone who'd like to try kicking should come on out thirty minutes early this one day. Well, I said, what the heck—I'll give it a try. So I did. And it seemed to be something that was very natural to me. From then on, I kicked off for Arkansas.

At the same time I was playing offensive and defensive end, the kind of thing you did in those days. The squads were just so much smaller. When I was with the Chicago Cardinals we were limited to thirty-three players on the roster, and with the Giants it was thirty-five. A team could not afford to have a specialist on its roster who did nothing other than kick or punt.

I had no thoughts of being a specialist back then. If you aspired to play professional football, the ultimate was to play the game, offense and defense. Kicking was just an additional element.

One of the highlights at Arkansas, I remember, was beating Texas my senior year [1951], and I got to kick the game-winning field goal that day. Beating Texas was the biggest thrill you could have down there in those days. Actually, field goals around that time were relatively unheard of. I kicked the most in college that year—just barely beat out Vic Janowicz of Ohio State, who won the Heisman Trophy—I kicked 4.

The following year I was drafted by the Lions in the fourth round. Detroit did not have a first or second choice that year. In the third round they took Yale Lary from Texas A&M, who, of course, went on to the Pro Football Hall of Fame as a safety and punter, and then they took me in the next round.

I played in the College All-Star Game in Chicago before the season. That was a big part of football at that time. There were, in fact, over a hundred thousand people at the game I played in. We had Janowicz and Ollie Matson and Hugh McElhenny and Babe Parilli, but we lost to the Rams [10–7]. The Rams were a wonderful team and had beaten the Cleveland Browns for the NFL title the year before.

Being with the All-Stars, I believe, hurt me to a degree because, as a result, I was behind when I finally got to training camp with the Lions.

I made the team, which I felt was a big accomplishment. The Lions were a very good team in 1952, with players like Bobby Layne, Doak Walker, Leon Hart, Pat Harder, Jack Christiansen. I played through the preseason but then broke my arm and sat out the whole year. [The Lions went on to win the NFL title that year, defeating the Cleveland Browns, 17–7.]

I went back to Detroit the next year thinking I would be a key part of the team. They had led me to believe that. But we had four kickers: Doak Walker, Pat Harder, Jim Martin, and me. The only time they'd let me try a field goal was from outside the 40. [Head coach] Buddy Parker had a system where Walker would kick from inside the 30 and somebody else inside the 40, and so I said to Buddy, "Hey, look, if I'm ever going to do anything, it's going to have to be on a regular basis."

He said, "Well, let me see what I can work out." He told me most of the players were happy, and he didn't want any player to be unhappy. So he traded me to the Chicago Cardinals.

There was a world of difference between the two teams. The Lions were quite a team, a real first-class operation. You came to the Cardinals and, boy, it was the opposite. The equipment was no good. Comiskey Park smelled.

You went from being a part of class to being a part of no class. The Cardinals in those days also had the policy of cutting the squad down when they found themselves out of the race, which was usually after about five games. I remember one year we ended the season with just twenty-five players when you could have had thirty-three. So it didn't take me long to figure out I had to do more than just kick. I played defensive end, I ran down under kickoffs, under punts, and I was on the punt-protection team.

Like the Lions, the Cardinals had some great players when I got there in 1953: Ollie Matson, Charley Trippi, Johnny O [Olzewski], Bill Fischer. But they weren't the team the Lions were. Where Detroit ended up winning their conference, we ended up at the bottom of the Eastern Conference in 1953 [a record of 1–10–1]. In fact, we didn't win a game until the last one of the season, when we knocked off the Bears at Wrigley Field.

I could see immediately what a wonderful back Charley Trippi had been. He could run, he could pass, he was excellent in the defensive secondary. But he was into his thirties, and by 1954 he wasn't really the fearsome runner he had been. But he was still a wonderful competitor. So they used him mostly as a defensive back, and that's when he was hit by John Henry Johnson of the 49ers and got his face shattered. It was a tragic thing, and even though he played another year his career, for all practical purposes, was over after that.

Later we got some other first-rate players. The Cardinals traded for Night Train Lane from the Rams, one of the best defensive backs ever; and there was Dave Mann, a halfback, and Joe Childress, a fullback—they were damn good ballplayers. Gern Nagler was a heckuva receiver; so was Don Stonesifer. Lindon Crow was a fine defensive back.

We had some outstanding players, but the problem was that after them there was a big dropoff down to some mediocre players and a lot of guys who shouldn't have been playing.

The talented toe of Pat Summerall. From 1958 through 1961, he handled all the placekicking chores for the Giants. The 313 points he contributed on field goals and extra points ranks eighth in Giants' scoring annals. During his ten-year NFL career, Summerall also played defensive end and occasionally offensive end.

We only had one winning season while I was with the Cardinals—that was in 1956. We won our first four games in a row, ended up 7–5–0 and in second place in the NFL East behind the Giants, who went on to win the championship that year.

I was with the Cardinals for another year after that. By that time I was contemplating getting out of the game altogether. It was such a depressing situation, such a miserable operation there in Chicago. After the 1957 season, Pop Ivy replaced Ray Richards as head coach, and in the spring of 1958 I called Pop and asked if he wanted me back and, if so, what he had planned for me, where would I fit in—that kind of thing. He told me, "You're a key part of the team, a key part of the operation. Yes! We want you back."

About a week later, I was over at the post office down where I lived in Lake City, and I picked up the afternoon paper and saw that I had been traded to the Giants.

I called Jim Lee Howell, who was the Giants' head coach at the time. I knew him from Arkansas—he went there, too. He was the athletic-dorm supervisor when I was there. He was in graduate school, and his job was to keep the young guys in line. I asked him what his plans for me were, and he told me that he wanted a kicker who could also play. They had Ben Agajanian at the time, who was getting up there in years and just wanted to come in on the weekends to kick in the game and stay home the rest of the week. So I asked him what weight he wanted me to come in at, and he said around 230, which is what I was [Summerall was 6′4″].

I became their kicker, played on most of the special teams, and was the third defensive end behind Andy Robustelli and Jim Katcavage.

Coming to the Giants was like going from the bottom of the heap to the top of the heap. I said to myself, Here we are again—this is class. That Giants team not only had some incredible players; they also had a couple of pretty fine coaches in Tom Landry and Vince Lombardi.

But don't forget Jim Lee Howell. He was the guy who had the presence of mind to say to Lombardi, "You run the offense," and to say to Landry, "You run the defense." He gave them the authority. But Jim Lee oversaw everything and coordinated the practices. He was the glue that held the entire team together. I've always felt it takes a pretty big man to realize what you have and to delegate the authority the way he did. There are an awful lot of executives out there who can't do that. No one on that team, however, had any doubt who held the ultimate authority, and that was Jim Lee Howell.

I finally felt truly accepted by the team and the fans after we beat the Colts midway through the season. It was a crucial game for us. We were a game behind the Browns [the Browns were 5-1-0, the Giants 4-2-0]. And, of course, the Colts were a helluva team who were on the way to winning their conference. It attracted the biggest crowd at that time in Giants history [more than seventy-one thousand] except for the game when Red Grange appeared with the Chicago Bears back in the 1920s. That was at the Polo Grounds—our game was at Yankee Stadium. It was a see-saw affair, and with about two minutes left the score was tied at 21 apiece. I got the chance to come on for a field goal. I made it [a 28-yarder], and we won. It was a very memorable game for me. And to top it off that day, the Browns lost, and so we ended up in a tie in the conference race at 5-2-0.

It is always a thrill to be put in a position where you can win a game for your team, although you don't think of it that way at the time. When the time comes to go into a situation like that—whether it's kicking a field goal, pinch-hitting, or shooting a free throw at the end of a game—you're totally oblivious to what's going on around you. It's almost like you're in a capsule. Everything around you is hazy; you aren't conscious that there are seventy thousand people out there ready to cheer you or boo you. You don't hear any of that stuff. You just get yourself mentally ready to do what you have to do. I always tried to stay calm; I knew

the more excited I got the less effective I'd be. Concentra-
tion is the key in a situation like that.

I had the chance, of course, to do it again in the last
game of the season that year against the Browns, a game
we had to win. They had it as a 49-yarder. I don't really
know how long it was because you couldn't see the yard
markings. Kyle Rote swears it was a 56-yarder because he
said he was standing on the sideline at the 50-yard line. All
I remember about it is that when I got into the huddle,
Charlie Conerly, my holder, looked at me and said, "What
the fuck are you doing here?"

I said, "We're going to kick a field goal." He was in
disbelief. But we did it, and it worked. I actually didn't see
it go through the uprights—you couldn't see that far
through the swirling snow. I could see the goalposts, but I
couldn't see the ball. I knew when I kicked it I had the
distance—you can just tell; like when you hit a golf shot
square, you know it—but you don't know whether it might
break to the right or the left. Fortunately it didn't.

The first person I saw when I came off the field was
Lombardi, shaking his head. We were all jumping up and
down and Lombardi came up and said to me, "You know,
you son of a bitch, you can't kick it that far." He had
actually been against trying it, but Jim Lee Howell made
the call.

There were some games in 1959, too, that I will never
forget. One to remember was the championship game,
again against the Colts. It was played in Baltimore. At the
time we were winning 9–7, just at the close of the third
quarter. After a second down, we had third and very long
and Jim Lee Howell said to me, "Get ready." Well, we didn't
make the first down. Now, on fourth down, I was between
him and Tom Landry on the sideline. I was about to go in

◀ *The* kick. Pat Summerall launches a 49-yarder—some say a 56-
yarder—through a swirling snowstorm to give the Giants a 13–10
victory over the Cleveland Browns in 1958. It clinched a tie for the NFL
East crown that year.

when Landry said to Howell, "Jim, the field goal's not going to help us. They're just about to break our defense. We need more than a field goal. Let's go for the first down."

Jim Lee went with Landry on that one—we tried for the first down and didn't make it. After that, everything broke down and the Colts scored 24 unanswered points in the fourth quarter and we ended up losing 31–16 [the Giants scored an inconsequential touchdown at game's end]. Looking back, you wonder if it might have been different had we kicked the field goal, but that's one thing you will never know.

Another game I got a great kick out of was not an NFL one. We played a touch football game in Central Park in New York, a kind of gimmick to celebrate the twentieth anniversary of the championship game of 1958. It started out lighthearted and then we all got kind of serious, pretty competitive. Johnny Unitas threw a couple of touchdown passes. They won, and I remember saying as we walked off the field, "I'll be damned—we couldn't cover Raymond Berry twenty years ago, and we still can't."

All the memories of those days with the Giants were good, positive ones. We were such a family—it was like thirty-five brothers. Some of them are gone from this life now: Phil King, who was my roommate; Don Heinrich, who was a very close friend; Jimmy Patton got killed in an automobile accident; Carl Karilivacz and Emlen Tunnell died of heart attacks. It's a loss to all of us who played with them; we all cared so much about each other.

I think when I got there what most impressed me was the intelligence of the players. There was, of course, an enormity of talent, but these guys were extremely intelligent on and off the field. That's why so many of them became major successes after football—guys like Frank Gifford and Andy Robustelli and Sam Huff and Kyle Rote.

As my career in football was winding down, I began another in broadcasting. The way it came about was that we had played the Green Bay Packers in a preseason exhibition game in Newark and were training at that time in Bear Mountain, New York, near West Point. The game was on a Friday night, and we did not have to be back at camp for practice until Monday night. So a bunch of us got together and went into Manhattan for the weekend. I was rooming with Charlie Conerly. I was lying on a bed watching television, and he was in the shower. The phone rang and I answered it, and this gentleman, who I didn't know, asked for Charlie. I said he was in the shower, and he asked, "Well, who is this?" I told him and he said to remind Charlie that he was supposed to come to CBS that afternoon at four o'clock to read for this radio show.

I was maybe an inch away from hanging up the phone when he said, "Hey, wait a minute. What are you doing this afternoon?"

My answer was, "I don't know. I'm either going to a movie or get together with the guys and go drink beer somewhere."

He said, "Well, why don't you come along and take the audition too?"

I said, "Why not?" As it turned out, there were four of us who went over there. And I ended up getting the job.

By the time I retired after the 1961 season, I'd been with CBS for several years. I guess I had always thought when I finally hung it up that I would go back home to Florida and tend to some business interests and maybe teach school. But when it became a reality, I said to my wife, "Look, I like this broadcasting business. It's something I think I can do. But to do it, we're going to have to move up to New York full-time." Which we did.

As it turned out, I didn't stray very far from football after retiring from the Giants. All I can say is, I've been very lucky to have both careers—football and broadcasting.

◙

Summerall's Moment in the Snow

Many unpredictable things have happened on professional football fields, but not many were less likely than Pat Summerall's miraculous 49-yard field goal in a dizzying snowstorm in 1958 to defeat the Cleveland Browns and clinch a tie for the NFL East crown. Gerald Eskenazi described the astonishing deed in his book *There Were Giants in Those Days.*

"I couldn't believe Jim Lee was asking me to do that," says Summerall. "That was the longest attempt I'd ever made for the Giants. It was on a bad field, and it was so unrealistic. Most of the fellows on the bench couldn't believe it either."

Meanwhile Wellington Mara was up in the press box in the upper stand . . . [and said] "I was sitting next to [assistant coaches] Ken Kavanaugh and Walt Yowarsky, and we all said, "He can't kick it that far. What are we doing?"

It is credited as a 50-yard [actually, 49-yard] attempt, but according to Summerall, "No one knows how far it had to go. You couldn't see the yard markers. The snow had obliterated them. But it was more than 50 yards, I'll tell you that. . . .

"I knew as soon as I touched it that it was going to be far enough. My only thought was sometimes you hit a ball too close to the center and it behaves like a knuckleball, breaking from side to side. It was weaving out. But when it got to the 10, I could see it was breaking back to the inside."

In the locker room after the game, Tim Mara was as happy as his sons Jack and Wellington, coach Jim Lee Howell, and Summerall all rolled into one. "What a kick," he said. "What a kicker. But what the hell, that's what I pay him for, and I'm glad to see he earned his money today."

◙

Mel Hein

People who witnessed Mel Hein's efforts on behalf of the New York Giants in the 1930s and early 1940s knew they were watching the best center in the game. On defense, at linebacker, he was outstanding both at bringing down runners and harassing pass receivers. And those who knew him swore there was not a finer gentleman associated with the sport. He could never be accused of playing dirty football, like so many others who inhabited the scrimmage-line trenches along with him; nor was he a brawler. He was simply a big, fast, and incredibly talented football player.

At 6'2" and varying between 210 and 225 pounds during his fifteen-year pro career, he was an especially mobile lineman, so mobile in fact that Don Hutson, the game's greatest and most elusive end of that era, claimed Hein made his life more difficult than any other player in the league. Bronko Nagurski said Hein was perhaps the surest, cleanest, and most effective tackler he ever encountered.

Mel Hein joined the Giants in 1931 and remained through the 1945 season. Extraordinarily durable, he played sixty minutes in practically every game—more than two hundred of them—and it is said that in fifteen years he never missed a game because of an injury. He has the unique distinction of being named All-Pro in eight consecutive seasons (1933–40). He was the team captain for ten years, during which time the Giants won seven divisional crowns and two NFL titles.

When it was rumored that Mel would retire after the 1940 season, the Giants staged a Mel Hein Day at the Polo Grounds late in the season. Mayor Fiorello La Guardia gave a speech, and the team gave him an automobile. However, the Mara family, the team owners, talked him into coming back for a few more years. When he finally left the game as a player in 1945, the Giants retired his number, 7.

Hein did not leave football, however; he coached for the Los Angeles Dons and later the New York Yankees of the old All-America Football Conference and for the Los Angeles Rams in the NFL. After that, he spent twelve years as an assistant coach at the University of Southern California. Later, he served as supervisor of officials for the American Football League, a post for which he was sponsored by Al Davis, who was then the general manager of the Oakland Raiders and today is the owner of the Los Angeles Raiders.

Mel Hein was one of seventeen charter members of the Pro Football Hall of Fame. He died on January 31, 1992.

When I was getting out of high school, football was not exactly the foremost thing on my mind. My ambition was to go to the University of Washington, not Washington State. The University is over in Seattle and, at that time, in the 1920s, they had good crew teams. Rowing is what I was most interested in then. The coach of the crew team gave a speech at our high school banquet, and I was very impressed. I made up my mind to go to the University of Washington then and there and to try out for crew. I lived right on the bay on Puget Sound [in Bellingham, Washington]; we had a rowboat, and from then on I'd go out every day and row—I wanted to build up my back. They did not give scholarships, and so I decided to stay out of school for a year and earn the money to go to Washington.

I had an older brother over at Washington State, however, who was on the football team, and he told the coach, Babe Hollingberry, about me and that I was a pretty good football player. Well, they looked up my records, and the coach made some long-distance calls to us in Bellingham. I told him I didn't want to go to Washington State. But finally he talked my father into it, and my father talked me into going there.

We had a championship freshman team, and most of the freshmen went on the next year to start on the varsity. We had a good season as juniors—only lost two games. And as seniors we went to the Rose Bowl. That was the last time Washington State played in a Rose Bowl game—1931—and we played Alabama. In those days, they selected teams from different parts of the country, not just the Pac-10 and Big Ten like they do today.

There's one thing I'll always remember from that game. Our coach, Babe Hollingberry, was somewhat of a showman, and he was superstitious. In the showman role he brought a lot of new bright crimson red uniforms for our appearance in the Rose Bowl—the headgear was red, the shoes were red, the stockings were red, everything was red. I think it scared us more than Alabama because we didn't play too good a ball game—they walloped us 24-0. They simply had a better team than we had.

The superstitious part of Babe Hollingberry came out when we got back to Pullman, the city where Washington State's campus is located, after the game. No one ever saw those uniforms again, and the story is that Babe had a big bonfire and burned them all. He didn't want any of his teams ever to wear those uniforms again.

I went from Washington State to the New York Giants, but I almost went with another team. Portsmouth [Spartans], out in Ohio, was in the league then—that was before the team moved the franchise to Detroit and became the Lions. They wanted me, and I had a contract offer from them. I had another contract offer from the Providence Steam Roller, out of New England, who were also in the

league at that time, and it was better than the one from
Portsmouth. I hadn't received anything from the Giants,
although I'd heard they were planning to make me an offer.
Well, Jimmy Conzelman, the Steam Roller coach, was push-
ing me, so I signed with Providence for $125 a game, which
was a pretty good salary for a lineman in those days. A lot
of the linemen when I started in 1931 were only making
$80 or $85 a game.

After I signed the contract, I went down to Spokane for
a basketball game, another sport I played at Washington
State. We were playing Gonzaga, and Ray Flaherty, the
captain of the Giants at that time, was coaching there
[basketball] during the off-season. He came down to the
dressing room after the game and asked me if I'd received
a contract from the Giants yet.

"No, I haven't," I said. "But if one is on the way, it's too
late now." Ray didn't know what I was talking about, so I
told him. "I signed one with the Providence Steam Roller
and mailed it back to them yesterday."

Ray said, "Oh, no. How much are they paying you?"

I told him and he said, "The Giants' contract is a better
offer, $150 a game. I know that's the figure, and I know the
contract's on its way to you. Damn!" A little later he came
back to me and said, "Why don't you go down to the
postmaster when you get home and ask him to send a
telegram to the postmaster in Providence to see if he would
intercept the letter?"

The next morning I went down there, but the postmaster said he wouldn't do it. He said that I could try myself
but that he truly doubted I'd get the letter back. So I sent a
telegram myself, and, sure enough, the letter with the contract came back, and in the meantime the contract from the
Giants for $150 a game had arrived. I signed with the
Giants and tore up the other contract with Providence. I
think at that time $150 was probably the highest pay of any
lineman in the league. It was pretty good money, even
though it would not sound that way now, but you could
buy a loaf of bread for a nickel and get a full meal for thirty-

five cents in the Automat back then. And you had no in-
come tax.

Tim Mara was the owner of the Giants at that time. Jack
Mara, his son, hadn't gotten involved yet. I believe my first
year with the Giants was Jack's last at Fordham; he had
been studying law and was a lawyer when he came on the
Giants' payroll. Tim Mara was easier to deal with as far as
a contract was concerned. Jack, being a lawyer, was a bit
tougher to get anything out of. I think Tim was a little more
generous and, needless to say, I preferred to deal with him
if I wanted to get a raise or anything like that.

Tim was a terrific fellow in many ways. He used to
travel with the team but was a New Yorker through and
through. In 1934, we won the world championship—we
beat the Chicago Bears in the famous "Sneakers Game." In
those days, the league champion always went to the West
Coast and played two or three postseason exhibition
games against an all-star team made up of different players
from the National Football League. So we went out there,
and we stayed at Pacific Palisades in a nice hotel overlook-
ing a golf course. It was very beautiful and very quiet, away
from the busyness of Los Angeles. Tim had come out with
us. Well, after two days in that hotel, he went home. He said
he had to get back to New York City. Why? Because it was
too quiet in California. He said the birds would wake him
up in the morning about six o'clock. Tim said he had to get
back to New York, where he was raised on the East Side—
and where he could hear the subway and the fire engines
and all the racket. He couldn't sleep unless he heard all the
noises of New York. So he never did see the game. After two
days he was all worn out from the quiet and had to get back
so he could get some rest.

Steve Owen was the Giants' coach when I joined the
team in 1931. It was his first full year as head coach.
Actually, Steve was player-coach that year, but he only
suited up for about three games. He was about thirty-three
or thirty-four then. Steve was a very good coach, though,

and all the players respected him. He made it harder on some of the rookies. That was just his way, his method. As a result, even the players wouldn't have much to do with the rookies. I didn't agree with that philosophy.

A couple of years later, when I was captain of the Giants, some of the rookies complained to me about the way Steve was treating them—a lot rougher, they said, than the way he handled the veterans. I told them that Steve was basically a very good-hearted, fair fellow, and that the reason maybe he was tougher on the rookies was because he wanted them to know that pro football was a very tough game and that they had to work hard to make the team. After a while, I assured them, they'd get into the spirit of the thing and everything would work itself out. Then I talked to Steve myself. We went back and forth some, but from that time on, I believe, Giants rookies were treated much more fairly and felt more like they were part of the team.

The closeness of the Giants team in the 1930s was one of the reasons we did so well. There was a lot of team spirit and togetherness. Most of the players lived in the same area—between 100th and 103rd streets around Broadway. We stayed in about three different hotels up there. I stayed the longest at the old Whitehall Hotel at 100th and Broadway, and a number of others did, too. It was a small hotel, and each room had its own kitchenette. Steve Owen lived there all year round with his wife; he had the penthouse. He liked to have his players nearby and usually tried to talk them all into staying at the Whitehall. After the season, of course, all the ballplayers went back to their hometowns. There were a few players who didn't want to live in a hotel, and they got apartments of their own; but still they were within two or three blocks of us. That worked out quite well in bringing us all kind of close, and we got to know each other personally and to know each other's families. It unified us in a way that a lot of other teams were not able to accomplish. That and the winning attitude that Steve gave to us was what made us a winning football team.

One of pro football's all-time greats, center Mel Hein was one of the
twenty-three charter members of the Pro Football Hall of Fame. He
was named All-Pro eight consecutive years (1933–40), and no Giant
has ever played more seasons than the fifteen glorious ones that Hein
turned in (1931–45).

As a rookie, though, I wasn't all that sure I was going
to make the team. If I didn't, I wasn't going to get that $150
a game, and I was a long way from the state of Washington.
I was married and had my responsibilities.

There were two veteran centers on the team, and teams
only carried twenty-five players then. Two of them would
be centers—certainly no more. Well, I made the team and

played behind Mickey Murtaugh, who had been there since 1926. He was out of Georgetown. But he got hurt in the second game of the season and I went in, and I guess I did okay because from that time on I was the Giants' starting center.

You learned about the pro game pretty quick in those days. It was very rough in the line—a lot of punching and elbowing and forearms and that sort of stuff. You had to stand up for yourself or you would be walked all over. A good example is the little encounter I had with George Musso of the Chicago Bears. He was a rookie in 1933 and played nose guard on defense. George was about 260 pounds and as strong as they come. I was about fifty pounds lighter than him. I was centering to the tailback on the single wing, who was about four yards behind me. Centering that way, I had to keep my head down, looking back at the tailback. Well, the first time George lined up opposite me and I snapped the ball, he popped me one right in the face. We didn't have faceguards in those days, and I said to him after the play that he'd better never do that to me again. Coming from me, about 210 pounds, it didn't make much of an impression on big George. On the next play, he let me have it again. So, on the following play, I was ready. I snapped the ball with one hand this time and at the exact same time delivered one heck of an uppercut with the other hand and got George square in the face. He really felt it, I could tell. He shook it off in a dazed kind of way and then smiled and said something like that was a helluva good shot. He never tried it on me again, and we became good friends. George was not a dirty player, and I never heard of him doing that kind of thing to anybody later. He was just massive and strong. We played against each other for more than ten years and I, for one, can say he surely deserved to be inducted into the [Pro Football] Hall of Fame.

One of our most colorful players in the early years was Shipwreck Kelly. He came up with us in 1932; he came from Kentucky and had this slow, southern drawl. I remember well the first time I saw Shipwreck. We trained in Magnetic Springs, Ohio, that year. It was a kind of health resort, with big hotels where elderly people went for the spas. Anyway, we were all there and Shipwreck drove up to training camp his first day in this huge Cadillac. I guess his family had a lot of money, and we thought, Gee, is this guy crazy, joining the team to play for peanuts, to get his head knocked around when he could travel in such style?

Kelly was not your ordinary ballplayer in those days, like those of us who lived for our little paychecks. He was truly colorful, a man about town. Still, he was a fine football player when he wanted to be. Steve Owen and Shipwreck clashed a few times. For example, Shipwreck would be back to punt—he was a pretty good punter. It would be fourth down and maybe two yards to go and he wouldn't punt. He'd just take off and run. I'm going to make that first down, he'd say to himself. And Steve would fume on the sideline. Once in a while he didn't make it. Steve would yank him out of the game, and they would have a big argument on the sideline. He was an erratic ballplayer but a good one, and he sure could run.

Ken Strong was one of the finest players in the early days. Ken graduated from New York University and played first for the Staten Island Stapletons, which we used to call Stapes for short. We always played them on Thanksgiving Day. The Giants would take the ferryboat over to Staten Island. They had a little field over there and people would stand along the sidelines to watch the game. We never did draw too many people—that's why Staten Island eventually had to give up football. Ken Strong was their whole team in those days. He carried the ball 90 percent of the time and handled the passing, the punting, the placekicking, and most of the tackling, as I recall. Then when they broke up, he came to the Giants. In his later years he didn't play as much, but he stayed with the Giants to do all the kicking.

We also had two of the best ends in the game during that time, and both are in the Hall of Fame: Ray Flaherty and Red Badgro. The only other two who would rank with them were Don Hutson, the great pass catcher with Green Bay, and Bill Hewitt of the Bears, who was as tough on defense as he was agile on offense.

Then there was Bronko Nagurski of the Bears. I learned that if you hit him by yourself, you were in trouble: if you hit him low, he'd trample you to death; if you hit him high, he'd take you about ten yards. The best way to tackle Bronko was to have your teammates hit him about the same time—one or two low, one or two high. He was the most powerful fullback that I ever played against in all my career. He had a big body and could get that body, that trunk, down and be able to throw his shoulder into you. If you didn't get under his shoulder, he just knocked you butt over tea kettles.

Another thing about Bronko was his blocking. The Bears had this little scatback in those days by the name of Beattie Feathers. Well, Bronko could open up the whole defensive line for him. He would burst it open, and Feathers would be right on his butt, following him through, and then he'd break one way or the other. It gave Feathers an advantage no other running back had, and he set a rushing record in 1934, over 1,000 yards [1,004], the first ever to do that. After that year we worked at special defenses to go up against that, and we were able to stop Feathers pretty well in later years.

Probably the greatest tackle I ever played against was Cal Hubbard of the Packers. We were playing up at Green Bay one time and the score was 0–0 at the half. Hubbard was the left defensive tackle, and he stopped everything. We used to like to run to our right from the single wing, running to the strong side of the line—that was our normal tactic out of that formation. But against the Packers that meant we would be running into Cal Hubbard's side of the line. So we changed it and were running everything to the left that day. Well, we were making yardage because we were running away from Hubbard. Between halves they decided to move Cal to middle linebacker. They had a seven-man line and set him up right behind them as a solo linebacker. From that position the son of a gun made tackles all over the field and they finally beat us, 6–0.

I've often been asked to select an All-Pro team from the players I actually played against, which is not an easy thing to do because there were an awful lot of excellent football players in the 1930s. But if I were to do it, I'd have to have Iron Mike Michalske of Green Bay at one guard and Danny Fortmann of the Bears at the other. My tackles would include Cal Hubbard, of course, and either Turk Edwards [Redskins] or Joe Stydahar [Bears]. Center, I guess, would be Bulldog Turner [Bears]. At ends, Don Hutson [Packers], everybody's All-Pro, and Bill Hewitt [Bears]. That takes care of the line. In the backfield, I would rate Sammy Baugh [Redskins] the best quarterback of that time and maybe any other time as well. Bronko Nagurski would be the fullback. And I think I would want Cliff Battles [Redskins] and George McAfee [Bears] as my halfbacks. Ace Parker, who played with the Brooklyn Dodgers, was so good a back that he deserves mention in that same class of ballplayers. So was Dutch Clark [tailback for the Lions].

I played in seven championship games over fifteen years in the NFL while I was with the Giants. The most famous, I guess, was the "Sneakers Game" of 1934, when we came back in the second half. We were losing 10–3 to the Bears at the half. Everybody was slipping and sliding all over the place, and Chicago was winning simply because they were bigger and stronger than us. They were actually a better team than us, but that didn't matter that day—not with those field conditions. Their size gave them an advantage in the first half, but the advantage we got from the traction provided by the sneakers in the second half was much greater, and that's why we were able to outscore them 27–3 in that period. Our passer, Ed Danowski, was able to stay on his feet and set up or scramble if he had to, and our receivers were able to get free. And Ken Strong was able to gain a lot of yardage running.

George Halas, their coach, shook his head throughout the whole second half. It was especially nice because we'd lost to the Bears in the championship game the year before [23–21]. The winner's share of that 1934 championship was $621 per player, a far cry from all the money a Super Bowl winner takes home today. But we thought it was a lot of money, that we were suddenly wealthy.

We got to the championship game again the next year—in fact, we have the distinction of having made it to the first three NFL championship games. In 1935, it was against the Detroit Lions, and they had Dutch Clark and Ace Gutowsky and Glenn Presnell, a wonderful backfield. It was an awful day—mud and snow and terrible winds. We could never get going. They beat us pretty soundly [26–7].

We played Green Bay for the title in 1938 and 1939— beat them in the first [23–17] and lost to them in the second [27–0]. They had Don Hutson and Cecil Isbell and Arnie Herber. Clarke Hinkle was their fullback—I've got a number of aches and pains to remind me what tackling him was like.

We were actually pretty lucky to have gotten into that championship in '39. We beat the Redskins out of the Eastern Division championship when Bo Russell kicked a last-minute field goal that could have won the game for them, but it was ruled no good. We were winning 9–7 at the time. I was backing up the line and the Redskins had worked the ball down to about our 25-yard line. There were only about forty-five seconds to go. Russell lined up and kicked the ball. It looked like it was good to a lot of people. But the referee, Bill Halloran, gave the signal that it was no good. Ray Flaherty, who was coaching the Redskins, and practically their entire bench came running out onto the field and raised the dickens about it. But Halloran paid no attention to them, and we won the game. I had a pretty good angle to see it, and it looked to me like he missed it. The Redskins sure didn't think so, however. The next year Halloran didn't come back as a referee. I think George Preston Marshall, the Redskins' owner, saw that he was fired. I don't know how he did it, but George Marshall had a lot of influence in the National Football League.

I retired after the 1945 season. But I'd almost gotten out earlier, in 1943. That was after twelve years in the league. I'd taken a job as head football coach up at Union College, in Schenectady, New York. I also taught physical education there—it was a fairly good-paying job because they made me an associate professor. They had to give me that in order to pay the money I wanted. Well, the war was underway, and many students were leaving the campus for military service. We had started with thirty young men on the football team and were down to about eighteen, so I called the president of the university and told him with that few players I didn't feel we could field a football team; others would certainly be going too. He said that I was undoubtedly right and agreed that we should disband the football team for the duration of the war.

Steve Owen saw the announcement in the *New York Times* sports section about Union dropping football, so he called me up and asked me to come back and play again for the Giants.

I said, "No, they're keeping me here to work with the civilian population in physical education, and we're getting some of the military trainees. The government is going to pay half my salary and the university the other half. It's going to be a year-round job."

Steve said, "That's too bad. I was hoping you'd come back because we're losing a lot of our men too." Then he said, "What do you think about just coming down to New York City on Sundays? You could stay in condition up there and just come for the games."

I told him that I did play touch football during the week and I was working out in the phys ed courses that I was running. And, of course, I did miss playing the game. "Let's give it a try," I said.

So I would go down on Friday night after my last class, work out with the team on Saturday, get the new plays, the

Ken Strong was *the* triple-threat back for the Giants in the 1930s. Run, pass, kick—he could do everything on the football field. He even came back from military service in World War II to kick for the Giants. Strong was enshrined in the Pro Football Hall of Fame in 1967.

defenses, and things like that, and then play on Sunday. For three years, I played sixty minutes of each game—no preseason games, just the league games for '43, '44, and '45—under those conditions, and then caught the train back to Schenectady after the ball game each Sunday evening. One of the sportswriters dubbed me the "Sunday center."

But it wasn't all that easy. I was getting up in my thirties at the time. In fact, I remember very well my first game. I went into it without any physical contact at all that year. We were up in Boston and our other center, who had worked out with the team in the preseason, was supposed to start until I'd gotten myself into decent shape. But he had gotten hurt in the last preseason game against the Chicago Bears. So I had to start. I played sixty minutes, and I think it was the hottest day Boston ever had. I tell you, it really took a toll on me. I could hardly get on the train to get back to Schenectady that night. It took me about three weeks to get rid of all that soreness and begin to get well. Still, the next week, I had to go the full sixty minutes again. It was a pretty tough time.

I stayed with the Giants all those years because I wanted to. I was satisfied with New York. The Maras treated me very well; but as far as salaries went, well, we went back and forth a few times. One year in particular, 1938, after we had won the NFL title, I asked for a certain amount of money, like $300 a ball game. I asked Jack Mara for it, and I got a telegram back from him: he offered me a contract, but the amount was not exactly what I'd asked for.

I said no. Then he offered me a season contract, flat sum for the year, but it also turned out to be less than what I'd wanted. So finally I got teed off and started looking around for something else. Well, the Los Angeles Bulldogs, out on the West Coast, was a pro team but not an NFL team, and the owner offered to get me a year-round job at a tire and rubber company out there if I played for the Bulldogs. Financially it looked pretty good. Well, after about five different telegrams from Jack Mara with offers, all of which I turned down, I finally sent a telegram to him that said, "Don't send any more telegrams or call me. My mind is definitely made up. I'm going to stay out on the Pacific Coast."

Right away, boom—I got another telegram from Jack with the salary I wanted.

Another time, I decided I wanted to get into coaching, perhaps on the college level. So I talked to Lou Little, who was head coach then at Columbia, which wasn't far from where we were staying in New York—up around 150th Street. Lou had been president of the coaches' association that year, and they were having their national meeting out in Los Angeles. I asked him if I could come out there and hang around the hotel and maybe meet some of the head coaches. He said, "Sure, Mel—come on out and hang around, and I'll find out if there are any positions that are open. I'm sure we can help you."

This all took place right near the end of our season. Well, the Giants had a breakfast at our hotel after the last game of the season, before all the players started heading back for their homes. Tim Mara, who knew I was thinking about going from a player to a coach, said to me, "Mel, I want you to sign a three-year contract with us for $5,000 a season."

That was real big money in those days. I couldn't believe it. I said, "Sure, glad to!"

I lived on the seventh floor of that hotel, and I ran up the stairs, didn't even wait for the elevator, and showed my wife a check for $500 and told her about the $5,000 contract. Then I called Lou Little and told him I wouldn't be seeing him out in Los Angeles. That's how you got your raises in those days; it was a little different from the way they do business these days.

◫

A Surprising Win . . . A Costly Pass

Tuffy Leemans, the Giants' second-round pick in the NFL's first
draft in 1936 who subsequently earned a well-deserved niche
in the Pro Football Hall of Fame, liked to tell this story of one
game he played for the Giants in 1942.

We were playing the Redskins at Washington. We
did not have a great football team because the war
was on and we had some wartime ballplayers. Steve
Owen said to me, "I don't want you to throw any
passes. I don't want you to ever throw the ball in this
game." I was the guy who called the plays from my
halfback position.

Well, we come out for the game, and, Jesus, here
over Griffith Stadium is the darkest cloud you've ever
seen. You know from the looks of that cloud that the
damn thing is going to let loose and rain all day. So on
our first play from scrimmage, I go into the huddle
and say to our center, Mel Hein, and a few of the
other old-timers, "Jesus, it's going to rain like hell. I
think I'm going to fake a reverse to [halfback Ward]
Cuff and run him wide and see what that Redskin
halfback over there does. And if he does what I hope
he will, then I'm going to pitch that ball to [end]
Willie Walls."

"Jeez," Mel Hein says. "Don't start throwing. If
they pick one off, Steve will blow his top."

"Mel," I say to him, "It's going to *rain*. We might
as well take a chance now."

I told Walls to head straight down and to the
outside. Then I ran Cuff wide on the fake, and this
Redskin halfback, Steve Juzwick, comes barreling up
there to stop Cuff. By the time Juzwick recovers, Walls
is out there behind him. I throw the ball to Walls on
the Washington 30-yard line, and he goes the rest of
the way. It's a 50-yard touchdown play to put us ahead
7–0. And now it rains. It rains and it rains and it rains.

Washington scores in the second quarter to make
it 7–7. Then in the third quarter one of our ends, Neal
Adams, drops off on one of their flat passes and picks

it off and goes 65 yards for a touchdown. We beat the Redskins 14–7.

But—this is almost unbelievable—our team never made a first down. We gained 50 yards on that touchdown I threw, and besides that we gained only *one* other yard [on offense] that day. The Redskins, meanwhile, gained more than 100 yards rushing and more than 100 passing, but we beat them.

After the game, Steve Owen said to me, "I thought I told you not to throw." Then he fined me fifty bucks for throwing that touchdown pass.

◻

It's All in the Game . . .

Was it a rugged game that they played back in the 1930s? Consider this account from the *New York Times* of the 1938 NFL title game between the Giants and the Packers:

What a frenzied battle this was! The tackling was fierce and the blocking positively vicious. In the last drive every scrimmage pile-up saw a Packer tackler stretched on the ground. . . . As for the Giants, they really were hammered to a fare-thee-well.

Johnny Dell Isola was taken to St. Elizabeth's Hospital with a spinal concussion that just missed being a fractured vertebra. Ward Cuff suffered a possible fracture of the sternum.

Mel Hein, kicked in the cheekbone at the end of the second quarter, suffered a concussion of the brain that left him temporarily bereft of his memory. He came to in the final quarter and finished the game. . . .

The play for the full sixty vibrant minutes was absolutely ferocious. No such blocking and tackling by two football teams ever had been seen at the Polo Grounds. Tempers were so frayed and tattered that stray punches were tossed around all afternoon. This was the gridiron sport at its primitive best!

(The Giants won the game, 23–17, with the winning touchdown coming on a pass from Ed Danowski to Hank Soar.)

◻

Y. A. Tittle

Y. A. Tittle was 34 years old when he came to New York after having quarterbacked the Baltimore Colts for three years (1948–50) and the San Francisco 49ers for ten (1951–60). In 1961, he took the starting job from veteran Charlie Conerly, who was 37 that year, and led the Giants to three consecutive conference titles.

After a fine college career at Louisiana State, Tittle displayed his talents in the pro ranks immediately: in his first game for Baltimore in the All-America Football Conference he threw four touchdown passes to lead the Colts to an upset victory over the New York Yankees. At the end of the season, he was named the AAFC Rookie of the Year.

When the Colts went out of business after the 1950 season, Tittle was obtained in a special draft by the 49ers, who had been absorbed into the NFL, and by 1952 he became San Francisco's premier quarterback, unseating another respected veteran, Frankie Albert.

By the time he came to the Giants, Tittle's passing talent and his on-field leadership were already well established. He often wondered if he might perhaps be approaching over-the-hill status; but instead, his quarterbacking talents were, in fact, peaking. And he brought a lot of excitement to New York Giants fans. As novelist Irwin Shaw later observed in an article for *Esquire* magazine, "He almost always seems to be in desperate trouble, and almost always seems to get out of it at the last fateful moment. Whether the record bears it out or not, the Giants always seem to be behind, and in the good days, at least, Tittle put them ahead when all hope seemed lost."

He quickly gained the affection and respect of his teammates. End Joe Walton, one of Tittle's favorite targets, said of him, "The greatest honor I've had in football is being a teammate and friend of Y.A.'s." And offensive tackle Rosey Brown remembered, "Y.A. worried about you like your wife worries about you. He had the interests of the whole team on his mind all the time."

When Tittle retired after the 1964 season, he held most of the NFL's career passing records: most completions (2,427), most touchdowns (242), most yardage gained (33,070), and most passes thrown (4,395). In 1962, he set the NFL record for the most touchdown passes in a season, 33, and then topped it the following year when he tossed 36. He was also named the NFL's Most Valuable Player in both 1961 and 1963.

Y.A. was inducted into the Pro Football Hall of Fame in 1971.

I was born and raised in Marshall, Texas, which is where I started playing football. It was in junior high—that was about 1938.

I ended up going to LSU. Marshall is right near the Louisiana border, and during the war my brother was going to Tulane in New Orleans—he was an outstanding blocking back. They were big rivals with LSU in those days. I went over to see him play at LSU in Baton Rouge, and I was impressed with the campus there.

But the main reason I chose LSU was because they let freshmen play on the varsity team in those days. The other colleges didn't. I felt I could play a lot the first year and, in fact, I did. I had offers from the University of Texas, Rice, Tulsa, TCU—but in those schools I couldn't play right off.

In 1948 I chose to go into the AAFC instead of the NFL. I hate to tell you how stupid I was then. College football was the big thing in the South in those days, and we didn't follow the pros. There wasn't any television or even radio coverage of the games, and so we didn't know much about them. As a result, I didn't even know there were two different leagues.

I was the first-round draft choice of the Cleveland Browns in the All-America Football Conference. Then two months later I was in Marshall during the January break, and the guy from the Detroit Lions in the NFL came by and said I was their first-round draft choice and wanted to talk about a contract. That's when I first found out there were two pro leagues.

I was on the Cleveland roster until about June, and then the AAFC commissioner balanced the league by taking some players from the top teams and giving their contracts to some of the weaker teams. They gave mine to the Baltimore Colts. Altogether they took about six players from the Browns and the New York Yankees, who had played for the AAFC championship the year before, and gave them to the Colts. It was a good break for me because if I'd stayed with Cleveland I'd have had to battle Otto Graham for the starting job; and that, of course, would have been very tough. With Baltimore I got the job the first year, and it enabled me to make Rookie of the Year. In Cleveland I would have spent most of the season on the bench watching Otto.

The league folded after the 1949 season. Only three teams were brought into the AFL—the Colts, Browns, and 49ers. So in 1950 I played for the Colts in the NFL, and we had a terrible season. We were the doormat of the league— won only one of twelve games. After that year, Baltimore folded. All the players on the Colts were then redrafted, and I was taken by the 49ers. So I was drafted three times—by Cleveland, Detroit, and San Francisco.

I was really happy with going to San Francisco. It was, in a way, like when I went to Baltimore. Their quarterback—the Colts'—was Charlie O'Rourke, and he was pretty

old by then, so I got the job. Out in San Francisco I also got
the chance to compete for the job with a much older quarterback, Frankie Albert, and working with him I got to
learn a lot, too, because he was a really fine quarterback.
He was not over the hill, but he was coming near the end of
his career. I was 24 years old and he was 31, and that was
pretty old for a quarterback in those days. We felt it was old
because a quarterback had to do a lot more back then—
run, block, as well as pass.

I got a good amount of playing time that first year—
almost as much as Frankie—in fact, more at the end of the
season. Then the following year Buck Shaw, our coach,
went to a system where he would start Frankie one game
and he would play the first and third quarters and I would
play the second and fourth. The next week I would start the
first and third and Frankie would play the other two. Toward the end of the year, we all decided it wasn't working
all that well—I mean, when you came in you were essentially cold. After that season Frankie retired, and I had the
job pretty much all to myself.

Frankie Albert taught me a lot, however. He was a
master magician as a quarterback in terms of ball handling
and leading the football team on the field. He was always
very sure of himself. When you start talking about quarterbacks, you have to remember how different it was then
from today. Today the plays are sent in from the sideline.
We had to be able to throw the ball like they do today, but
we had to do a lot of faking, a lot of trickery, and we had to
get in the huddle and run the offense; we had to be thinking about what we were going to be doing the down after
this as well as this down and make the decisions ourselves.
And Albert was probably the best quarterback I saw play in
terms of this. I don't mean to say he could play quarterback
in the NFL today—he probably couldn't because he didn't
throw the ball that well. But in that period he was a true
leader. He had what a lot of others didn't have—he could
fake and bootleg and punt, and he was a great team leader.
I'm disappointed he's not in the Hall of Fame.

I guess my first friends out there were the others who

came in new that first year. Billy Wilson, an end, was a newcomer that year, and we became good friends. There was also Jim Cason, a defensive back and one of the better ones in the league, who had been a teammate of mine down at LSU. And there was Joe Perry, our great fullback, and Bill Johnson, our center. Hugh McElhenny came the next year, 1952, and as a result we had quite an offense.

One game I particularly remember was back in 1957 when R. C. Owens caught the alley-oop pass against Detroit in the last five seconds to give us a 35–31 win. They had all those great defensive backs there—Jack Christiansen, Yale Lary—two Hall of Famers covering him, but he goes up between them and comes down with the ball. It was a spectacular catch. The Lions went on to win the Western Conference that year. They beat us in a playoff game—we both ended up with 8–4–0 records that year—but still we beat them with the old alley-oop in the regular season.

Then there was that game in 1953 with the Los Angeles Rams in San Francisco when McElhenny ran through the entire Rams team to set up the winning field goal. Everyone on Los Angeles had a crack at him, but he ran it down to about the 10-yard line. Gordie Soltau kicked the field goal and we won, 31–30.

I was going into my fourteenth season in 1961 when the 49ers decided to trade me to the Giants. I had very mixed feelings about it. I didn't know whether to retire or not to retire. One of the reasons I was thinking about retiring was that in the 1960 season I had a groin pull that bothered me from about the fourth game on and it seems I never could get well. I'd lay off a game and then I'd come back, and it would come back. So I had a miserable season.

Then Red Hickey, our coach, was using the shotgun offense exclusively—not just occasionally like teams do today, but on every play. The quarterback was like a tailback in the old single-wing offense. It was more suited to the talents of John Brodie, who was more mobile than I was. So with the switch to that, I thought there was a good chance I'd be traded; and, of course, I was.

I went up to the Giants' training camp in '61, which

was held in Salem, Oregon, back then, and I still had the groin pull. It bothered me and I was concerned about it. I didn't want to tell the trainers about it. In fact, I would actually go into the toilet and tape myself so they wouldn't find out about it. I'd flush the toilet while I was tearing the tape so no one would hear it. Then I'd get the tape on and go out and get some practice.

They asked me to play in the first game that year, an exhibition game against the Rams down in Los Angeles. On the first play I was in for, I fumbled the snap from Ray Wietecha. Their linebacker—I think it was Jack Pardee—came down on me and his knee got me in the back, and I ended up with a couple of broken bones there. They took me out of the game after that play. I was out for six weeks. During that healing time I'd get in the hot tub every day, and it healed my groin injury too.

Everything was fine after that. I moved to New York—didn't bring my wife, just got an apartment near Yankee Stadium for the season. I roomed there with Del Shofner, who had also come to the Giants on a trade—they got him from the Rams, and it was one of the Giants' best trades ever.

Charlie Conerly had been the starting quarterback for years when I got to New York—since 1948. We came into the pros the same year but Charlie was about three or so years older than me. He'd spent his whole career with the Giants. And Charlie was a fine gentleman; we became good friends. I'm sure he felt some pressure when they brought me in. We were both old—he was 37 and I was 34.

That first year we shared some playing time early in the season. He'd been starting there for thirteen years and so I'm sure it gnawed at him that the Giants went out and

◄ Y. A. Tittle (14) in a familiar pose. Tittle came to the Giants in 1961 from the San Francisco 49ers. He guided the Giants to three Eastern Conference championships in his four years with New York (1961–64). The Bald Eagle, as he was sometimes called, was inducted into the Pro Football Hall of Fame in 1971.

traded for me. But Charlie had a lot of class. When I did something well in practice or in a game, he'd often come over and say something like "Well, you're looking pretty good, Y.A."

After the Redskins game, the third of the season, which Charlie started, I started most of the rest of the games, although Charlie came in and relieved me on several occasions. After that season Charlie retired.

Del Shofner was my favorite receiver. He was just so good—he had blazing speed and great hands. Most receivers don't have both, but Del did. He just never dropped the football—if it was there and he could get his hands on it, he caught it. Billy Wilson, the player I went to most often in San Francisco, had great hands too. He was probably the best short-pass receiver I'd ever seen, but he couldn't go deep as effectively as Del because he didn't have the speed.

Kyle Rote was also very good. He played the opposite flanker spot for us in New York. He was very shifty and had great moves. He didn't have great speed because he had bad knees. And Frank Gifford—he played flanker in 1962 and 1963. He had come back out of retirement—he stayed out the 1961 season after he got that concussion in '60 when he collided with Chuck Bednarik of the Eagles. And Joe Walton was another who I liked to throw to a lot—he was very sure-handed.

I suppose one of the best games I remember from the New York days was the one in 1962 against the Redskins. That was the one where I threw the 7 touchdown passes, which tied the NFL record [and still is the NFL record]. I wasn't even supposed to start that game. The week before we'd played Detroit, a real tough game; and Detroit, of course, had a great defense—players like Joe Schmidt and Alex Karras and Night Train Lane and Yale Lary. The game was a real battle. We won 17–14 but it was rock 'em–sock 'em in the trenches. I hurt my right arm and ended up with a huge contusion.

I couldn't throw the following Tuesday, Wednesday,

Thursday, or Friday. I didn't throw a ball that whole week. I limbered up a little on Saturday, but I still couldn't throw very well. On Sunday morning Allie Sherman, our coach, said to me, "Why don't you go out and give it a try? See what you think." So I threw a few look-ins, short passes; it hurt. But I'd found out in my career that you can be hurting pretty bad, but when they blow the whistle you just forget about it.

Football is an emotional game, and sometimes you can do amazing things when you're hurt. I remember once I went into a game with two sprained ankles. I could barely walk into the huddle. But once I got under that center I was cured on the spot. In 1953, I played a game with a shattered cheekbone and completed 29 passes. I pulled a hamstring muscle with San Francisco in 1957 and was supposed to be out for three weeks, but John Brodie went bad in the first half the next week against Green Bay, and [coach Red] Hickey asked, "Can you play, Tittle?" What does a ballplayer say in a situation like that? I tried. I got out there and threw a couple of touchdown passes and we won 27–20. You never want to tell a coach you can't do it because there's always someone else on the sideline waiting for a chance, and he might just go out there and do it.

Anyway, that day I told Sherman I thought I could do it. But it didn't look like it when I got out there. The first seven passes I threw were incomplete and I thought I would be out. But he didn't take me out, and when I went back in I completed twelve passes in a row. And there were some long ones too. There was a bomb to Gifford for over 60 yards and a 50-yarder to Shofner.

I had a shot at an eighth touchdown that day. There were about four minutes left in the game, and we had the ball on about the 20-yard line. All the guys wanted me to go for it, but I didn't really want to take any chances throwing the ball. Norm Snead [Washington's quarterback] had already thrown four touchdown passes that day, and they had Bobby Mitchell, who was always a threat—he was a real speed-burner. Snead could throw him a little hitch and

he could be off 70 yards for a touchdown. So I decided to keep the ball on the ground and be sure we won the game. I just didn't think it was right throwing for the record—that's just glory-seeking.

I played against a lot of great teams. The Detroit Lions in the 1950s were a great ball club and we [the 49ers] always had some heavy battles with them. Those were the years when they had Bobby Layne and Doak Walker and Leon Hart, and, of course, that great defense.

The Cleveland Browns were another very tough team to go up against in the early '50s—all those Hall of Famers: Otto Graham, Lou Groza, Marion Motley, Bill Willis. And in the late '50s the Giants were rugged. Charlie Conerly was in his heyday then, and their defense was outstanding with Huff and Robustelli and Katcavage and Grier and all the others.

When I came to New York, I thought their offense was not as good as the one I had just left. After all, we had had Hugh McElhenny and Joe Perry in the backfield out in San Francisco. But great defensive teams are the ones that win. And that's what the Giants had. There were a lot of Hall of Famers on that team. They had great pride, and deservedly so. And there's something about New York and Yankee Stadium itself. Bill Johnson [49ers center] used to say, "Every time I'm introduced in Yankee Stadium I feel I'm already seven points behind." It was just that you were playing in this awesome structure—The House That Ruth Built and where winners like Gehrig and DiMaggio had played and where Joe Louis had fought.

And the Giants had a tradition of winning. When I got there they hadn't had a losing season since 1953, and

◀ Y. A. Tittle's favorite target, Del Shofner (1961–67), gathers one in during the conference championship season of 1963. The beaten Philadelphia defender is Irv Cross. Shofner set a Giants' record in 1963 when he gained 1,181 yards on pass receptions, and Tittle was the NFL's leading passer that year.

they'd been in two NFL championship games in the previous five years [1956 and 1958].

We got to throwing the ball a lot when I joined the
team—that's because the Giants had added Shofner and Joe
Walton the same year [1961]. We really had a great corps of
receivers. And Allie Sherman gave me total freedom in the
huddle—I could do anything I wanted to do. He let me
make up plays, let me play football the way I loved to play
it. If it was third down and four and I wanted to run a hook-
and-go, well, I'd just do it. And if it didn't work, Sherman
wouldn't say anything. It was a very comforting feeling, the
faith he had in me, instead of having a coach on the sideline second-guessing everything you did out there. The
players never second-guessed either. We were a well-drilled
team and a closely knit one, too.

Nineteen sixty-three was the last good season we had.
We won the Eastern Conference—won eleven of our fourteen games—beating out the Browns by a game. We had
the best offense in the entire league that year. Our passing
attack was just about unstoppable, with Shofner, Gifford,
Walton, and Aaron Thomas and with Phil King and Joe
Morrison coming out of the backfield. We certainly had a
better offense than the Bears, who we had to play in the
championship game.

Our problems that day were that it was brutally cold
and windy in Chicago and I got hurt early in the game, all
of which severely hampered our passing game. I don't want
to take any of the credit away from the Chicago Bears. They
were a good team. They had a great defense. But in my
heart I felt we were a much better all-around football team.

We didn't really have all that great of a running attack,
however. And we hit a day that was geared for a running
game, not a passing one. I hurt my knee when [Bears
linebacker] Larry Morris tackled me—and I couldn't move

◄ A standard production number of the early 1960s: Y. A. Tittle (14)
hands off to fullback Alex Webster (29).

well. I was just a sitting duck back there. It took so long for me to drop back and set up I ended up throwing balls I didn't want to throw because I had to get rid of the ball. And so we lost [14–10].

The next year I got hurt probably the worst of all my seventeen years in pro football. I got hit by John Baker of the Steelers in the second game of the season and it crushed all the rib cartilages; they were all torn. It was really hard to breathe after that, and every time I got knocked down it was really hard to get up. I played, but I was a sitting duck again. You couldn't get novocaine in there, so I was really limited in what I could do; as a result I had a very poor year.

After that, I knew it was time to quit—especially when I saw our other quarterback, Gary Wood, was wanting to date my daughter.

After football, I opened my insurance business in California, and I helped coach the San Francisco 49ers.

◙

Tittle's Day

The game was at Yankee Stadium, October 28, 1962, against the Washington Redskins, and it was to be one of the most memorable afternoons ever to thrill the hearts of Giants fans. It was to be Y. A. Tittle's day.

Losing 7–0 in the first quarter, Tittle engineered a touchdown drive in the first half with passes to Del Shofner, Frank Gifford, and finally the six-pointer to Joe Morrison. Then, after Erich Barnes intercepted a Norm Snead pass on the next Washington possession, Tittle again went to the air with two passes to Shofner and a short lob to Joe Walton for Y.A.'s second scoring toss of the day. As the two-minute warning approached in the first half, Tittle completed a 53-yard pass to Shofner and, after two futile running plays, fired a bullet to Joe Morrison in the end zone, and the Giants had a 21–13 lead.

On the first play following the Giants' kickoff to start the second half, Snead launched one to Bobby Mitchell for an 80-yard touchdown, his third of the game as well. On the next New York possession, Tittle moved a stride ahead of Snead by throwing his fourth touchdown pass of the afternoon.

The thirty-six-year-old balding New York quarterback was back at it again after the next Washington drive stalled and the Giants took over at their own 49-yard line. Tittle completed three consecutive passes, the last to Walton, who carried it into the end zone for passing touchdown number 5.

In the press box, reporters were scrambling through their media guides to see just which records Tittle was approaching. Two loomed as possibilities: Y.A. had completed 11 passes in a row at this point, and the NFL record was 13, set by Minnesota's Fran Tarkenton the previous December; and there was the long-standing NFL mark of 7 touchdown passes in a single game, set by Sid Luckman of the Chicago Bears in 1943 (against the Giants at the Polo Grounds) and tied by Adrian Burk of the Philadelphia Eagles in 1954 and George Blanda of the Houston Oilers in 1961 (later also tied by Joe Kapp of the Minnesota Vikings in 1969). Midway through the third quarter, Tittle was two completions shy of both records.

Tittle completed his twelfth consecutive pass, this one to

Alex Webster, when the Giants got the ball again, but he lost his bid for the record when the next pass fell incomplete. He made up for it on the succeeding throw, however, a bomb to Frank Gifford that resulted in a 63-yard touchdown. Then, in the fourth quarter, came Tittle's record-tying pass. First, a 50-yard completion to Shofner brought the ball to the Redskins' 15-yard line. A few plays later, the Bald Eagle tossed a 5-yarder to Walton, who, after racing across the goal line, tossed the historic ball high into the air.

When the record-setting day was over, Tittle shared the NFL standard of 7 touchdown passes in a single game and established a Giants record of 505 yards passing (27 completions in 39 attempts), a mark that would stand until Phil Simms eclipsed it in 1985 when he threw for 513 in a game against the Cincinnati Bengals.

Late in the game, fans screamed for Tittle to go for touchdown number 8, but he never did. "It would have been bad taste," Tittle was quoted in the *New York Times* the next day. "If you're leading by so much [the final score was 49–34], it just doesn't sit right with me to fill the air with footballs. I'm the quarterback. It would be showing off."

Sam Huff

Sam Huff came to the New York Giants in 1956 as a two-way tackle from the University of West Virginia; he was a third-round draft choice that year. Defensive coach Tom Landry, looking at the 6'1", 230-pound Huff, wisely converted him to a middle linebacker. Huff quickly established himself as the best in the league at that position. He won the starting job as a rookie and added a new dimension to the position during his eight years in New York. Never had the Giants had such a hard-hitting, aggressive, instinctive linebacker. His head-to-head collisions on the field with running backs such as Jim Brown and Jim Taylor reverberated throughout NFL stadiums.

While the Giants' front four of Andy Robustelli, Rosie Grier, Dick Modzelewski, and Jim Katcavage dismantled offensive lines, Huff moved in for the kill on running backs of all sizes. He was such a devastating tackler and so visible on the field of play that CBS television made a documentary in 1960 entitled "The Violent World of Sam Huff." In it, he was wired with a microphone, which enabled a national television audience to hear firsthand the brutal impact when body meets body in the NFL trenches. The program also drew widespread and unprecedented attention to the defensive side of football.

In his eight years with the Giants, Huff played in six NFL championship games. He went to five Pro Bowls and was named the outstanding defensive player in one (1961). The Pro Football Hall of Fame Selection Committee named him to the All-Pro Squad of the 1950s, along with fellow linebackers and future Hall of Famers Joe Schmidt of the Lions and Bill George of the Bears.

To the surprise of New York Giants fans and the chagrin of Sam Huff, he was traded to the Washington Redskins after the 1963 season. He played in Washington for five years, the last under Vince Lombardi, who had been an assistant coach with the Giants when Huff first arrived in New York.

Sam Huff was inducted into the Pro Football Hall of Fame in 1982. His presenter at the ceremony in Canton, Ohio, was Tom Landry, the defensive coach of the Giants in the 1950s who helped mold him into one of the best linebackers the game had yet seen.

After football, Huff went to work for the Marriott chain of hotels, where today he serves as vice president of special marketing, residing in the Washington, D.C., area.

Football has been a part of my life for about as long as I can remember. I was born in a little coal-mining town named Edna Gas, just outside of Morgantown, West Virginia. It was a company town, and it no longer exists. I started playing football when I was in grade school there, and we had some organized games. Then I went to a Class B high school in Farmington, a little town of about seven hundred people, and that's where I really started playing the game—that was in seventh grade. In those days, the seventh and eighth grades were in the same building as the high school. As a freshman, I dressed for the varsity, and as a sophomore I became a starter.

The University of West Virginia recruited me when I was a senior. Art Lewis was the head coach there then, and he came and talked to me about coming to West Virginia. He came to our house and to the high school; he was very professional about recruiting. However, the first to talk to me was an assistant coach, Harold "Toad" Lahr, who left shortly thereafter to take the head coaching job at Colgate.

Both the University of Florida and Army were also interested, and I visited both campuses. Florida, in Gainesville, was really nice. You had to like it there with the weather, the palm trees—especially coming from West Virginia. But I really wanted to go to West Virginia, which is in Morgantown—that was always my dream.

I played both ways in college—offensive and defensive tackle. I didn't switch to linebacker until I got with the Giants. They thought I was too small to play tackle in the pros, and rightly so.

I was really surprised that the Giants drafted me. They were one of the few NFL teams I hadn't heard from. Almost all the others at least wrote me a letter, but not the Giants. So it surprised the hell out of me when they called and said they'd taken me in the third round [of the 1956 NFL draft].

Wellington Mara was the first to contact me. He called me down in West Virginia, told me about the draft, and said he wanted me to come up to New York. And he was the person I dealt with in regard to a contract. We didn't have agents in those days, so you had to handle the negotiations yourself; needless to say, the teams had the advantage.

When we met in New York, he said, "We'd like to sign you to a contract as soon as possible."

I said, "How much?"

"Seven thousand dollars," he said.

"That sounds good," I said, "but I promised Coach Lewis that I wouldn't sign any contract without consulting with him."

He said, "That's no problem. Why don't you call him from here?"

So I did. And coach Lewis said, "They're going to pay you $7,000 for playing? That's like stealing. Wow, $7,000 for playing football! You sign that contract!"

I signed it, and then Wellington Mara asked me if I needed any money right then. And I said I did, I could really use $500 to pay off my furniture. So he wrote me a check. When I got my first paycheck, which was after the first regular-season game, the $500 was deducted. I thought it was a bonus, but I found it was an "advancement." They had signing bonuses back then, but I didn't get one. Gifford and Tittle got them, I believe.

The owners essentially knew what they could get away with in those days, and they took advantage of it—all of them did it; that's just the way it was. You even had to come to training camp with your own shoes. The team wouldn't buy any for you.

We won the league championship that year [1956]— destroyed the Chicago Bears in the title game, 47-7. I was named the NFL's Defensive Rookie of the Year. And Wellington Mara offered me a five-hundred-dollar raise for the next year.

The NFL Players Association exists today because back then it was so one-sided. As a player, you hardly had a chance; you were not even allowed to talk to a lawyer. It was a true monopoly. There was no such thing as hospitalization programs—if you got hurt you only got paid what was in your contract; there were no guarantees of anything.

There were only twelve teams in the league [in 1956] and therefore there weren't a lot of places to go if you wanted to play professional football. Only about thirty-three guys on a team—they had a death grip on you. If you were going to play, you were going to play for what they wanted to give you. And that's why in the 1950s the Players Association was started.

It's hard for a lot of the older ballplayers to understand the ballplayers of today—guys making millions of dollars who have agents and business managers and attorneys. Take a linebacker today—a good one is making a million, maybe a million and a half a year, and he only plays on first down, doesn't play on second down or third down. Back in the '50s you played on all four downs. I'm not saying the guys shouldn't get it; if the team wants to pay it, I say great. We were just there at the wrong time. Hell, when I was on the cover of *Time* magazine, I was making $9,000 a year playing football.

Tom Landry was the defensive coordinator when I got there. He was a marvelous man. Tom and Vince Lombardi were both there; they were two of the finest men that I ever met. I learned something from them—I learned what makes coaches great: one word—credibility.

[Dolphins coach Don] Shula has credibility. [Redskins coach Joe] Gibbs has it. Only a handful of coaches have credibility. And those who don't have it are basically a bunch of losers because they lose the respect of their football team. And once you lose the respect of that team you never gain it back. Landry and Lombardi always had the respect of their ballplayers.

When I came to the Giants, my good friend Don Chandler, who I played in the College All-Star game with, came too. He was a great punter, and we were roommates until they traded me to Washington eight years later. They traded him to Green Bay the year after they traded me. I remember he was so upset that they traded me, he made it clear they had to trade him too.

All of us on defense were close. We got along, went around together, all of us: Robustelli, Grier, Modzelewski, Katcavage. It's like a platoon in the army—you live together, fight together, depend on each other. That's what it's all about.

That was a great year, that first one [1956]. I'd always been with a winning organization—high school, West Virginia University. We beat Penn State three years in a row; no college ever did that before. And so I was just used to it. I felt that that's the way things were supposed to be, so it didn't really surprise me when we just kept winning that year. As it turned out, though, that was the only championship team I ever played on. In my eight years with the Giants, we played in six NFL championship games, but we only won that one in '56.

In those days, it was truly the two best teams who met

for the title. There were only twelve teams then, and routinely you got the two best football teams in the league to face each other in the championship game. That isn't necessarily true today. You've got twenty-eight teams and often it is *not* the best two who match up in the Super Bowl.

The Bears and the Giants were truly the two best teams in the NFL in 1956, however. We had a superior football team, I felt, and we were playing in Yankee Stadium. We had a lot of advantages. The field was frozen that day, but it didn't affect them any more than it did us. What the hell, look where they were coming from—Chicago. They were used to cold weather and icy fields. We wore sneakers that day, but so did the Bears.

We had everything going right from the start; they had everything going wrong. We just controlled the game. They couldn't stop us, and we stopped them flat. Hell, the only touchdown they got was when [Emlen] Tunnell fumbled a punt return [on the Giants' 25-yard line]. We were up by like four touchdowns at the half [the Giants actually scored four touchdowns and two field goals in the first half to lead 34-7]. The final score was 47-7.

Don't get me wrong—the Bears were a fine team, but they weren't that particular day.

We had another good year in 1958. In fact, I'd say the 1958 and 1959 teams were as good as any football team that ever played in New York. The unfortunate part is those were the greatest teams they ever had in Baltimore, too. Some people feel the Colts of that time were the greatest football team ever to play in the NFL. They had four Hall of Famers on their offensive team alone—Johnny Unitas, Raymond Berry, Lenny Moore, and Jim Parker—and two more on the defensive unit—Gino Marchetti and Art Donovan. And they also had guys like [Alan] Ameche and Big Daddy Lipscomb.

They beat us in '58, but it was in overtime, sudden death. We were winning by 3 points with about two minutes left; that's when Unitas took them about 85 yards and they got a field goal to tie us. There were only seven seconds left when they kicked that field goal. They had the momentum then, and Unitas drove them down the field again in overtime, and they beat us [23–17]. They were a better team than us at the end of that game; that's all there was to it. The difference was Johnny Unitas.

We had to play some very good football to get to those two championship games in '58 and '59. We had to beat out the Browns, and they had a very good team, what with Jimmy Brown and Bobby Mitchell and players like that. And, of course, Paul Brown was one of the most highly regarded coaches in the league. But we beat them three times in 1958, one of them a playoff game. We were a better team, though. They built their whole offense around Jim Brown, but we shut him down. [Defensive coach Tom] Landry had analyzed them perfectly; we simply stopped Brown and therefore shut down their offense. They had a great placekicker, Lou Groza, but so did we—Pat Summerall. Pat kicked that field goal in a snowstorm to win one of those games that year, probably the greatest kick I ever saw. And we beat them both times we played in 1959, the second time by a huge score [48–7].

I got myself up for every game, not just the big ones. It was just a natural competitive spirit—I think we all had it on the Giants' defense. We put those helmets on and we could feel the challenge. Defense is especially a game of mental attitude—desire and determination, that's what makes the difference. When I went out on that football field, it was the greatest feeling. I played the game for me because I loved the game, I loved to practice. I believe it's America's game and nobody plays it like we do. Some coaches even said to me, "You're a sick man." I said, "Why?" They said, "Because you love it to be hot, you love it to be cold, you love lousy conditions, you love it to be miserable, you love misery." But football was never misery to me. It never got too cold to play, it never got too hot. We didn't care about mud or rain or snow. Hell, just strap it on and let's go out there and play—that's the way we felt. We didn't have any heaters on the sideline, oxygen masks, things like that.

I was broadcasting a ball game not too long ago, and I'd heard the Redskins had some ballplayers who were not considered "cold-weather" ballplayers. Out in Green Bay that day it was *so* cold—one of the coaches shook his head and said to me a couple of the Redskins were so wrapped around the heater it looked like they were making love to it.

Speaking of Green Bay, they had a great team under Lombardi. They also had one guy I loved to hit and that was [fullback] Jim Taylor. He was a ferocious ballplayer. It's interesting how an offensive guy is never considered ferocious, but defensive players are. Well, that just isn't the case. A guy like Taylor is every bit as competitive and vicious as a defensive player. We really went at it. I remember denting my helmet hitting that sucker.

People often say, "But you were still friends?" When were you friends with Taylor when he was playing against you? Did Taylor have any friends? Did [Bears linebacker Dick] Butkus have any friends? Did [Packers linebacker Ray] Nitschke have any friends? Linebackers don't make friends very easily.

Actually, the 1961 and 1962 Green Bay Packers were as good as any team ever put together. We lost two championship games to them those years. They really beat up on us in the first one [37–0]—that's when Paul Hornung had a really great day. He scored nineteen points himself. The next year at Yankee Stadium I think we should have won. We held them to sixteen points, we outgained them by about fifty yards, but we couldn't score. We got our only touchdown when Erich Barnes blocked a punt and we recovered it in Green Bay's end zone.

Two of the best teams ever to play the game—the Colts and the Packers—beat us four out of the six championship games I played in. It was very frustrating. We had a team that ranked right along with them, but we lost. You lose, you don't get the money, you don't get the ring, you don't get the recognition. They may have been great teams, but, believe me, there is no pride in losing.

The last championship game I played in we lost too. That was in 1963 against the Bears. What I remember most about that game was that the Bears never crossed the 50-yard line offensively. Our offense turned the ball over to them seven times in that game. Two of the turnovers—interceptions—set up their two touchdowns, both on quarterback sneaks by Billy Wade. We outgained them, we got more first downs than them; we just didn't get more points.

The Bears, I believe, were a very inferior team to us that year. In that game, they were one of the luckiest teams that ever played the game. Granted, they had a great defense—they gave up only a little over 10 points a game in the regular season. But so were we, and we had a better offense than they did. Y. A. Tittle was hurt, and that was what caused a lot of the turnovers. He just couldn't move or maneuver like he normally could, and so he had to get rid of the ball quicker than I'm sure he wanted to on various plays.

At halftime we were leading 10–7, and I said to Tittle, "Y.A., *don't* play anymore and we got 'em." I was sure our defense could shut them out. But he said, "I've gotta play. This may be the only chance I ever have to win an NFL world championship game."

I said, "Stay out!" But he didn't, and the coaches played him. He threw another interception deep in our own territory and they snuck it in and that was it [final score: 14–10, Bears].

And who did our coach, Allie Sherman, blame? The defense. He traded it away the next year. He traded me to the Redskins. He traded Dick Modzelewski to the Steelers. He traded Erich Barnes to the Browns. Rosie Grier was already gone to the Rams on a trade.

Guess what happened then? The Giants were 2–10–2 in 1964 and went in one year from first place in the Eastern Conference to last place. They went to the outhouse in one short jump.

It isn't pretty down there on the field, as reflected in this portrait of the Giants' Sam Huff. The great middle linebacker toiled in the trenches for the Giants from 1956 through 1963. He was elected to the Pro Football Hall of Fame in 1982.

I was very ticked off about the trade. Still am. I make no bones about it. When you do that—trade away your defense, your strong point, and your team comes up winning only two games after it—you deserve to be fired as a coach. Wellington Mara—and I love Wellington Mara—instead gave him a ten-year contract. He said it wasn't Allie's fault. The hell it wasn't.

It just came as a helluva surprise. I was twenty-nine years old. In eight years with the Giants, I'd never missed a game. And the next thing I know I'm on my way to Washington.

But I was able to get even with Allie. Nineteen sixty-six—a day of infamy. I predicted the outcome of that game, live, on the radio, over WNEW in New York. Before the game, I said to Kyle Rote, who was broadcasting the Giants' games then, that we would score *over 60 points*. I said this is a day of reckoning for Allie Sherman, who traded away the best defense the Giants ever had.

I had watched the films of the game two weeks earlier

when they played the Los Angeles Rams in L.A. and the Rams scored 55 points. It was absolutely the worst defense [the Giants'] I'd seen. The Giants gave up the most points in their history that year [501, an average of almost 36 points a game]. And we had Sonny Jurgensen at quarterback and receivers like Charley Taylor and Bobby Mitchell and Jerry Smith. We had a hell of an offense—a scoring machine—and I just knew we were going to annihilate them.

Well, as it turned out, I was right in what I told Kyle. We did score more than 60 points—we scored 72, the most ever in an NFL regular-season game. That record still stands today.

After the game, I couldn't have been happier. It's not that I didn't like the Giants. I love the Giants—I still do to this day. It was Allie Sherman, who traded me, traded away the rest of the defense. He's not my favorite person, and he knows that. And he doesn't like me either. I just felt good that he got what he had coming that day in Washington [final score: 72–41, Redskins].

I guess what I loved most about the game was tackling. I loved going up against guys like Jimmy Brown and Jim Taylor. I'd look across the line of scrimmage and I'd see those guys in the backfield, and I knew they were going to get the ball. That was the challenge—I was going to get the chance to hit them. They were great and powerful, and they were the ultimate challenge for me. I loved it.

I retired in 1967, and that was a helluva difficult decision. It wasn't that I wanted to. It was very frustrating down in Washington under Otto Graham. I don't think Otto really liked coaching. Otto is a great guy—there is no finer man than he—but I think he really would have preferred playing golf or tennis to coaching football. In that, I don't think he had everything quite straight. He said one time to me, "You know, every time I say practice is over, you're one of the first ones into the locker room. From now on, when I say practice is over, you don't leave the football field."

"Why?" I said.

"Well, because I want you to stay out like the other guys and work on your specialties."

I said, "If I played eleven years, what would you think my specialty is?"

He said, "I don't know, but when I say practice is over, don't leave the field."

I said, "Do you want me to find something to do? Is that it?"

So, I stayed out there with Charlie Gogolak, our kicker—he only practiced five minutes a day. Our center, Len Hauss, would snap the ball back to the holder, and Gogolak would kick it; another player would catch the kick and throw it back to me, and I would hand it to Len Hauss. That was my specialty—after practice—catching the throw-back and handing it to Hauss. But it made Otto happy. What he really meant when he said practice was over was not that practice was over; he meant that portion of practice was over and now everyone should stay out and work on their own.

So I just finally said, I'm out of here.

I went back to New York and worked for a textile company. But then the following year Vince Lombardi took over as head coach of the Redskins, and he asked me to come back down there. I really wanted to play for Lombardi, so I signed on in 1969 as a player-coach.

Lombardi turned it around in a year. The Skins were 5-9-0 in Otto's last year [1968], and Lombardi got them up to 7-5-2 the next. But, of course, he died of cancer before the next season.

It was really a difficult thing being both a player and a coach at the same time. On one hand, you have to do everything a coach does; and on the other, you have to do everything a player does. You're kind of caught right in between. I wouldn't recommend it to anybody. I would never do it again. And under Lombardi you had to do every single thing right. He worked you to death in training camp. After a morning session, you wondered how in hell you would get through the afternoon session. He was so different in his football philosophy and his approach to conditioning than Otto Graham. Lombardi was my kind of coach. He made you feel like a team, and you all thought he was God and you were his disciples.

After he died, I coached one more year under Bill Austin in Washington and then I got out of the game. Actually, Austin got fired and all of us [assistant coaches] got fired along with him. It was okay—I was ready to get out of football, anyway. Edward Bennett Williams, the owner, wanted somebody with a name, so he hired George Allen away from the Rams. Allen came to Washington and brought practically his whole team—especially the defense, which was his specialty. Hell, he even brought his secretary, towel boys, everybody. He had that philosophy: the future is now! It was a good time to look at the rest of my life, put football aside, and see what else was out there in the world.

So, after 1969 I went with the Marriott hotels, and I've been with them ever since, although I still stay in touch with football from the broadcast booth. It's a wonderful sport, and I loved every minute of it when I was on the field.

◻

Thanks for a Late Plane

One of the most often told tales among Giants nostalgics concerns a pair of twenty-one-year-old disheartened rookies in 1956—linebacker Sam Huff and punter Don Chandler, whose professional careers almost ended before they ever began.

Huff, a third-round draft choice, and Chandler, a fifth-rounder, were not happy with the way things were going at the Giants' training camp up at St. Michael's College in Winooski, Vermont. Huff had played tackle at West Virginia, but, at 6'1" and 230 pounds, he was considered too small for that position in the pros. The rumor that a few of the coaches thought he was too slow for any other position got back to him, and he was, in his words, "disheartened, miserable, and homesick." Chandler was suffering from an injured shoulder and not doing well in camp and therefore was often the butt of Jim Lee Howell's "bellering," as the players called the coach's remonstrations.

One day after workouts, the two decided it was hopeless and that they might as well go home. Line coach Ed Kolman heard about the situation and cornered Huff. "You'll never forgive yourself if you leave now," he told him. "You'll feel like a quitter."

Huff shook his head. "It's not working out. I'm just wasting my time here."

"I've seen some great ones," Kolman said. "And I think if you stick it out you could be one of them in a few years. You've got talent, and I mean it. Don't throw it away by leaving."

The vote of confidence was enough to persuade Huff to stay, but when the linebacker tried to talk Chandler out of departing, he couldn't. So Huff agreed to accompany his friend to the airport in Burlington, Vermont. What happened there is described by Don Smith, former publicity chief of the Giants, in a book he wrote in 1960.

> There they were informed that Chandler's flight would be late. It might be an hour or more before he could leave. The players drifted into the hot waiting room and plopped down on a bench. As the minutes

ticked by, Huff began to wonder if he had made the right decision; whether or not he should get his bags and join Chandler as they had originally planned. Despite Kolman's comforting words, Sam was losing his confidence again.

Just then a station wagon roared up to the terminal and out bolted [then Giants assistant coach Vince] Lombardi. He dashed through the waiting room and pursued Chandler almost to the revved-up plane, which had just taxied up to the passenger gate.

"Hold on," Lombardi shouted in a voice that was disturbingly familiar to all Giant rookies. "You may not make this ball club, Chandler, but you're sure as hell not quitting on me now. And neither are you, Huff, in case you've got any idea about running out." With that he packed the rookies into the station wagon and delivered them back to camp.

"If that plane had been on time," Huff recalls, "Chandler would have been on it. And maybe I would have gone with him."

Tom Landry

Tom Landry is surely best remembered as the jut-jawed, stone-faced coach who revealed neither a smile or a scowl as he paced the sidelines those twenty-nine years with the Dallas Cowboys, an era in which he established himself as one of the greatest NFL coaches in history.

But he was also an integral part of the New York Giants, and his tenure there as both player and defensive coach in the 1950s was instrumental in the development of his coaching career.

Football had always been a major part of Tom Landry's life. Born and raised in Mission, Texas, a small town near the Mexican border, he played fullback on a team there that during his senior year went both unbeaten and unscored upon, defeating their opponents by a collective score of 322 to 0.

After a semester at the University of Texas, he joined the U.S. Army Air Corps and, as a copilot of a B-17 bomber in World War II, eventually flew thirty missions over German-occupied Europe and survived one crash landing. When asked about his wartime experiences, with characteristic underplay he told his biographer, Bob St. John, "Oh, we got a few holes in our bomber every once in a while, but nothing much happened really."

After the war, he returned to the University of Texas and resumed his football career as a defensive back and as a backup to All-American quarterback Bobby Layne.

With a college diploma in hand, Landry matriculated to the pros in 1949, signing with the New York Yankees of the All-America Football Conference. After the demise of the AAFC the following year, he joined the New York Giants in the NFL, which would be his home as both a player and coach throughout the 1950s.

Landry started as defensive left halfback for the Giants from 1950 through 1955. He became a player-coach, handling the defense, after Jim Lee Howell took over as head coach of the Giants in 1954. Vince Lombardi was hired to handle the offense. The tandem of Landry and Lombardi stands as the greatest assistant-coaching partnership in the history of the NFL.

The innovative Landry defenses, carried out by such stellar players as Emlen Tunnell, Andy Robustelli, Sam Huff, Rosie Grier, and a host of other talents, were a major part of the Giants' successes in the last half of the 1950s. In the last four years (1956–59) of Landry's coaching career with the Giants, the club won the Eastern Conference title three times and the national championship once (1956).

As a defensive back, Landry ranks sixth in the Giants' record book in pass interceptions, snaring 31 and returning 3 of them for touchdowns. He was also known as one of the smartest, most instinctive defensive backs of his time.

Landry, of course, went on to greater fame in Dallas. With the Cowboys—their only coach from the club's birth in 1960 until he left twenty-nine years later—he won 270 regular-season games against 178 defeats and 6 ties. He took the Cowboys to five Super Bowls, two in which they triumphed: Super Bowl VI, 24–3 over the Miami Dolphins, and Super Bowl XII, 27–10 over the Denver Broncos.

The third-winningest coach in NFL history, behind only George Halas and Don Shula, Tom Landry was enshrined in the Pro Football Hall of Fame in 1990, his first year of eligibility.

Today, out of football—at least actively (Tom Landry could never be divorced from the game of football)—he devotes his time to a variety of charitable interests and works with his son in Dallas at their company, Landry Investments Group.

I t was in the summer of 1950 when I officially joined the Giants. I was twenty-five years old at the time, a little old for a rookie in the NFL, but there were several things that had come up before my entering the NFL.

I had attended the University of Texas after playing football in high school down in south Texas along the border there, a town called Mission. There was an oilman in our town who was a Texas U. graduate, and he was the one who got me an interview with the university.

In those days, D. X. Bible [also known as Dana Xenophon Bible] was the coach there, and they had a tremendous program under him. That was around 1941 and 1942. They were anticipating a national championship in 1941, and *Life* magazine featured them in a big article as the nation's top team. After that they lost three games.

I came there the next year, and D. X. Bible was still the coach. I played in 1942 but then I went into the Army Air Corps in February 1943. I came back and reentered school at the university in the spring of 1945. So my sophomore year was actually the 1946 season. That, as it turned out, was D. X. Bible's last year—he had actually been coaching in the college ranks since 1913.

When I came up into the varsity that year, we were playing D. X. Bible's single wing and I was pegged at fullback and defensive back. The next year Blair Cherry took over as head coach, and he moved me into a quarterback position behind Bobby Layne. So I played first-string defensive back and second-string quarterback. But I busted up the thumb on my right hand and the joint kind of froze up on me, so I couldn't play quarterback anymore. Coach Cherry moved me back to fullback then. But let's face it—nobody was going to beat out Bobby Layne at quarterback.

We didn't think much about pro football in those days. There weren't any teams in the South or Southwest. They were all in the East and the Midwest back then. In fact, the only information we ever got about the pros in Texas was maybe a filler in the sports pages, maybe something as a trailer at the bottom of a big story about a college game.

On the other hand, baseball we followed all the time. And my team had always been the New York Yankees. Again, we didn't have major-league baseball anywhere in the South or Southwest then either. The Yankees were such a wonderful, winning team, however—excellence was the only word to describe them. So I was always rooting for them.

Then, in the All-America Football Conference, there was another Yankees team, owned by Dan Topping, who also owned the baseball Yankees. That team I had heard about. There were some ballplayers who had gone up from Texas to play for the Yankees in the AAFC: Jack Russell from Baylor, Martin Ruby from Texas A&M, Pete Layden from Texas, and Bruce Alford from TCU. We had heard about them. So it was just a natural for me to take on with the Yankees, which I did, in 1949. At the time, I didn't know anything about the Giants in New York and had never heard from them. So, I just said what the heck and signed with the Yankees.

I remember I started out playing offensive halfback for the Yankees, and backup defensive back to Harmon Rowe. Then in the second game of the year Harmon got hurt, and they put me at defensive right half. Well, we were playing the Cleveland Browns and I had to cover Mac Speedie that day, and he set an All-America Conference record for yardage on pass receptions. He turned me every way but loose. That's when I got the sudden message I had to learn how to key on offenses and know what they were going to do before they snapped the ball. It was quite an initiation.

Well, the AAFC went out of business after the '49 season. And the way the thing worked was that the Maras, the family who owned the Giants, had territorial rights to New York City in the NFL.

Dan Topping gave up his AAFC franchise and so our Yankees team was gone. There was another Yankees team the NFL allowed to be brought down from Boston which was owned by the singer Kate Smith and her agent [Ted Collins]. But with the NFL territorial rights in the hands of the Giants, to keep them happy the Maras were allowed to pick six or so players from Topping's Yankees. I remember they took almost all defensive players—Arnie Weinmeister, Otto Schnellbacher, Harmon Rowe, me. I think they took only one offensive player.

The Giants weren't nearly as flamboyant as the Yankees had been. The Giants were in an older league, well entrenched; you could just feel it. Topping's Yankees had been much more free-spirited in the way in which they were run. There was much more freedom in the upstart league. But you knew with the Giants this team was going to be around for a long, long time. It was an exceptionally well-run organization, and everyone inside was dedicated to making it work.

Steve Owen was my coach when I signed on with the Giants, and he was a dedicated coach. He'd been there since the 1920s, an old-line coach who had foremost in his mind the motivation of his players—get them fired up and send them roaring out onto the field. Like in the old Rockne speech: "Go out and win this one for the Gipper."

Steve was like most of the coaches in the NFL in those days—besides motivating the players the emphasis was on a sound defense and not a lot of attention was paid to detail. It wasn't a precision type of football, which is what the game was just emerging into. Paul Brown, over at Cleveland in the AAFC, had launched that, and it was to become the wave of our future in the NFL.

I remember when the Browns came into the league everyone was saying, "Well, the NFL will show them!" Well, they didn't. Cleveland's first game in the NFL was against the Eagles, who were a very good team and the defending NFL champ. With guys like Steve Van Buren, Pete Pihos, and Tommy Thompson, the Eagles were going to show this AAFC team. Well, the Browns beat the hell out of them [35–10].

At any rate, the help the Giants got from the Yankees on defense really shaped the team in 1950, and we won ten of our twelve games that year.

I remember the first time we faced Cleveland that year. At that time in the NFL almost all defenses were a 5-3 type [five men on the line, three linebackers, three defensive backs]. Steve came in early in the season and said we're going to play a 6-1 defense. Well, all of us looked at each other and wondered what was going on; what kind of defense was a 6-1?

It was the beginning of the umbrella defense Steve had invented—one we would use pretty effectively for a couple of years. We had six men on the line and just one line-backer, who was John Cannady—a big, tough guy who would line up like a middle linebacker today—and four defensive backs in an arc, or umbrella shape, behind him.

"We're going to vary it," Owen said. "On one down, we're going to bunch up and the six linemen are going to rush them. On the next down we're going to send the ends out in the flat, and the next we're going to bring them back against the run or the hook." And that's really all he told us.

Teams had only a few assistant coaches in those days—I think we had three. So that's how I really started coaching. I was playing left defensive halfback, and I thought someone really had to coordinate us back there. I mean, if the end moved out into the flat, I had to know where I was going and where Em Tunnell was going to go, and so on. So I kind of just took it upon myself at practice to direct a lot of things.

I remember when we went into the meeting before the game over in Cleveland, which was our second of the year. Steve got up before the blackboard and started talking about the defense we were going to use and then said, "Here, Tom, show 'em what we want to do." And here I'm a player, and I didn't hardly know what to do, but I got up there and did what I could.

Well, the umbrella worked. We shut out the Browns 6-0 that day, and that was a team that featured Otto Graham and his great receivers Dante Lavelli and Mac Speedie and fullback Marion Motley and halfback Dub Jones and kicker Lou Groza. They would average over 30 points a game that year. It was unheard of to shut out the Browns [the Browns had never been shut out during their four years in the AAFC and, in fact, would not be again until the Eastern Conference playoff game of 1958, when the Giants would once again shut them out, this time 10-0].

We beat them a second time in 1950, this one at the Polo Grounds. In this game, Steve switched the umbrella to a 5-1-5. We had five linemen rushing all the time and Cannady keying on their big fullback, Motley, and five defensive backs out there. Again it confused Paul Brown, because he was so precise in his preparation and he wasn't expecting this. We won 17-13. Those were the only two losses Cleveland suffered that year.

Well, we only lost two games in the regular season too. So we met the Browns in a conference playoff game. It was on a very icy field in Cleveland, and a very windy day. This time they won—the score was 8-3. It was a great defensive game, and they didn't win it until there was less than a minute left—Lou Groza kicked a field goal to break a 3-3 tie, and then they got a safety which didn't really matter. Actually, we should have won it because Charlie Conerly threw a touchdown pass to our end, Kelly Mote, in the fourth quarter, but he was ruled offside and the touchdown was called back.

We had some really top-flight defensive players that year. We could do almost anything we wanted to because we were so talented at each position. Besides Arnie Weinmeister and Otto Schnellbacher and Harmon Rowe, who came from the Yankees, we had John Cannady, Ray Poole, and Al DeRogatis and, of course, Emlen Tunnell. [The Giants of 1950 gave up a total of 150 points, an average of only 12.5 per game.]

I was a straight defensive player my entire career in pro football, except for one instance—actually two instances. It was in 1952, the year we were getting beaten up pretty bad—physically, that is. Charlie Conerly was our quarterback and Freddie Benners, who had played down at Southern Methodist with Kyle Rote, was our backup. In this one terrible game near the end of the season, against the Pittsburgh Steelers, Conerly had to leave the game because of a shoulder injury. Then Benners got knocked out of the game in the second quarter. The Giants didn't have anybody else, so they sent me in because I was the only one who could legitimately take a snap, having played quarterback for a while at Texas in college. Steve Owen said, "Okay, you're the quarterback." So I just went in. They didn't send in any plays. I was just lucky because we were playing at Pittsburgh and the field there was mostly dirt, so I could draw the plays on the ground with my finger. I'd just draw where I wanted the receivers to go and they'd shrug and go off and try to get there. I finished the rest of the game, but by the time I got in it didn't really matter because we were losing something like 35–0 [the Giants ended up losing 63–7].

I quarterbacked again the next week against the Redskins, and it wasn't quite so bad. We lost 27–17. That game we played at home, and when we got there we couldn't get on the field—we had to scrape the snow off just to get into the Polo Grounds. But that was the extent of my offensive play in the NFL. I was much more comfortable playing defense, as I think you could imagine after my 1952 experiences. Charlie Conerly's job was never in jeopardy.

A truly great team around that time and one that really put the test to defensive backs was the Los Angeles Rams, with Bob Waterfield and Norm Van Brocklin and Elroy Hirsch and Tom Fears—all four of them are in the Hall of Fame, and deservedly so. That group was like the run-and-shoot today. With Waterfield throwing short or Van Brocklin throwing long and Hirsch and Fears always there to catch the ball—plus, they threw to backs coming out of the backfield—they were something special. The Rams and the Browns were the two most difficult teams to try and handle in those days.

I got into coaching on a formal basis after Steve Owen was released. His replacement, Jim Lee Howell, took over

Tom Landry, toting the ball here, played defensive back for the Giants from 1950 through 1955 and was acknowledged as one of the finest in the league. He was named All-Pro in 1954. Landry served as player–defensive coach in 1954 and 1955 and as full-time defensive coordinator from 1956 through 1959 before leaving to take over the head coaching duties at the newly enfranchised Dallas Cowboys in 1960.

in 1954. He had been coaching at Wagner College over on Staten Island, and he had also been coming over afternoons to coach our ends.

Jim Lee didn't really want a head-coaching job. They went back and forth a bit, and finally he said he would take the job if they put me on as defensive coach and let him hire another coach for the offense. They agreed. So Jim Lee then got Vince [Lombardi] from Army, and from that point on Vince and I coached side by side, even though I was still playing at the time.

I had complete responsibility for the defense, and that wasn't all that easy because there weren't any other assistants to help. There was Ed Kolman, who handled the offensive line, and Ken Kavanaugh, who was brought in to coach the receivers; but that was about it, as I remember. I'd practice with the defense but at the same time coach them.

One must remember that in those days football was a fairly simple game. We had maybe a couple of offensive formations, a couple of defensive changes. That's all we had. So we didn't spend a lot of time like the staffs do today. We would come in and practice in the morning, and then the coaches would meet right after lunch; then most would go home. In 1954, however, I would keep the defense there in the afternoon. I was devising the 4-3 defense at the time, and it was a new concept that needed additional work from the players. That new defense took a lot of time, and so we were always there late after the offense had already gone home. I don't think the players really liked it too much, but that's the way it was.

We got the 4-3 installed and were using it, but we didn't get to be a really good defense until 1956, when we got Robustelli, Huff, Modzelewski, and Katcavage. We'd gotten Rosie Grier the year before. Now we really had the talent and, of course, it showed; we won the NFL championship that year.

I had such a wealth of defensive talent to work with in those years between 1956 and 1960, the year I left to go to

Dallas. As good as they were, I shouldn't forget Arnie Weinmeister, who played with me before that era. Arnie came to the Giants from the Yankees with me in 1950. He was such a devastating player. When he played for us, he was our left defensive end in the 6-1 defense. He pretty well controlled the entire left side of the defensive line. He was so fast he could outrun almost every player on our team. And he was about 245 pounds, which was big in those days. A natural player—a tremendous player, in fact—but he just couldn't ever get along with the Maras all that well. He was always having arguments about salary. Of course, he ended up after football in the union business on the West Coast, and the Giants, I think, gave him a good background in negotiating things like salary contracts.

Emlen Tunnell was, of course, there around the same time. He came as a walk-on and walked his way into the Hall of Fame. I played side by side with Emlen. I was the left corner and he was the left safety. He was a very talented football player. He never really played the defensive position exactly the way I liked to see it played. I used to kind of look at him when the ball was snapped to see where he was going. Then I had to quick figure out where I was going. He was exceptional at playing the ball—that's why he was such a great interception man in the secondary. He was also such a great return man. Emlen was truly an All-Pro.

Then in 1956 we got Andy Robustelli, a wonderful defensive end. The thing about Andy was that he was such a smart player. The thing that made our teams later on, when we were using the 4-3 defense, was that we had players who really worked together. They didn't just worry about their own jobs—they were concerned about taking care of the team. They all worked together. The nature of our defense demanded very disciplined football players. And the one who so often pulled them all together, kept them together, was Andy Robustelli. He was a natural team leader on the field. It was because he was so smart. He always took such good advantage of the keys we used.

Then there was Sam Huff, who came to us in the draft as a tackle—played that both ways at West Virginia in college. He was a little on the small side, and I made him a middle linebacker. Since our defenses were so simple in those days, it was easy to convert him even with his lack of experience in the pros. And he became a great one. After I left, the 4-3 was changed and he had to go up against Vince's Packers. By that time, however, he was an excellent player who could do so many things on his own. He was also a very, very tough player, a tough competitor.

Rosie Grier was the most likeable guy I had ever seen. He was also a giant of a player, about 6'5", an easy 275 pounds. He had great spirit on and off the field. I remember when we used to have training camp out in Salem, Oregon, and at the end of the day when everyone was really tired he would play the piano for everybody after dinner. He wasn't just big and strong—he had an instinctive football talent.

Jim Katcavage came in 1956 too. Jim was a good disciplined player, a great team player. He and Dick Modzelewski played the left side of the line—Katcavage at end and Mo at tackle. They really worked together so well.

In 1959, we got Dick Lynch. He'd played at Notre Dame. There was only one Dick Lynch. Very talented. The hardest thing I had to do was get him to concentrate on the receiver and not on the quarterback. As it was, he could cover just about anybody. Once I could get him to discipline himself he could go up against anybody. He could stay right with a Raymond Berry or somebody as fast and elusive as that—if he would just keep his eyes on the receiver and break with him. He was a real gambler as a defensive back and made a lot of great plays.

There were so many good ones there in that 4-3 defense. Dick Nolan was an excellent defensive back. He later coached for me for many years down in Dallas and then went on to become a head coach for the 49ers and later the New Orleans Saints. Another excellent defensive back was Jimmy Patton. There were also Harland Svare and Cliff Livingston, a couple of fine linebackers. There was a lot of defensive talent on those Giants teams of the late '50s.

It was something to coach with Vince during that time too. There was no stronger disciplinarian than Vince Lombardi. He demanded so much from people. He was that way in New York, and he'd become even more famous for it when he moved on to Green Bay. I used to call him "Mr. High-Low." I tell you, when his offense did well he was sky high; but, boy, when they didn't do well, you couldn't speak to him. None of us could—maybe not for two or three days. He was such a competitor. The best thing that could have happened to him was to get the job at Green Bay. Vince needed to run the whole show, and when he got the opportunity he showed how successful he could be.

I stopped playing after the 1955 season. The next year I just coached, and that was the year we beat the Bears for the NFL championship [47–7]. And I will say both our defense and offense were superb that day. I stayed on as defensive coordinator for three more years.

In the off-season, I was living in Dallas. I'd moved there in 1955. I was very familiar with the people who were starting up the Dallas Cowboys—Clint Murchison, the owner, and Tex Schramm, who was going to run it for him. I believe it was Clint and some others behind the team down there in Dallas who got Tex to come to me about taking the head coach job there in their first season, 1960. I don't know whether Tex might have gone that way—after all, I was just an assistant coach, and I think maybe he might have wanted an experienced head coach to get the new team off the ground.

At the time, too, I was actually thinking about getting out of football altogether. During the off-season a while back I'd gotten a degree in industrial engineering in addition to my degree from the University of Texas, and so I was thinking about a life other than football. But then Tex came out and we talked, and he offered me the job. I said to my wife, "Oh, well, we might just as well try it. We'll probably be fired in two or three years, but what the heck." So I agreed and we signed a contract. And my days with the Giants came to an end.

◘

A Record-Setting Rout

The Giants, their collective eye still on a playoff berth as a wild card, rampaged into Yankee Stadium on November 26, 1972, to play the Philadelphia Eagles. With quarterback Norm Snead, running back Ron Johnson, and receiver Bob Tucker all in top form, it was hardly a contest. On New York's first possession, they scored on a 15-yard pass from Snead to Tucker. The next time the Giants had the ball they scored again, this time on a 35-yard run by Johnson.

On the first play of the second quarter, Snead passed to fullback Joe Orduna for a 5-yard touchdown. Not much later, Pete Gogolak nailed a 25-yard field goal. Tucker then made his second touchdown reception of the day on a 29-yard pass from Snead, and Johnson subsequently added yet another touchdown on a 1-yard run. At halftime, the score was 38–10, New York.

Later in the game, reserve quarterback Randy Johnson took over for Snead, and a host of other Giants replacements took to the field. For Philadelphia it was just one of those days. In the final eighteen minutes of the game, Johnson hit Don Hermann twice in the end zone with touchdown passes and ran another one in himself.

The final score, 62–10, set team scoring records for the Giants and the Eagles as well. Philadelphia had never before allowed so many points in a single game. Pete Gogolak also set a team game record when he kicked his eighth extra point. Ron Johnson rushed for 123 yards before he was pulled in the third quarter. Tucker caught 8 passes for 100 yards.

A group of disgruntled Philadelphia fans planned to use the game as evidence in their lawsuit against the Eagles. The season-ticket holders went to court demanding their money back because they alleged that the Philadelphia team failed to provide football entertainment at a big-league level.

◘

Harry Newman

With the NFL's adoption of new rules in 1933 that would en-
courage the passing game, the New York Giants were in critical
need of someone to replace Benny Friedman, at that time the
game's best passer, who had defected to the Brooklyn Dodgers
the year before. So they went after the youngster reputed to
be the best passer coming out of college football: an All-
American from the University of Michigan, Harry Newman.

In those years before the NFL draft, every college player
was fair game, and the Giants landed Newman with a most
unusual contract offer. He was to be guaranteed a percentage
of the gate receipts, the most potentially lucrative offer since
C. C. Pyle worked out a similar kind of deal for Red Grange
with the Chicago Bears back in 1925.

Newman proved his worth that rookie year by guiding the
Giants to a divisional title (11–3–0) and to the first official NFL
championship game. He led the league in three key passing
categories that season with 53 completions, 973 yards gained,
and 9 touchdowns. He was named the All-Pro quarterback of
1933.

Harry Newman, 5'8" and 175 pounds, was one of the small-
est players in the game in those days, but he was known as an

exceptionally rugged player on defense as well as offense. Besides his impressive statistics as a passer that rookie year, he was considered a fine runner, both from scrimmage and as a kickoff-return specialist.

Newman stayed with the Giants for only three years, 1933–35, during which they won three division titles and one NFL title (although Newman did not play in that championship game). But by 1935 his contract deal with the Giants had gotten out of hand, management felt, and the Mara family and Newman could not come to terms. So he left in 1936 to help found the second ill-fated American Football League, never to return to either the Giants or the NFL.

I t was actually Benny Friedman who was most instrumental in getting me to go to Michigan and play football. He had been a great quarterback there in the 1920s, and when I was a senior [in high school] he was already established as the best passer in the NFL.

Benny had a summer camp out in New Hampshire, and a lot of kids from Detroit and Cleveland went to it. I was one of them. It wasn't a football camp like they have these days—just an ordinary summer camp. Benny was the head counselor. He was a very nice guy and took an interest in me. He thought I would have a good college football career and told me I would be better off at Michigan than anywhere else. And it was Benny who taught me how to pass. We worked on it a lot. I think I may have thrown two passes in high school and that was all. Benny felt if I was going to make it to the top in college I needed to be a good passer as well as a runner. And, of course, he was right. Later on, Benny stopped working at that summer camp in New Hampshire, and I got the job as head counselor.

So I enrolled at Michigan, and I began playing football there my freshman year. We had some mighty good football players the years that I was at Michigan, quite a number of All-Americans. We had the first of the Wistert brothers, but he didn't go on to play pro football like his brother

Al did later on. Bill Hewitt was a fine end and, of course, he had a terrific pro career with the Chicago Bears and Philadelphia Eagles and was put in the Pro Football Hall of Fame. Ivy Williamson went on to become a coach and athletic director at Wisconsin. In my sophomore year, there was a center and linebacker by the name of Doc Morrison, who made All-American; he played a couple of years with the Brooklyn Dodgers. In my junior and senior years our center was Chuck Bernard, and he was an All-American, too; he later played for the Detroit Lions.

I had been what they called a "junior All-American" in my sophomore year [1930] at Michigan—had a real fine year. But as a junior I broke an ankle, and I played most of the year with it until we found out it was in fact broken. It slowed me down a lot that year.

In my senior year, we earned a share of the national championship [Michigan, with a record of 8-0-0, shared the title with Southern Cal, 10-0-0]. We also won the Big Ten title that year. We beat Northwestern, who used to have great teams around that time. They had Pug Rentner, an All-American halfback—and he was very good in the pros too, with the Boston Redskins.

My ankle was fine my senior year, and I had a great season. A lot of our games were close—and the last one was really a tough one. It was up in Minnesota and the temperature was six degrees below zero. They had Biggie Munn then, who would become a great coach, and Jack Manders, who was a fine back and kicker and would later play for the Bears—"Automatic Jack" they used to call him, because he was such a consistently good kicker. We just barely got by them to save our perfect record. I kicked a field goal, and that was the only score of the game.

I was named to the All-America team, and that meant an awful lot to me. I also won the Douglas Fairbanks Trophy that year, which was sort of like the Heisman Trophy. The Heisman didn't come along until a few years later [1936]. And I was given the *Chicago Tribune* trophy for most valuable player in the Big Ten.

Actually, we lost only one game in the three years I played at Michigan. In my sophomore year, we won eight games and were tied once. Then in my junior year—that was the year I had the bad ankle—we lost once to Ohio State. They had Sid Gillman that year, who was to go on to become a famous coach in the NFL. The only reason we lost it was because Jack Heston, one of our key running backs, got hammered on the opening kickoff. Jack was the son of Willie Heston, one of the all-time great football players at Michigan who played for Fielding Yost back in the early 1900s. Anyway, Jack was totally stunned—he was really unconscious—but he functioned, and we didn't know his condition until later. So he stayed in the game. But he fumbled the ball three times, each somewhere around our 20-yard line. On two of them they scored afterwards. That's really why they beat us. I wasn't able to play the entire game either because my ankle was bothering me too much. But that was really something—only one loss in three years, and we played many of the very best teams in the nation.

After I got out of college, I had several offers to go with the pros. I wasn't very big, and that was a drawback. I was only about 175 pounds in college and I was only 5'8". But George Halas of the Chicago Bears came up with an offer. It wasn't a very good one. The New York Giants came up with a better one. I talked with Tim Mara and I got the feeling they really wanted a passer and that I'd fit in with them right away.

The contract deal he came up with was that I was actually to receive a percentage of the gate. That was a very good deal in those days. As I remember it, the first year I was supposed to get 10 percent of the gate after $11,000 had been deducted for expenses. The second year I was to get 20 percent.

It was kind of a foregone conclusion, I guess, that I was to be the starting quarterback—or tailback, I think you'd call it. So I really wasn't treated like a rookie when I showed up there. We had our training camp at Pompton

Lakes over in New Jersey back then. And from the time I got there I was starting. We had two sessions each day at camp, and I think that was the first time they started that; but it was turning into a different kind of game with all the passing we were going to do—a lot of new plays and all that.

I roomed with Kink Richards when I first joined the Giants. He was a helluva blocking back for us. Ken Strong came to the Giants that year too; he'd been playing with the Staten Island Stapes before that. Ken, of course, was a magnificent football player and a fine guy. I used to pal around with him quite a bit. Some others who were good friends then were Mel Hein and Ray Flaherty and Red Badgro. Mel was a true All-Pro at center, and Flaherty and Badgro were two of the best ends in the league.

When training camp was over, I lived in New York at a place called the Broadway View Hotel. Then I moved to the Terrace Hotel, which was over on Ninety-sixth and Riverside Drive. We didn't do too much carousing in those days. Some maybe, but during the season we were all pretty dedicated. We wanted to win, and we knew we were a good enough team to win.

And we did win that year, at least we won the Eastern Division. We only lost three of fourteen games. In one game we set a record when we beat the Philadelphia Eagles 56-0. We split with the Chicago Bears during the regular season—they beat us at Wrigley Field in Chicago [14-10], and we won at the Polo Grounds [3-0]. They won the NFL West and we played them in what was the first official championship game in the NFL—it was the first year the league was broken into two separate divisions. They had Bronko Nagurski and Red Grange and Jack Manders—a really fine team.

That [championship] game was really something. I think the lead changed hands six different times. There was one play in it that Bob Considine, the New York sportswriter, said was the greatest play he had ever seen. It wasn't a planned one, though. It was just an ordinary play, a

Harry Newman took over as quarterback for the Giants in 1933 and guided the offense the next three years. An excellent passer and runner, he led the league in completions, passing yardage, and passing touchdowns and was the team's top rusher during his rookie year. He led the Giants to a divisional title that season and to an NFL championship the following year.

handoff by me to Ken Strong, who would then buck into the line. Well, the hole was all plugged up, just nowhere to go, so Ken spun out of the line. As he did, he saw me standing back there in the backfield and so he lateralled the ball back to me. I was surprised, and suddenly all the Bears were coming after me. They chased me over to the right side of the field. I was hoping to get around end for some yardage but there was no way to do it—too many Bears in front of me. Then in just a flash I saw Ken down the field. After lateralling to me, he had raced down the field and was now in the end zone with no one near him. I threw it back to him, and we had a touchdown. It was in the fourth quarter and I believe that put us ahead 21–16.

There was another famous play from that game. I got it from watching two of my nieces playing football, believe it or not. It was a little touch game—one of them was the quarterback and the other the center. One centered the ball to the other in a kind of T formation setup, and then the quarterback just handed the ball back to the center, right back through her legs, and she took off with it.

I thought that might be a helluva play, a trick play we might pull off some day. So I went to Steve Owen, our coach then, and between the two of us we worked it up. We'd line up with just an end next to Mel Hein, our center, on one side; then just before the snap the end would shift into the backfield, which would make Mel eligible as a receiver. Well, we pulled it off against the Bears. After I had handed it back to him, I spun around, faking as if I had the ball, and then pretended to trip. Well, all their linemen were convinced I had the ball, and several of them landed on top of me. One of them, big George Musso, who was about 270 pounds, was the first one to land; as he was getting up, he suddenly got this puzzled look on his face and said, "Where the hell's the ball?"

I just looked at him and said, "Next time you want to see me do some card tricks?" I think Mel got maybe 30 or 40 yards on the play.

Well, for all our surprising plays, we still lost. They got

a touchdown in the closing minutes and beat us 23–21. But it was one of the greatest games ever played in terms of excitement. I completed 12 passes in that game [for 201 yards], 2 of them for touchdowns. It was a tough one to lose.

We won our division again the next year. For me, it was really a rugged year. In one game, I carried the ball 34 times, which then was a league record and, as I think about it, pretty stupid for a quarterback. It wasn't because I wanted to. The reason I had to carry it so often was that Ken Strong had a broken toe, Bo Molenda had a bad back, and there seemed to be something wrong with everybody else who ordinarily carried the ball. We were playing Green Bay that day at the Polo Grounds, and we beat them 17–3. At the same time, Strong couldn't kick the ball, so I did all the placekicking that day as well. I also returned punts and kickoffs. It was one of the longest, most bruising days I ever encountered in a football uniform.

One of the reasons it was so bruising was that they had a guard named Iron Mike Michalske, and he was a tough tackler. Before that, Green Bay had the most brutal lineman in the game, Cal Hubbard. He played tackle and was about 6'5" and maybe 250 pounds. He played with the same kind of intensity that Dick Butkus did later. We used to say of Cal that even if he missed you he still hurt you. When he tackled you, you remembered it. I do to this day.

The next week, in a game against the Chicago Bears, I suffered two broken bones in my back, and that did me in for the season. Ed Danowski, a rookie out of Fordham, replaced me at tailback. The team went on to win the NFL championship that year. They beat the Bears in that game where they wore tennis shoes because the field was frozen. I was there but I wasn't in uniform.

In 1935, I had a contract dispute with the Maras. I decided to hold out. In that last game that I played in, in 1934, the one against the Bears, we filled the Polo Grounds. Because I was on a percentage, they had to pay me a lot of dough. As a result, they wouldn't give me the same kind of contract for the next year.

Also that year before, they had a fund-raising game for Mayor Cavanaugh—I think that was his name. He was a famous World War I hero, and it was a benefit for him and charity. They had a sellout for it, and I donated my entire salary for that game to the benefit. They [the Maras] never said anything about that when contract negotiations came around.

I held out, but it didn't do me a lot of good. The season started, and I kept myself sort of busy scouting for Coach [Harry] Kipke of Michigan. I scouted teams like Columbia. But finally I had to do something, so I came back and played out the year with the Giants. I alternated with Danowski that year, but I felt my days with the Giants were over. They were never going to pay me the money I wanted. I knew that.

So the next year I got out of the NFL altogether. Along with a couple of others, I started the American Football League. Ken Strong came along into the new league, and so did Red Badgro. We had teams in six cities: New York, Brooklyn, Rochester, Cleveland, Pittsburgh, and Boston. I started the team in Brooklyn and we called ourselves the Tigers. The second year of the league, 1937, my franchise moved up to Rochester. We didn't have many big-name players—most were right out of college, and they were the ones who didn't make the NFL. We didn't draw very well either in Brooklyn [perhaps because they were 0-6-1] or Rochester. [After that season the Rochester franchise folded.] Those were still the Depression years, and we just couldn't make a dent in the NFL—which, incidentally, wasn't doing all that well either.

After the Rochester team went under, I left football. I went back to Detroit, my hometown, and went to work for the Ford Motor Company. I was in the sales department at first, but soon I worked into a position where I represented the company over at the state capital in Lansing. I was basically a lobbyist for Ford at that time.

In 1946 I opened my own Ford dealership in Detroit. A few years later I opened another one in Denver, Colorado.

I played on a few very good teams in the 1930s. We knew what it was like to win, but we truly worked for it. We were very serious about the game. I still love the game, but because I'm retired now and living in Florida, I guess I watch the Miami Dolphins more than any other team. I watch the New York Giants too, but I don't have the allegiance to them that I probably should have. When I look back on it, they treated me fairly well when I was there. I probably wanted more money than I should have gotten, and I can understand now why I didn't get it. But that's just the way it was in those days.

◘

Team Poet Laureate

On the occasion of "Tim Mara Day" at the Polo Grounds in November 1932, Westbrook Pegler, in his syndicated column "Speaking Out," observed a new Giant in the fold:

> They have hired cheerleaders from time to time, and yesterday a poet laureate bobbed up in the literature of the official program (price, 15 cents) with a new alma mater song dedicated to Tim Mara, entitled "My Song."
> The new alma mater song, struck from the lyre of poet Thomas J. McCarthy, runs about a hundred lines, which is somewhat longer than the formula for such works. . . . A few lines will serve to tell you about the new song:
> *Each fall my joy is without bounds,*
> *On Sundays at the Polo Grounds.*
> *For when our football Giants play,*
> *Just try to keep this guy away.*
> It is little better than most college songs, but, then, the college poets are amateurs, like the college players, and cannot be expected to write as well as the pros.

◘

Andy Robustelli

Andy Robustelli came to the Giants in 1956 with five years of NFL experience, all of them with the explosive Los Angeles Rams of the early 1950s. Small by today's standards for defensive ends at a mere 6'1" and 230 pounds, he was a formidable giant on the field in both Los Angeles and New York.

During his fourteen-year NFL career, Robustelli missed only one game. He was named All-Pro five times as a Giant and twice with the Rams, and he went to seven Pro Bowls. During his nine seasons with the Giants, they won six Eastern Conference titles, and during his five years in Los Angeles the Rams won two Western Conference titles.

A graduate of tiny Arnold College, with an enrollment of 350—a school that does not even exist anymore—he was the nineteenth-round draft choice of the Rams in 1951. He played both offensive and defensive end in college but was pegged for the defensive line in the relatively new two-platoon system in pro football.

With the Giants, Robustelli and fellow defensive end Jim Katcavage and defensive tackles Rosie Grier and Dick Modzelewski made up the most-feared front four in the game in the late 1950s and early 1960s. Robustelli was especially respected for his intelligence and enthusiasm on the field of play. As one coach described him, "He studied the game. He studied films. He diagnosed opponents. He diagnosed plays. He came to every game ready to play."

He had the much-deserved honor of being inducted into the Pro Football Hall of Fame in the class of 1971. His enshrinement prompted one writer to observe, "He has the added distinction of being the only Arnold alumnus to ever make it to the Pro Football Hall of Fame."

Robustelli returned to the Giants in December 1973 to serve as the club's director of operations and remained in that capacity through the 1978 season. When he announced his resignation, it prompted Giants president Wellington Mara to remark, "What made this year so hard to accept [was not the 6–10–0 record] but the knowledge that we were losing Andy."

Today Andy Robustelli is a prominent businessman, owner of a marketing and travel services conglomerate of nine companies known as Robustelli Corporate Services, based in Stamford, Connecticut.

Most kids who like football start just about the time they find out they can throw one. That's the way it was with me. I started in Stamford, Connecticut, where I grew up. We lived in a neighborhood where, when we were twelve or thirteen, we hung around a church which was kind of the hub for getting together, and we played makeup football games outside there. We also hung around what we called "night school" because we would go back to school at night to play basketball or some other sport.

Back then you played all different positions. You played what you were told to play—nobody specialized. If you were good enough, and tough enough, to be the captain, however, you played the position you wanted and you told the others where they were going to play. I think I played quarterback, halfback, end, lineman—you name it.

I played football in high school, and after that I went into the navy. I was eighteen at the time and this was

during World War II. I ended up a water tender, a snipe—
that's one of the guys below deck who fires the boilers. I
was in for two and a half years and spent most of the time
on a ship out in the Pacific.

After the service I went to a little college in Milford,
Connecticut, named Arnold, which no longer exists. I got
out of the service about six or seven months after the war
ended, early 1946. Most colleges around were crowded
with veterans who had already returned from the war. I
think I could have gotten into Fordham, but they wanted
me to go to a prep school to pick up a couple of credits. I'd
gone from high school before graduating to LaSalle Military
Academy for three months before going into the service. I
had to wait until I was eighteen before enlisting, so by
doing that I missed a few high school credits, and that's
what Fordham wanted me to make up.

A couple of my buddies were going up to Arnold College because they were having difficulty getting into the
better-known colleges too. I went along with them. I was
on the GI Bill of Rights, and so at Arnold they said come on
in. It was primarily a phys ed school, but before there were
about 200 girls and only about 40 boys. With the veterans
now coming in, it ended up with more boys and less
girls—about 350 students in all.

I decided to enroll, and once there it gave me the
opportunity to play any sport I wanted to. So I played
football and baseball. We played football against schools
like the Coast Guard Academy, St. Michaels' in Vermont,
Adelphi on Long Island, and a lot of teachers' colleges. It
wasn't the greatest competition in the world, but still it was
tough football.

I was headed more toward baseball when I was at
Arnold, and I thought—or hoped—I might get something
in that sport when my college days were over. As it turned
out, I did have the chance of going with the baseball Giants
in New York. There was an offer. They had a Class B team
in Knoxville, Tennessee, which is where I would have
gone.

As for pro football in those days, you might get a letter from the teams that were interested in you and a questionnaire to fill out. And that was about the only contact you ever made with a pro team, especially if you were from a small college.

The Los Angeles Rams were the farthest thing from my mind at that time. I thought I might be drafted by the Giants, who were the closest team, but they didn't show much interest. The Pittsburgh Steelers seemed the most interested in me.

But when it got down to the nineteenth draft choice in 1951—in those years they had thirty picks, unlike the twelve of today—the Rams took me. They told me later that that far down in the draft they were merely looking for special features in a player. Well, I had blocked a lot of punts and, as they told me, they felt anyone who could block punts well was worth taking a look at. Basically I was drafted on that alone.

So I had the choice of the Giants' minor league team, a couple of high school teaching job offers, and a tryout with the Rams. I decided to go to California and try to make the team. After all, I was twenty-five years old that year and I felt I had to get something going, something that would lead somewhere. Pro football was a make-it-or-break-it situation. In the minor leagues you could flounder around for years and never get to the major leagues. As far as teaching was concerned, that was something I figured I could always go to later. When I made the team in Los Angeles, that made the decision for me.

I signed with the Rams—no signing bonus, just a plane ticket to get out there. My first-year salary was $4,250, about $350 a [regular season] game.

I was more of an offensive player in college than defensive, but that was changed the first year with the Rams, and I became a 6'1", 220-pound defensive end. It wasn't something etched in stone in those days. I mean, you might play offense too. Or if you were a linebacker, you were a linebacker, not a right outside linebacker; you'd play where you were needed at a particular time. If you could play more than one position and had specialty skills, you had a much better chance of making the team. You had to be a little more flexible than the players of today. Only about three or four rookies would make the team in those days, sometimes less, so it really helped the more versatile you were. But defensive end was the right place for me. After all, we had Tom Fears and Elroy Hirsch as our offensive ends.

It was quite a change from Arnold College in Milford, Connecticut. Los Angeles was so huge, sprawling; and there was also the awe of Hollywood. It kind of distracted you from the awe usually associated with football. In those days, Bob Hope owned a percentage of the Rams, and a lot of the Hollywood people, friends of his, were great fans of ours. We used to train at Hollywood Stadium, and the Rams' office was in Beverly Hills. There were always a lot of movie stars around. And, of course, there was Bob Waterfield's wife, Jane Russell, and that was a major distraction to a kid coming from Arnold College—turning around and seeing her in the front row or on the sideline.

We had a great group of ballplayers out there then. Besides Waterfield, we had Norm Van Brocklin. If one of them wasn't on, the other would be. We also had Hirsch and Fears for them to throw to. And we had that great set of running backs: the powerhouses—Tank Younger and Deacon Dan Towler and Dick Hoerner. And we had Glenn Davis. It was really a spectacular team, and the Rams were riding high in those days. My rookie year we won our conference and then beat the Cleveland Browns [24–17] for the NFL title, and the Browns were the defending champions [they had defeated the Rams 30–28 in the 1950 title game].

This was a time when they were changing the whole philosophy of pro football with the forward pass, and the Rams were a great advocate of it for obvious reasons: Waterfield, Van Brocklin, Hirsch, and Fears.

I played for the Rams for five years, and we never had

a losing season. In fact, we won another conference title my last year there, 1955, but that year we lost in the championship game to the Browns [38–14].

After that, I was traded to the Giants. Sid Gillman, who had taken over as the Rams' head coach in 1955, decided to shake things up because of that championship-game loss. A number of the players were traded away. Besides me, Big Daddy Lipscomb and Ed Hughes from the defensive unit were dealt away too.

What happened in my case was that I would ordinarily go home after the season was over, back to Connecticut. Well, in those days guys would straggle into training camp—it wasn't as regimented as it is today. But for 1956, Sid said we all had to be there at the very start, to get going, so we could wipe out the defeat we'd suffered in the title game of '55.

We talked by telephone before camp and I said to him, "Coach, I can't. I need a couple extra days. We're going to have another child any day, and I need to be here for that and be sure everything's okay."

He said, "No, you're coming out here or I'm getting rid of you."

I said, "Well, if you're going to do that, okay, but I'm not going to be there." And the next day he traded me to the Giants.

The Giants were a great contrast to the Rams—a completely different organization. The Rams were glitzy, Hollywood style—everything was kind of show business. The Giants were more the hard-nosed football team, and that entire conference was that way. The attitude was hard-nosed on all levels. The ballplayers did not get pampered as they did in Los Angeles or with the 49ers out on the coast. You got your own socks and your own jocks; you did everything yourself, whereas with the Rams everything was sort of laid out for you. It was quite a difference.

It really was the best thing that could have happened to me, however, to come home to New York. I could live at home in Connecticut and commute. We still weren't making much money—this was my sixth year in the NFL and I think I was earning $7,500.

Like my first year with the Rams, my first year with the Giants we won the NFL championship. I had been privileged to play in two title games with Los Angeles, but none of the other Giants had ever played in one before. Hell, the Giants hadn't been to a championship game since 1946. So it was just a big thrill for me to be there again—three times in six years.

We played the Chicago Bears, and they were a good team, with guys like Rick Casares, Harlon Hill, Doug Atkins, Stan Jones. I still can't believe we beat them as bad as we did [47-7]. There was a point in the game when you knew you just had it. I mean, we were beating them 34-7 at the half.

There were a lot of great guys who came to the Giants that year, the core of the defense: Sam Huff, Jim Katcavage, Dick Modzelewski—we were all first-year men in New York—and Ed Hughes, a defensive back, who came out from Los Angeles along with me. We all became good friends. The defense stuck together, and they were the guys I palled around with.

We were very parochial in those days, our social lives pretty simple. Being out late was not something you did a lot, and very rarely was anybody fined. Modzelewski would sit around and sing in Polish, Grier would play his guitar all night until you might want to kill him, and we'd go out for a couple of beers, but that was about the extent of the excitement. Some of us used to go to Toots Shor's, however. That was the one place that most of us liked to go. Toots always liked the athletes and looked after us—getting us a table, things like that. He made you feel like you were a little special.

We got into another championship game two years later, in 1958. That year we had to beat the Browns back-to-back at the end of the year—the last game of the regular season and the playoff game [both teams ended up with

9-3-0 records]. Both the games were at home, at Yankee Stadium.

The first was just an awful day—snow, wind, frozen field. That's the one which came down to Pat Summerall's field goal in a blizzard. It was a miraculous kick under the conditions. It was a tough game, but then all the games with the Browns were tough. But we won it, 13-10. We were always fired up for the Browns. Then we beat them the next week 10-0, which got us to the championship game against the Colts.

That game, I believe, was a crystallization of what pro football was all about. It brought out a lot of the drama of the game to the public. We were losing 14-3 at the half but came back and took the lead, 17-14. They tied it with a field goal after Unitas led a march down the field. Then, of course, they won it in sudden-death overtime [23-17].

That game was on national television and, from what I heard later, more than ten million homes had the game on their televisions that day. It was blacked out in New York, however, and with the way it turned out maybe that was for the best. There was also a newspaper strike in New York, so New Yorkers couldn't even read about it the next day. But it really turned the country on to pro football. I don't think pro football was nearly as popular in the United States before that game as it was just after it.

We should have won it, but we didn't, and therefore it's not going to be one of the most memorable games of my life.

The Colts were a great football team. They had perhaps the best player I ever went up against, [offensive tackle] Jim Parker. We were playing a defense that was a

◀ The mighty front four of the Giants—Dick Modzelewski (77), Andy Robustelli (81), Rosie Grier (76), and Jim Katcavage—do battle while Jim Brown waits in the flat for a pass from Frank Ryan (13) in this game against the Cleveland Browns. The Giants and the Browns waged war quite a few times for the NFL East crown in the 1950s and early 1960s.

little different—basically a five-man line, and then we started to get into the four, and sometimes the three. We played a changing defense. And it put people like me and other defensive ends, who were relatively light—I was about 235 by then; so was our other defensive end, Jim Katcavage—in a position where Katcavage and I had to go up against interior offensive linemen who were much bigger. Parker, for example, was 6'3" and 270 pounds and still very agile and quick, and I often ended up playing off him. He was outstanding.

We not only had to contend with enormous linemen but often a total of three players who were out to prevent us from doing what we were supposed to do. Besides the lineman, there was a back who could come up close to the line of scrimmage and also a guard who might pull out.

Another very good ballplayer was Lou Creekmur, who played on the offensive line for Detroit. He was somewhere around 260 pounds. Lou Groza of the Browns was another one. He's probably best remembered as a placekicker—and, of course, he was one of the all-time best—but he was also an exceptional offensive lineman. He never really got the credit he deserved for his play on the line because it was overshadowed by his kicking.

Later, in the 1960s, I played against the Packers, and they were an exceptional team. They had guys like Willie Davis and Henry Jordan in their defensive line who were very good. I think it's probably a toss-up as to which was the better team I ever played against: the Packers of the '60s or the Colts of the '50s.

The two teams were different—and so were the players. For example, take Bart Starr. He was not a John Unitas, but he got the job done for the Packers in a very meticulous, Vince Lombardi sort of way.

We went to another title game in 1963, and my most vivid memory is cold, cold, cold. It was a very brutal game. I thought we played an outstanding game defensively. They [the Bears] only scored twice, and both of those were set up by interceptions and were on quarterback sneaks by Bill

Wade. Unfortunately, Tittle got hurt early. Had he not, I believe we would have won the game.

They had another exceptional ballplayer I went up against—[tight end] Mike Ditka. I knew him pretty well because in those days I had a sports marketing business on the side, and Mike and several other athletes worked for us in the off-season. We were friends, but not on the field; every opponent was a mortal enemy to Mike on the field. But off the field we were good friends and still are today.

In those days, pro football was so much less a business than it is today. There was a wonderful fellowship and loyalty and togetherness among the players then—there was no selfishness or jealousies over how much someone else was making. The average ballplayer makes so much money today; it is a different situation. It would have been absolutely inconceivable to us to think we could ever make money like that playing football.

I didn't have any trouble with the decision to retire. In 1964 we had a bum season [2–10–2] and I was 38 years old and it was my fourteenth year in the NFL. I knew it was time. My biggest decision was whether to stay in football in some other capacity. My business in the off-season [sports marketing] was doing well. I'd started it my first year out in Los Angeles, 1951. It began as a sports store. I started it with the championship-game check I got that year when we beat the Browns. It was small and I didn't take a salary. But it got bigger, branched out, once I moved to New York. It kept me busy during the off-season.

I decided to devote my time to the business rather than stay in football. I did, however, come back to serve in the Giants' front office in the 1970s as director of operations.

Moving Day, 1956

The Giants moved from the Polo Grounds, their home field since the team was born in 1925, to Yankee Stadium in 1956.

The last sporting event New Yorkers were treated to at Yankee Stadium before the Giants made their debut in that illustrious edifice had been the fifth game of the 1956 World Series, the one in which Yankees hurler Don Larsen pitched the only perfect game in World Series history.

When this fact was mentioned by one of the Giants coaching staff to the players during a session devoted to extolling their new home, one player remarked to head coach Jim Lee Howell, "And you want us to top that?"

When Howell did not respond, the player added, "Do we get more than one game to do it?"

Dick Modzelewski

Little Mo, as he was affectionately called, was far from little. As a defensive tackle in the National Football League of the 1950s and 1960s, Dick Modzelewski stood six feet tall and weighed somewhere in the vicinity of 260 pounds. He was as durable as he was menacing to opposing offenses. When he retired after the 1966 season, he took with him the NFL record for consecutive games played, his 180 eclipsing the 174 Leo Nomellini of the San Francisco 49ers had set in 1963.

Born and raised in a coal-mining town in western Pennsylvania, Modzelewski was an all-state tackle in high school. He chose the University of Maryland, for whom his older brother Ed—Big Mo—a year ahead of him, was playing fullback. A varsity starter for three years, he earned All-American honors in 1952, his senior year, and was awarded the Outland Trophy, which honors the most outstanding interior lineman of the year.

Little Mo was the second-round draft choice of the Washington Redskins in 1953 and promptly won the starting job at defensive tackle. After two years, he was traded to the Pittsburgh Steelers and played out the 1955 season there.

In 1956 he was traded to the Giants, joining fellow new-

comers Sam Huff, Andy Robustelli, and Jim Katcavage and
such veterans as Rosie Grier, Emlen Tunnell, Jimmy Patton, and
Harland Svare to form the foremost defensive unit in the NFL.
With their help, the Giants went on that year to win their first
national championship since 1938.

During the eight years Modzelewski played for the New
York Giants, they won six conference titles. Their collective
regular-season record for that period was 73 wins, 25 losses,
and 4 ties.

After winning the Eastern Conference in 1963 and then
losing the title game to the Chicago Bears, Modzelewski was
part of an Allie Sherman housecleaning and was dealt away
along with Sam Huff and several others. He went to Cleveland,
where he played the final three years of his fourteen-year NFL
career. During that career, Modzelewski played in eight NFL
championship games—six for the Giants and two for the
Browns—and he has one championship ring from each of those
teams.

After his playing days were over, Little Mo served as an
assistant defensive coach for various NFL teams for twenty-two
years before finally retiring in 1989. Today he is enjoying that
retirement in New Bern, North Carolina.

We were truly a football family. My older brother
Ed, who they called Big Mo, played for Maryland
just like I did. He was a fullback and went on to the
pros with the Steelers and then the Cleveland Browns.

We were from a little town called West Natrona, Pennsylvania, which is thirty miles east of Pittsburgh. It was a
coal-mining town and a steel town. My dad worked in a
coal mine for thirty-three years. During summer breaks
from college my brother Ed and I worked at the Allegheny-
Ludlum Steel Company. There was also a chemical company in town, and I worked there one summer. There were
factories all over town. Most of the people in town were
Polish, and most worked in the mines or the mills or some
factory.

Western Pennsylvania, where we were from, produced some great football players—Joe Montana, Mike Ditka. . . . In high school, we played teams from all over the area, and we played to capacity crowds. There was a great amount of interest in football there.

The way they did it around there was if a kid was big enough and the coach wanted him to play, he would go and ask the parents about it. If they would allow you to play, you played. I remember one kid, a big kid, who didn't want to play. The coach went to see his father, and the father said to the kid, "You are *going* to play." And he played, even though he really didn't want to. He ended up getting a scholarship to college for football, however.

Ed was two years older than me, but he was only one year ahead of me in school. The reason was that when he was fifteen he lied about his age so he could join the merchant marines in World War II. Well, he went off, and my mother eventually found out what had happened. She learned he was in Sheepshead Bay, New York, and she called somebody—a councilman, maybe—and said to get Ed's ass out of there because he was too young. They sent him back, and he lost a year of school as a result.

We got our nicknames, Big Mo and Little Mo, while we were playing football in high school. When Ed was a junior and I was a sophomore, Ed weighed more than me. He weighed 195 pounds and I was about 175 pounds, but as time went on I got a little bigger. I had a younger brother who played too, Eugene, and they nicknamed him "No Mo." He went to New Mexico State on a football scholarship but didn't play in the pros.

Ed and I went to Maryland. I had a number of offers because I'd been all-state my senior year. Notre Dame was interested in me; so were Tennessee, Pittsburgh, and South Carolina. I'll never forget South Carolina. My dad was home one day—my dad was an immigrant, and all he could write was his name—and a coach from South Carolina pulled up in front of our house in a brand-new 1949 green Oldsmobile convertible. And I was told if I went to school down there, there was a good chance I'd get me a car like that. Well, my old man about flipped. He said he couldn't believe it, him working in the coal mines all those years and here is his son, a senior in high school and they're offering him a car like that. It was hard to turn down, but I did.

Coach Jim Tatum came over from Maryland and talked to my parents, and I think he did a good job selling them. Part of it, of course, was how good it would be with my brother already there. So that's where I went, and I'm glad I did. I had the benefit of a great coach [Tatum] there.

Coach Tatum always said my father was Maryland's good-luck charm. When Ed and I were playing there, a friend of mine, Dom Corso, used to bring my father to all the home games. He would wait for my dad to come from the coal mine on Friday, drive him to College Park, and then after mass on Sunday drive him back. After a while, Coach Tatum had my dad sit on the bench each time he came. Tatum loved my dad.

My dad said his proudest moment was when my brother Ed and I were invited to a big sports lunch at the White House. This was at the end of my senior year, 1953, and my brother was in the air force at the time. Ed got his invitation out at Hamilton Air Force Base in California and told his commanding officer he had to go to Washington for this lunch at the White House with Dwight D. Eisenhower. His CO just laughed at him, but when he showed him the invitation they got a jet ready and flew his butt to Washington for the lunch. It was a big affair, with people like Rocky Marciano and Joe DiMaggio and Florence Chadwick there. It was a big thrill for Ed and me, and I think maybe even bigger for my dad getting to tell everyone around town where his two boys were having lunch.

In 1953, the Washington Redskins drafted me. It was no big surprise. There was an article in the *Washington Post* that said the Redskins were interested in getting our quarterback, Jack Scarbath, and me. We had both made All-American our senior year and, sure enough, they did draft us, Jack in the first round and me in the second.

The first contract the Redskins offered me—I remember Herman Ball, one of their assistant coaches, came over to my dormitory at Maryland and handed it to me to sign—it was for $3,800. I told him, hell, I had to make more than my father was making in the coal mine, and he was making $6,200. And the year before, my brother had signed with the Steelers—and he got $10,000 and a $3,000 signing bonus.

George Preston Marshall, the owner of the Redskins, was never known to pay on any fancy scale. I argued like hell, refusing to sign, and they finally came around and made it $6,500. I said okay, but I also wanted a $1,500 signing bonus. Well, hell, Marshall thought I was crazy, like I had a gun and was robbing his bank. Well, I held out for a couple of weeks and I finally got it. Other guys with the Redskins who had been there a while were only making about $4,500. Marshall used to pay us in cash. We used to have to go down to his office each week, which was in a laundry he owned, and his secretary would pull out an envelope with your name on it and inside would be the cash.

After the 1954 season, I decided I was going to go to Canada, where our line coach at Maryland had become the head coach of the Calgary Stampeders. When I said that was what I was going to do, Marshall sued me. We only had one-year contracts in those days, but there was this thing that said they owned perpetual rights to you in terms of playing pro football. If you tried to play anywhere else without the permission of the team who had the rights to you, they could sue you. The Canadians finally told me that I'd better go back because it would probably take a couple of years before they and Marshall got through all the court proceedings, and it just wasn't worth it.

When I decided to stay in the United States, I told

Marshall that you and me are never going to get along and that you better trade me. So he traded me to the Pittsburgh Steelers, where my brother was playing. They turned around and traded my brother to the Cleveland Browns. The Browns ended up winning the NFL championship that year, and we were stuck in last place in the NFL East.

We had a coach that year who was really something else—old Walt Kiesling. He'd played in the 1920s and '30s, and he worked our asses off like nobody ever had. In training camp, we had two hours of really head-to-head scrimmages in the morning, two more hours of it in the afternoon. We were okay going into the season; but he just kept it up, and we were so beat up it was a disaster. That was the same year Kiesling cut this young quarterback named Johnny Unitas.

A lot of things developed there that year in Pittsburgh. I thought the world of Art Rooney, the Steelers' owner, but I had some other problems with the team. During the year, my wife was going to have a baby, and I went in to see Kiesling and asked if I could go home—she was due with our first kid any day. He told me if I went it was going to cost me five hundred bucks. At that time, it was a lot of dough—I was making maybe $7,000-something.

I thought about it and finally said, "Oh, go to hell," and got dressed and went home. As it was, I missed the delivery of the baby. Kiesling, as it turned out, didn't fine me—but only because Art Rooney told him not to. When my next year's contract came up, I didn't have any heart for it. I told them I wanted a million dollars, that's what it would take to get me to come back and play for Kiesling— otherwise, trade me.

They took me up on it. It was a convoluted deal: I was traded to the Lions, and they sent me to the Giants. I was with Detroit for two days, and they sent me to New York for Ray Krouse, who had played for my alma mater, Maryland, and had been with the Giants since 1951. I remember getting a call from Wellington Mara after the deal sending me to Detroit, and he said something like, "Don't get too comfortable there." Well, moving on to the Giants was the best thing that ever happened to me in pro football.

I had to report to St. Michael's in Winooski, Vermont, where the Giants were holding training camp in 1956. I met up with Andy Robustelli, Jim Katcavage, Sam Huff, Rosie Grier. Most of us were new to the Giants that year except for Grier, but after about two weeks I said to my wife, "This is a winning ball club. I can just tell." We really melded into a family.

It was very different from the Steelers. Jack Mara, who was running the operation then, the coaches, and the veteran players all made you feel welcome, that you were a real part of the team. And in training camp we were out there in shorts and baseball caps in the morning, pads in the afternoon. During the season we never wore pads at practice. And consequently we did not get beat to hell by our own team as we had in Pittsburgh.

This was also the year that Tom Landry took over as full-time defensive coordinator. He had just retired as a player—and, incidentally, he was one fine defensive back when he played. After the first meeting or two we had with Tom Landry we all had the feeling he was going to be one helluva coach. Before Landry, the Giants had been using the old six-man front or the 5-4, and he introduced the 4-3, which was unheard of at the time. But it sure worked for us. The man never got excited, you never heard him swear, but I believe he proved he was one of the greatest coaches ever in the NFL.

The one person I had known before coming to the Giants was Walt Yowarsky, one of our defensive ends. He and I had played together in Washington. We became roommates in New York. We palled around with Robustelli, Katcavage, Huff. After Yowarsky left in 1957, Robustelli and I roomed together. We also hung around with a lot of the offensive players too—guys like Jack Stroud, Ray Wietecha,

On the sideline—waiting. Three of the famous front four: Jim Katcavage (75), Andy Robustelli (81), and Dick Modzelewski (77).

Rosey Brown. We weren't a bunch of carousers, but we'd go out for a bunch of beers, things like that.

I was probably the biggest jokester on the team—along with Sam Huff anyway. I remember in 1956 before the championship game my brother Ed drove my car in from Pittsburgh, and he stayed a night or two with us. We were not staying in the hotel at that time; we were on our own until Sunday morning. There was a bunch of us—Sam Huff, Bill Svoboda, Ed, and some others—who stayed up playing poker. And Ed kept saying, "Aren't you guys going to bed? You're playing for the championship tomorrow!"

He was in the locker room before the game the next

day and most of us were clowning around. He just kept shaking his head. Ed was with Cleveland then, and he kept saying Paul Brown would never let this go on. Finally he said to me, "You guys are gonna get the shit beat out of you today. You're nowhere serious enough." Instead, we went out and beat the crap out of the Bears [47-7].

Every time we played at Pittsburgh, my mother would have a lot of us from the defense over for dinner the night before the game. She'd put on this big Polish feast: kielbasa, pierogi, stuffed cabbage, Polish ravioli stuffed with cheese and eggs, soup made from duck's blood.

The best season I can remember in my entire football career was 1958. We had to beat Cleveland three times, which would seem to be impossible—but we did it. Top it off with the sudden-death championship game against Baltimore. It was such an intense, suspenseful year. Too bad we couldn't have ended it on a better note by winning the championship. We deserved it that year.

They had some tough linemen, the Colts; so did the Browns around that time. You'd never forget going up against Jim Parker of Baltimore or Lou Groza of Cleveland—everybody remembers him as a kicker but he was a hell of an offensive lineman too.

One of the truly toughest I went head-to-head with, however, was on our own team—Jack Stroud. We'd go at it in scrimmages, and he would beat the hell out of me. I remember one time when Jim Lee Howell blew the whistle and yelled, "All right, last play." Well, we'd been going at it for some time and both of us were really tired. I said to him, "Jack, just fall down and I'll fall on top of you, and we can get the hell out of here."

"Good idea," Stroud said.

So Charlie Conerly drops back to pass and Stroud falls down. I just jumped over him and nailed Conerly for a sack. Howell must have chewed Jack's ass off for ten minutes. Stroud never forgot that, which is probably one of the reasons he came on so strong in our scrimmages.

Another guy who was always tough was John Nisby of the Steelers. He didn't get a lot of publicity, but I'll tell you—out there on the field he never quit coming at you. Vince Promuto of the Redskins, who came along in the 1960s, was tough as hell too. The best center I ever played against was Jim Ringo of Green Bay. He was smart and so damn quick.

Talk about tough: a guy I teamed with on the Steelers, Ernie Stautner, set the standard. I never had to play against him, fortunately, because he was a defensive tackle too. I remember one time we played the Pittsburgh Steelers, and after the game Jim Lee Howell said, "I want to congratulate Rosey Brown and Darrell Dess, who did a great job of containing Ernie Stautner today." They both rolled their eyes; the next day both of them were in the treatment room. They couldn't practice for the next two days because Ernie had just beat the living hell out of them.

The best backfield I think I ever went up against was the 49ers in the 1950s. Hugh McElhenny was a great runner, one of the hardest to nail who ever played the game. And they had that great fullback, Joe Perry, and Y. A. Tittle at quarterback. The one play they used so well was Tittle dropping back and dumping a screen pass to McElhenny. It was very effective. Tittle used the same kind of pass a lot when he came to the Giants in the 1960s.

The best running back—no question—Jim Brown of Cleveland. One time they showed film after a game with the Browns, and here was Jimmy Brown going up the middle and there are about six or seven of us on him, underneath him, everywhere, and we could not bring the son of a bitch down for about ten yards. The only way to stop Brown was to gang-tackle him.

I played a total of eight years with the Giants, and in six of them we won our conference. And the other two years we were second once and third the other time. That's the kind of team the Giants had.

After the 1963 season, the one when we lost to the Bears in the title game, I was traded. So was Sam Huff. Allie Sherman was the coach then. I was living in Cleveland at the time because my brother and I had a restaurant and cocktail lounge there. One day after the season, Sam Huff came over to Cleveland. We were sitting down having dinner and he gets a telephone call. He comes back to the table and I said, "What the hell's wrong? You look kind of funny."

He said, "I've just been traded to the goddamn Washington Redskins."

I couldn't believe it. Sam was an All-Pro. He was only about twenty-eight years old, had a number of good years ahead of him. Then about two weeks later I get the telephone call from Allie Sherman. He tells me I've been traded to Cleveland. I couldn't understand that either. I must admit I was very hurt.

After I told Sam I got the call from Sherman just like him, Sam told all the other Giants to stay out of my restaurant or else they'd probably get traded too.

As it turned out, it was a good thing. The Giants collapsed in 1964 [2–10–2] and the Browns won the whole thing, whipped the Colts 27–0 for the title. On top of that, my family was in Cleveland, my brothers and a sister were there, we had the business.

I played three years with the Browns and then retired after the 1966 season. It was time. I'd been in the league since 1953. As Charlie Conerly said, "When you're sore the day of the game, it's time to quit." I was sore the day of every game in 1966.

The restaurant Ed and I owned—Mo and Junior's was the name of it—was a success. We had it for sixteen years. When the Giants would come to town to play Cleveland, they would all come to it for dinner. We'd have people lined up in the streets to see the guys like Gifford and Robustelli and Summerall. Then in the summer when the Yankees would come to play the Indians, we used to get a lot of their ballplayers coming in: Yogi Berra, Mickey Mantle, Moose Skowron.

After I quit playing, I did some scouting for the Browns. In 1968, I got calls from the 49ers, the Steelers, and Art Modell of the Browns about coaching their defensive lines. I signed with the Browns and coached there for ten years. After that I was an assistant coach with the Detroit Lions and Cincinnati Bengals. I coached a total of twenty-two years, and the last eight of them I was the defensive coordinator.

I've been associated with a lot of different teams in the NFL, playing and coaching. But even though I got traded and was mad as hell about it, I still look upon myself as a New York Giant. And I'm proud to be able to say it.

◨

The Pits

The day the Giants would most like to forget in a history that now spans almost seven decades is Sunday, November 27, 1966. That was the day they went down to Griffith Stadium to take on the Washington Redskins. It was the day the Giants set an NFL record, one that still stands in ignominy.

Otto Graham, the former renowned quarterback of the Cleveland Browns, was coaching the Redskins, and they were having a poor year (5–6–0 at the time of the meeting). The Giants were having a much worse year, having won only one of their ten games thus far that season. The one game in which they had triumphed had been against Washington, 13–10 at Yankee Stadium.

This late in the season, it was dubbed as a contest of the losers and garnered little attention in the nation's press.

Until. . . .

Sonny Jurgensen quarterbacked the Skins to a 13–0 first-quarter advantage and then a 34–14 halftime lead (the 34 points Washington scored was more than it had in any full game so far that year).

Redskins linebacker Sam Huff was especially joyous. He had less than fond memories of the day three years earlier when Giants coach Allie Sherman had implied he was over the hill and summarily traded him to Washington after eight illustrious years playing in New York. Huff approached Graham at halftime. "Show no mercy, Otto," he said. "Promise me no mercy."

Graham carried out Sam's wishes as the Redskins scored five more touchdowns in the second half. Then, with seven seconds remaining in the game and with a 69–41 lead, Graham called a time-out and then sent Charlie Gogolak onto the field. The little soccer-style kicker booted a 29-yard field goal.

With the final score of 72–41, three NFL records were logged, and all of them remain today. The 72 points scored by Washington is the highest ever in a regular-season game (the 73 scored against the Skins in 1940 by the Chicago Bears was in a postseason game), and the total of 113 points is the most ever scored in a regular or postseason game. And, of course, the Giants are stuck with the NFL mark of having given up the most points in a regular-season game.

After the game, when reporters asked Otto Graham the inevitable question—why had he added a last mortification in the waning seconds of the game?—he shrugged and with a straight face said, "Gogolak needed the practice."

Charlie Conerly

George Preston Marshall, owner and founder of the Washington Redskins, was never known for his acumen in drafting football players (except when he took Sammy Baugh in 1937). In 1946, for example, he selected in the first round halfback Cal Rossi of UCLA, only to discover that Rossi was still a junior and therefore ineligible for the draft. The next year he again chose Rossi in the first round, unaware that the now-eligible young back had no intention whatsoever of playing professional football.

True to form, Marshall traded away the rights to tailback Charlie Conerly to the Giants before the 1948 season—he had drafted Conerly in 1945, but Conerly at the time was still serving with the U.S. Marines in the South Pacific. Marshall's largesse was greatly appreciated by the New York Giants and their fans over the ensuing fourteen years.

Coming from a small town in Mississippi, Conerly went on to the University of Mississippi where, after his stint in World War II with the marines, he led the Rebels to their first Southeastern Conference championship in 1947 and earned consensus All-American honors in the process.

Charlie Conerly joined the Giants in 1948 and immediately

became the core around which Steve Owen solidified a new offensive attack—one that now involved throwing the football. Working first out of an A formation, a derivative of the old single wing, Charlie was eventually converted to a T formation quarterback. From that position, he instituted a passing game the likes of which the Giants had never seen before.

When Charlie Conerly finally retired after the 1961 season, he had staked claim to every career passing record in New York Giants annals. He threw the most passes (2,833), completed the most (1,418), gained the most yards passing (19,488), and tossed the most touchdown passes (173).

From 1948, his rookie year, through 1959, Conerly guided the Giants' destiny on the field. If a quarterback were credited in points for the touchdown passes he threw, Charlie Conerly would have accounted for 1,038 points with his arm alone, almost 400 more than the club's accredited scoring leader, kicker Pete Gogolak, who scored 646 with his foot.

Only Hall of Fame center/linebacker Mel Hein played more seasons than Conerly (fifteen to fourteen). Charlie played under Steve Owen, Jim Lee Howell, and Allie Sherman and was acknowledged as one of the finest quarterbacks of his time. In the words of the late Vince Lombardi, who was Conerly's offensive coordinator in New York for a number of years, "If you want dependability, if you want someone who truly knows the game and has the instinct to lead on the field . . . you want a Conerly."

After football, Charlie Conerly went back to his native Mississippi, where he still resides today.

I was born and raised in Clarksdale, Mississippi. Went to Clarksdale Bobo High School there—I don't know what the Bobo stands for; somebody, I guess, just named it that.

In 1941 I went to Ole Miss—the University of Mississippi. Then in 1943 I went into the marines. I was overseas for a little more than two years and got out early in 1946.

I was supposed to have graduated from college in 1945, and that year the Washington Redskins drafted me.

Only problem was that I was over in Guam. They sent me a telegram down in Mississippi, which my mother got. She wrote me about it, and I said to myself, "Well, I'd be happy to come back right away." But, of course, I couldn't.

After I got out of the marines, I went back to Ole Miss and finished up there after the 1947 season. I played football in the fall of 1946 and then again in 1947. My senior year [1947] we won the Southeastern Conference. I happily remember we beat Tennessee that year. Ole Miss had never beaten them before. [General Bob] Neyland was their coach. We played them up in Memphis and beat them pretty good [43–13]. Because we won the conference we should have gone to the Sugar Bowl, but earlier that year they announced a new bowl, the Delta Bowl, and Ole Miss accepted an invitation to it midway through our season. So we couldn't go to New Orleans—Alabama went instead to play Texas. We beat Texas Christian at the Delta Bowl [13–9], although we would've preferred beating Texas at the Sugar Bowl. But, all told, it'd been a real good year.

During that year the Redskins, I guess, decided they didn't want me anymore, and so they traded the rights to the Giants. I think they got Howie Livingston, a halfback, for me. Wellington Mara, I remember, came down to see me and watched our last game of the '47 season.

So I saw I was going to New York, which wasn't all that bad. After all, the Redskins had Sammy Baugh at the time. And I also felt New York was the place to be if you were going to be playing professional sports.

There was the story, too, around that time about me and the Brooklyn Dodgers and Branch Rickey, who owned that team in the AAFC. They had drafted me—they had their own draft then and didn't care about the NFL's draft. They offered me some money—a little more than the Giants, as I recall—but they were a new team, and I just felt the Giants had been playing football, what, twenty-some-odd years, and that sure seemed like a safer place to go. They wrote it up in the papers that the Dodgers were going to give me a $40,000 bonus or some such. Well, if they were

I might have taken it. That was a lot of money in those days. There was all this stuff in the papers about money—big money, $15,000 a year for so many years—but it was all talk. It was written up that Branch Rickey was offering a package like more than $100,000, but figures tend to get all messed up between what they were offering and what the newspapers said they were offering. There was a gentleman who was a baseball scout for their baseball team who came to visit me, but that was almost all the contact I'd had with them. At any rate, I felt I made the right decision signing on with the Giants.

My first encounter with the pros was in the College All-Star Game that summer in Chicago. We were up there to play the Chicago Cardinals, that team with Charley Trippi and Pat Harder and Paul Christman. Our coach was Frank Leahy, and he had a horde of his Notre Dame players on the All-Stars—Johnny Lujack, George Connor, Zig Czarobski. I think there were about eight of them altogether. We had all kinds of great backs on that team: Bobby Layne, the Michigan boys—[Bob] Chappius and [Chalmers "Bump"] Elliot.

Because of Leahy and all his ballplayers from Notre Dame, we knew we weren't going to play a whole helluva lot. So we spent a lot of time up there going to Zig Czarobski's restaurant and bar about every night. That's my biggest memory. Oh—and I did get to punt once in the game. We were really hungry to get to our training camps, and all of us were glad when the game was finally over [the All-Stars lost 28–0].

So I went on to New York. I always liked New York. When I was a teenager, me and this friend of mine hitchhiked up there from Mississippi to go to the World's Fair, and I remember once we got there going to the Polo Grounds to see a Giants baseball game. It was really something, I thought.

When I moved up there to play for the Giants we lived on the West Side, around 100th Street and Broadway. Ray

Poole was a year ahead of me with the Giants, but he'd played down at Ole Miss with me—an end and a fine one, one of the best—and we roomed together in that apartment there when I first got to New York. We were just a couple of country boys. We would catch a subway to go to practice at the Polo Grounds, which was where we were playing in those days. We always kept saying, "Hey, this is a little different from where we come from!"

When I got there I was a single-wing tailback, which I'd been in college, but down there at Ole Miss it was different that last year. Our coach was Johnny Vaught—it was his first year—and he wanted to throw the football. I would be in a position every time I got the ball to throw it. We made all kinds of records passing because Barney Poole [brother of Ray Poole], who had come back down from Army, was an end—and one of the finest—and we just had a kind of natural thing, me throwing to him.

I also played out of a thing they called the A formation, which gave me all kinds of options. I would get the ball on each play—unless we had a trick play where the ball was centered directly to the wingback. I could pass, run with it, hand off and go down to catch a pass, all kinds of things. But most of it had been throwing the ball. I had to block a little too, which I wasn't all that fond of.

Well, up at New York under old Steve Owen we also played an A formation. It wasn't for a couple of years until we switched to the T formation. And that's what saved my life. Hell, I only weighed about 180 pounds back then [on a 6'1" frame]. It was just too tough playing out of the A with all the blocking and running that went along with it.

We did pass a lot, though, after I joined the Giants. That first year [1948], in fact, when we played the Pittsburgh Steelers, I threw so often that day I completed 36 passes [out of 53], which was an NFL record at the time; and, hell, we still lost the game [38–28]. So I always felt the record didn't mean much of a damn because we lost the game; you weren't out there to set records, you were out there to win the darn ball game.

I was blessed with some great receivers when I came to the Giants. Bill Swiacki was one. He came from the Ivy League—Columbia—made that famous catch to upset Army in '47. He was a rookie with the Giants, same as me, in 1948. He wasn't all that speedy, but he sure could get open. And we had Ray Poole at the other end; and Choo Choo Roberts, coming out of the backfield. They were the ones I most liked to throw to then. Later, of course, Kyle Rote came up, and after him Frank Gifford. You couldn't ask for better than those two.

As much as we might pass, we were still a defensive team. Steve Owen coached defense, that was the emphasis from '48 through '53. His philosophy was if we could beat somebody 3-0 or 6-3, he loved that. Just stop the other team. Then he got the boot and things began to change with the Giants.

When they finally switched me from tailback to a T formation quarterback, it was all new to me. I must say, it wasn't all that easy making the adjustment. You must remember in those days we just came to camp a couple of weeks before the season started, and that's all the time we had to work at making the change. Bobby Layne [with the Detroit Lions] was going through the same thing at the same time, and I know he found it the same way—difficult. It was, in the end, much better for me than the A formation. And I must admit I was happy with it. It's what enabled me to play so long. That and, of course, the guys who did such a good job blocking for me. That's what kept my career going as long as it did. I believe Sid Luckman and Sammy Baugh said the same thing: switching to the T, where you didn't get hit every play, lengthened their careers too.

I remember once after we were using the T formation that, for one game, Steve Owen had us go back to the old A formation. It was against the Chicago Cardinals, and we really confused them. They just didn't know how to defense the A because nobody was using it. We whipped them bad that day [51-21, in 1950].

Vince Lombardi came down from Army just after Steve

left and Jim Lee Howell had taken over. We all hit it off from the start with Vince—the backfield, that is. We would listen to him and he would listen to us. We'd go over to his house, eat pasta, and talk football with him regularly—me, Gifford, Rote, Webster, and some others.

I remember one time when we were in training camp—this was later on—and Vince came up with this play. We were supposed to work it out of a split T. We ran through it in practice. It was one where I was supposed to fake the handoff, fake a pass, and then run it myself. We were in an exhibition game and Frank [Gifford] came in from the sideline and said, "Lombardi wants you to run that play where you keep the ball."

Well, I wasn't crazy, so I didn't do it. He sent the play in a couple of other times, but I never did run it. After the game, Lombardi said to Gifford, "How come Charlie won't run that play?"

Gifford said, "Hell, Charlie don't want to run the ball."

We did use one of Vince's trick plays where I ended up running with the ball once in an important game, though. It was in the playoff game against the Browns in 1958. In the first quarter we got down to about the 18 or 19 of Cleveland, and Vince sent in the play. I handed off to Alex Webster, and he started to sweep around one end but then handed a reverse to Gifford, who went around the other end with me trailing behind him. Well, Frank got about 10 yards and was about to be tackled when he wheeled around and lateralled the ball to me. Everybody was on him, and I just took it on in for the touchdown.

Their coach, Paul Brown, said after the game, "The double reverse didn't surprise me. But the lateral to Conerly? What the hell was he doing there?"

Well, I was supposed to be there. The lateral was an option. Vinnie set it up that way. I was just supposed to be there if Gifford needed me. I don't know how long it'd been since I'd scored a touchdown, but it was great for an old guy like me to run it in [Conerly was 35 at the time].

It was the only touchdown we scored that day. Pat

Charlie Conerly (1948–61) was the quiet, reserved quarterback for the
Giants during the 1950s. Throwing to receivers such as Kyle Rote,
Frank Gifford, Alex Webster, and Bob Schnelker, he set every career
passing record in Giants' history, all of which stood until Phil Simms
came along in the 1980s.

Summerall kicked the extra point and then a field goal in the next quarter and we beat the Browns, 10-0. So we won the Eastern Conference and went on to play Baltimore for the championship that year.

Vince was a great coach for us in those days, and, of course, he proved it again when he went on to Green Bay.

During the years I quarterbacked the Giants, we never had any real speedsters as receivers. We had Gifford, who could do just about everything out there—run, catch the ball, pass. And we had Kyle Rote, who had a bum knee. He was a great receiver but he couldn't go deep because of his knee. Fact is, the only real speedster came my last year there [1961], Del Shofner, but by that time Y.A. [Tittle] was doing the throwing. But we did just fine throwing short and had a lot of different patterns to suit that style of passing game.

The players would often come into the huddle and tell me they thought they could get open or this or that—Gifford and Webster especially, and Rote too. And a lot of times I'd go with them. There were some other guys who'd come in and say they could get open; but they'd say it all the time, and I usually ignored those guys. The linemen had some good input too. They'd tell me if they thought they could block a player one way, things like that.

They would occasionally send a play in from the sideline, but ordinarily I would call the plays in the huddle in those days. It's not anywhere like that anymore—now they've got computers and coordinators and coaches working things out, and then somebody runs the play in and that's it.

One thing I'll always remember about my career with the Giants was the way we used to be able to beat Cleveland. In those days almost nobody could beat the Browns. They were just such a great team [joining the NFL in 1950, the Browns won six consecutive conference titles and three NFL championships]. Those were the days when they had Otto Graham at quarterback. They couldn't stop Otto in those years, the early '50s, but we could. Hell, that first year they won the league championship—lost only two games all year, and those were to us. And later, when they had Jimmy Brown, we were about the only team who could shut him down. We just had something special when we took on the Browns, and they knew it.

But the game that sticks in my mind most was the overtime championship game in 1958. We played so well against the Baltimore Colts that day, both the offense and the defense. We were losing at the half [14–3], but then we came back. In the third quarter, our defense made a great goal-line stand and stopped them. That really fired us up, and we marched on them. I threw a pass to Kyle and he went some 60 yards with it and fumbled, but Alex Webster picked it up and got all the way to their 1-yard line. We scored [fullback Mel Triplett bucked it in]. A little while later we moved on them again, and I got the ball to Gifford for another score. We were winning [17–14] with just about two minutes left and we had them back on their own 15-yard line. But then ol' Johnny Unitas got going and took them all the way down the field, and their guy [Steve Myhra] kicked a field goal to tie it.

Ol' Johnny did the same thing in overtime and we lost out, but it was one great ball game all the way.

It was in that game that their Gino Marchetti got his leg broken. He was a great one, big and fast. He got it broke in the fourth quarter. In the hullabaloo that followed, they mismarked the ball where Gifford had been brought down. It was a third down and Frank was sure he'd made the first down. But in the confusion and yelling they placed it differently, about a foot and a half behind where it should have been. So instead of a first down we punted, and that's when Unitas brought them all the way back to tie us.

I was pretty lucky when it came to injuries. I had very few in the fourteen years I was with the Giants. It wasn't until 1960 that one really got to me. I hurt my elbow that year and couldn't throw the ball, so I missed a good portion of the season. George Shaw did much of the quarterbacking that year. That was a bad year all around for injuries: Alex Webster was out most of the year with a bad knee, Gifford got that concussion and was out the whole next year as well, and [Jim] Katcavage from our defense got a broken shoulder.

Two things helped me. I got great blocking the whole time I was there. Our offensive line was fierce, and they protected me very well. And later, as I was getting older, Jim Lee Howell spelled me from time to time because we had a fine backup quarterback, Don Heinrich, who unfortunately just passed away [in 1992]. Don came in 1954 and stayed through 1959, and he could take over very well any time he was called upon.

After each season I'd go back to Clarksdale. There weren't any kind of decent jobs you could get for half the year, so I just played golf every day. I also had bought a little farm from the bonus money I got when I first signed, and my dad farmed it.

After the 1960 season and the problems I was having with my elbow, when they asked me if I was going to come back, I said, "Well, I don't know. I think maybe I've had enough." I'd been with them through thirteen years by then. But we talked, and I finally said I would come back for 1961 but then that would be it.

So in '61 they traded to bring Y. A. Tittle to the Giants. Y.A. and I had played against each other in college—he was at Louisiana State when I was with Ole Miss. Then we'd been playing against each other after he went with the 49ers.

I'm glad they did bring Y.A. in because he was a mighty fine quarterback. I started the first game that year; but in the second, I threw a pass out in the flat and it was intercepted. Allie Sherman, who was our head coach then, pulled me out. Y.A. came on and threw a bunch of passes to Del Shofner and brought the team back so Pat Summerall could kick a field goal for us to win the game.

It was the right thing to do. I was about thirty-eight years old by that time, and Y.A. was just a fine quarterback with a few more good years ahead of him. And he certainly was a big help to the Giants for the next three years. I still to this day cannot understand why San Francisco let him go. But I'm sure glad they did, and so were the Giants.

After I left the Giants I didn't do anything much for the next year. Then I went into the shoe business down in Mississippi, which turned out to be just fine for me, and I stayed with that until I retired in 1984.

Now I'm just taking it easy down here in the same town where I was born—Clarksdale. My wife and I do some traveling, and I get together with some of the old ballplayers in different places, and I get back to New York for some of the Giants' games and some of their alumni functions. I like to see them all. We can still kick around the stories about the way it was.

I played golf the other day with Wellington Mara over in Florida. That was really nice. And I'll be damned—I didn't know he could play that well.

◙

Distant Replay

The ambulance that stood in New York's Central Park was not needed, despite the ninety-degree heat, as the stars from the Colts and Giants 1958 championship game played touch football on July 7, 1978, a game that was to be broadcast later in the season by CBS television.

Colts players included Johnny Unitas, Alan Ameche, Gino Marchetti, Lenny Moore, Ray Berry, Jim Parker, Art Donovan, and Steve Myhra. The Giants players hoping for revenge from the 23–17 loss they suffered two decades earlier included Charlie Conerly, Frank Gifford, Kyle Rote, Alex Webster, Rosey Brown, Ray Wietecha, Dick Modzelewski, and Pat Summerall.

Myhra brought a six-pack of beer to the Colts' bench for pregame refreshments, but soon referee Sonny Jurgensen had the players, six to a side, on the field. After just a few plays from scrimmage, Unitas threw a scoring spiral to Lenny Moore in the end zone. Jurgensen declared the score 7–0 without a point-after attempt.

Conerly's first pass was intercepted. "Same old Charlie," cracked Alex Webster.

To round out the scoring in the first half, Unitas hit Raymond Berry on two touchdown bombs.

Frank Gifford took over the quarterbacking chores for Conerly, who was now nearly sixty years old. In the third quarter, the Giants resorted to subterfuge to get on the scoreboard. Kyle Rote hid on the sideline and just before the ball was snapped ran into the end zone, where he pulled in the pass from Gifford. Later Gifford threw another touchdown pass, this time to Webster, and for a time it looked as if the Giants might pull off an upset by tying the game.

But with less than one minute to play in the second thirty-minute half, Unitas intercepted a Gifford pass and ran it back all the way for a touchdown.

And the Colts had won again.

◙

Shipwreck Kelly

John Sims "Shipwreck" Kelly arrived in New York City in 1932 and soon after engraved a truly inimitable imprint everywhere from the Polo Grounds and Ebbets Field to the Stork Club. He came from the rolling hills of central Kentucky, from a wealthy family—owners of a 3,000-acre dairy farm, among other things—and he was unawed by Manhattan and its sophistications.

An All-American halfback at the University of Kentucky, who was dubbed in his college yearbook as "the fastest man in the South" because he ran the 100-yard dash in 9.8 seconds, Shipwreck was equally as adroit, he quickly proved, moving through New York's café society.

Shipwreck signed first with the New York Giants and played one season with them (1932). The following year, in partnership with Chris Cagle, the All-American from Army who also played in the Giants' backfield in 1932, Shipwreck, at age 23, bought the Brooklyn Dodgers NFL franchise. He was a fine if unpredictable football player, and in fact led the NFL in pass receptions in 1933 (22, including 3 for touchdowns).

When Shipwreck was not in a locker room or on a football field, he could usually be found in places like El Morocco or "21" or perhaps out in the Hamptons or up in Newport. His closest friends included people such as Dan Topping, Jock Whitney, and Bing Crosby. He dated Tallulah Bankhead and various Broadway starlets, and he married New York's most glamorous debutante, Brenda Frazier.

The setting for the following interview gives some idea of how much Shipwreck Kelly's lifestyle differed from that of the other young men with whom he played the game of football. It was conducted in the trophy room of Shipwreck's home, "a little place I have on the water," as he referred to it, which was in actuality an eighteen-room mansion on the shore of Long Island Sound that F. Scott Fitzgerald might very well have had in mind when writing The Great Gatsby.

The trophy room was not one to house mementos from his successful careers in football and track, however. Instead, it was an enormous room filled with relics of an incredible life. The trophies were the mounted heads of animals he had hunted and killed: lion, tiger, caribou, elk, impala, moose, puma—practically every form of big game. Draped across chairs and tables everywhere were skins of leopard, cheetah, bear, jaguar; on the floor was a huge polar-bear skin rug and the skin of an enormous maned lion, both with mouths gaped open in fierce snarls. On one wall was an original Grandma Moses painting, and in one corner was a poker table covered in leopard skin—instead of the traditional green felt—where, according to Shipwreck, Jock Whitney once staged a game of poker in which each chip was worth $10,000.

And throughout the room were framed photographs of Shipwreck and his friends. Here was Shipwreck golfing with the Duke of Windsor, there he was in the south of France with Aristotle Onassis and Maria Callas, at a bullfight in Spain with Pablo Picasso, hunting with Ernest Hemingway in Africa, crouched over a freshly slain mountain lion in Idaho with Clark Gable. Many others posed with Shipwreck, making a kind of scrapbook of the celebrity register of the mid-twentieth century: Irving Berlin, J. Edgar Hoover, Richard Nixon, Bob Hope, Bill Paley, Casey Stengel, Fred Astaire, and on and on.

An unframed letter from J. Edgar Hoover attests to and thanks Shipwreck for his service as an undercover agent for the FBI during World War II.

Surely one of the most colorful men ever to be associated with professional football, Shipwreck Kelly died in 1986 at the age of 74.

I went to the University of Kentucky, and I thought I was hot shit—but they didn't. I knew I could play football and that I could run like hell. But the coaches there hardly ever let me play.

Finally they put me in during the last freshman game of the season against Centre, which was a smaller school in Kentucky. I made three touchdowns after they let me in the game that day, and from that time on they knew I could play.

It was while I was at Kentucky that I got the nickname "Shipwreck." Around that time there was a man who was known as Shipwreck Kelly, an old sailor who went around sitting on flagpoles. He came to Lexington one day and climbed up and stood on a flagpole, and people thought that was very funny. I guess I was a junior or senior then and a pretty big hotshot. Well, after we won a game, somebody said something like, "You can sure play football, but you can't sit on a flagpole like Shipwreck Kelly."

I said, "Bullshit." And I climbed up on a flagpole and stood there on top for a few minutes. Then I started down and somebody yelled, "What are you coming down for?"

"I have to piss," I said.

By the time I got to New York, after I graduated, I was known mostly as Shipwreck because I had climbed that flagpole.

It was Percy Johnson who wanted me to move to New York. He was from Kentucky and like a father to me. He was chairman of the board of the Chemical Bank, a guy like J. P. Morgan—wealthy as hell. When I was in school, he used to come down to Kentucky and watch me play football. He had a son who was my age and in the same class, and we were great friends. I used to go up to New York every summer and stay with them. Then after I graduated, Percy Johnson said, "Come on to New York."

So in the summer of 1932 I came and he gave me a job at the Chemical Bank. I worked there two weeks, I think it was. I saw what it was like and decided I wanted to play pro football. I went to see the people at the Giants, and they offered me a contract, a shitty contract like they all were in those days, but I played. Tim Mara was the man I talked to there, the owner. There was also Jack Mara, his son, and a kid called Wellington Mara, but Tim Mara was the whole thing then.

Steve Owen was the coach, a nice friendly sort of guy; too friendly, in fact, and a lot of the players used to bullshit him a lot because he was too nice sometimes. His brother Bill played on the team and was a pretty good tackle.

I didn't get to play until the second game of the season. It was against Green Bay, and we weren't doing a thing. The Giants hadn't scored a single point in their first game that year, and against Green Bay we hadn't scored one either. So Owen sent me in. I broke a couple of runs, one was about 30 yards, and I caught a couple of passes that day, but we still didn't score a point. But I became a starter after that. I played about six or seven games with the Giants that year, but then I quit because the doctor told me I wasn't in shape for it. I had a small touch of rheumatic fever, and I didn't feel very good—and they weren't paying me very much money anyway. I had some money myself, and so I went back to Kentucky.

After the season, Chris Cagle, who had been the Giants' best back that year, called me up on the phone and told me there was a football franchise for sale, the Brooklyn Dodgers; Bill Dwyer owned them and he wanted to sell out, Cagle told me. So I called up Percy Johnson and asked him what he thought about it. I told him I might want to buy the team. He said, "Well, if you think you can make it go, come on up and I'll help you." So I went back to New York and I bought the Brooklyn Dodgers with Cagle.

New York was a great place to be back then. I had a helluva life. I really was a protégé of Percy Johnson—and if you're a protégé of someone like that you can tell everybody to kiss your ass. I met all kinds of people through him—the socialites, the big people on Wall Street. . . . I nearly married Bill Woodworth's daughter around then. Bill

The raucous and colorful halfback Shipwreck Kelly (left) poses with one of the early game's greatest quarterbacks, Benny Friedman. Kelly played for the Giants only one year before buying the Brooklyn Dodgers NFL franchise. Friedman quarterbacked the Giants for three years (1929–31).

Woodworth was one of the biggest bankers in the world then—had houses in three or four places.

I was having a great time. [Dan] Topping [who would later own the New York Yankees baseball team] and I were all over Broadway. He loved the showgirls.

There was another guy, another millionaire, that I was good friends with too: Ed Madden. He bought me a LaSalle so I could get around New York easier. After a while I shit him around. I said, "You mean you want me driving around in a car like this?" So he took it back and got me a Cadillac instead. Madden also got me to run for the New York Athletic Club. I ran the 100 and the 220 in a lot of those big relays in New York, Philadelphia, Pittsburgh, quite a few places. I tried out for the 1936 Olympics, but I lost out to Jesse Owens and Ralph Metcalf in the sprints.

We used to go to the nightclubs around New York all the time too, but not during the times I was playing football—at least not a lot. I was serious about football. The one that was my favorite was the Stork Club because Sherman Billingsley liked me. He owned it and he had piles of money. I used to go in there and if I wanted any money he'd give it to me and say, "Pay me back when you're ready." He did the same thing for Walter Winchell and a lot of other people who went in there.

The hot-shit place of them all, though, was El Morocco. I knew John Perona, the owner there, and he was very nice to me. The big thing was to get into the nightclub; and even then only if you were a hot shit would you be sitting where the hot shits were. If you were not, they'd put you in the back or in a corner somewhere out of the way.

I remember one night in the El Morocco when I was with four or five people at one table. In walked this guy with a beard—there weren't many beards in those days—and John Perona came over and said to me, "Do you know who that guy is?"

I said I didn't.

"It's Orson Welles, the actor."

On second thought, I said, I thought I'd seen a picture

of him somewhere. So Perona brought Orson Welles over to the table and introduced him to us. I tried to be a smart aleck, like I did a lot of times in those days. I said, "Gee, Mr. Welles, it's nice meeting someone like you." He didn't know who I was or that I played football or anything about me. But he was very pleasant. Then I said something like, "Why do you cultivate something on your face that grows wild on your ass?"

"Mr. Kelly," he said, "you are new in New York, and if I were you I wouldn't tell my friends how much you know about my ass."

I felt like shit and got up and left.

Another time I remember was at the Stork Club. I took Tallulah Bankhead there. I used to date her a lot around that time. In walked this beautiful young girl, Brenda Frazier, one of the richest, most famous debutantes of the time, with three young men, and they sat down on the floor near the table Bankhead and I were at.

Well, the waiters were giving out balloons and one of them was supposed to have a hundred-dollar bill in it. It was something Billingsley used to do every once in a while. I think this time it had probably been fixed because Bankhead got the balloon with the hundred dollars in it. She got up and walked over to where Brenda Frazier was sitting on the floor and handed it to her. "Here, my dear," she said. "I think you'll need it. I've been reading in the papers lately how broke you are all the time."

"Thank you, I can use it," Brenda said. "I don't get my money until I'm twenty-one."

I didn't let that crap interfere with my football playing, however; I kept the two apart. You had to because it was a rugged game, much tougher than college ball. The sons of bitches in the pros were bigger and stronger, and all of them were pretty damn good, whereas in college only two or three players on a team might be worth a shit.

Two of the toughest I remember were Bill Hewitt of the Bears and Father Lumpkin, who played for Portsmouth and

Detroit and then came with the Dodgers. They both played without headgear. Harry Newman of the Giants was a helluva ballplayer too [Kelly only played against Newman, not with him on the Giants]. He was very small but tough. Probably the greatest I played against was Dutch Clark. He played for Portsmouth and Detroit too.

The greatest I saw after I left the sport was Sid Luckman [quarterback for the Bears]. I ran into him on the street one day in New York and we talked a little. He told me I had been his hero when he was a kid growing up in Brooklyn. I really appreciated it, him remembering me for playing football. I get tired of all those people remembering me because I married a rich girl and was in the café society thing all the time. Football was important to me. One thing I'm especially proud of is that I never made a fair catch of a punt. Never. I'd take it on the run no matter what.

I quit playing after the 1934 season. But then the coaches asked me to come back in 1937. One of their backs got hurt or something and the team was doing shitty. I guess they thought I could run like I used to. Potsy Clark was the coach [of the Brooklyn Dodgers] that year. Anyway, they had to persuade me to come back, but I wasn't the player I was before. I wasn't in shape; I couldn't help them on the field.

After that I got out of football for good. Then I married Brenda Frazier. And after that I did that work for the FBI. I traveled everywhere for them. You see, I could because of the society that I hung around in. I mean, I went to Europe, to Cuba, then to Mexico, to Peru, to Chile, and when we got in the war I spent a lot of time in Argentina. I could meet people at parties and things—the big shots there—because of my connections. An ordinary person didn't have access to them. But I did. There were loads of rich Germans in Argentina and high-ranking officers, all in that same international society. I would try to find out about the ships, the submarines—things like that—that were off our coasts. And there were a lot of them. A lot of those people knew where they were. I kissed everybody's ass in Argentina to find out things like that, and I found out a lot. I also found who the others who were sympathetic to the Germans were, others in that society. I worked at it all the way through the war for Hoover. Then I got out of that part of it. He [J. Edgar Hoover] and I were good friends, did things together many times in the years after the war.

But football was great. It helped me in a lot of ways. I tried to do my job right in the years I played. And it's nice to be remembered for that part of my life.

◻

A Brief Career

New York sportswriters John Kieran and later Barry Gottherer wrote of the arrival of Shipwreck Kelly at the Giants in 1932 and his departure later that same season.

It was in the summer that a big, lanky, redheaded chap came into Tim Mara's office on Twenty-third Street.

"Ah'm Shipwreck Kelly," explained the visitor.

"What?" said Mr. Mara. "The fellow who sits on flagpoles?"

"No, suh," said the visitor. "Ah play football. Played foh Kaintucky."

Mara, who had been given a list of the top college prospects by his sixteen-year-old son Wellington, suddenly realized who his visitor was. "Welcome," said the Giants' owner, smiling and offering a chair. "I've heard of you, my boy. Here, look at this." Opening his drawer, Mara pulled out a folder crammed with clippings detailing the exploits of Shipwreck Kelly of Kaintucky.

"I've seen them all," said Kelly, "and I'd lak to play football this fall with yah Giants. Ah hear it's a right smart team, suh."

Mara and the Giants needed Kelly, but not at his price—a percentage of the gate similar to the deal Red Grange had [with the Chicago Bears] back in 1925. "I'd love to have you, but I can't afford you," said Mara. "Well, the news about the Depression will get back to the hills of Kentucky sooner or later, and you might as well be the one to carry the word."

The Giants had not heard the last of Shipwreck Kelly.

Totally unannounced, the drawling, redheaded halfback reported to the Giants training camp at Magnetic Springs, Ohio.

"Glad to have you," said [coach Steve] Owen, "but really we weren't expecting you."

"That's why I came," drawled Kelly. "I do the most astonishing things. Nevah know why myself. Now, coach, there's nothin' to do but give me the ball and let me get going."

Shipwreck got the chance to prove himself early in the 1932 season and proved to be an exciting, elusive runner as well as a fine punter. After six games he quickly became the focus of the fans at the Polo Grounds. But . . .

For the Portsmouth game, Kelly's picture was on the cover of the program. Only one thing was missing—Kelly himself. When he didn't show up by game time, the band started playing "Has Anybody Here Seen Kelly?" but Shipwreck obviously had better things to do for the afternoon.

"What happened to Kelly?" a writer asked Owen after the game.

"Maybe he's sitting on a flagpole," quipped one of the Giants.

"As far as I'm concerned, he can sit on a tack," said Owen. "He's suspended." And colorful John Sims "Shipwreck" Kelly, who never fully explained his mysterious absence, never played another game as a Giant.

Actually, Shipwreck Kelly does explain his absence in the interview on the preceding pages, which was given a few years before his death in 1986: "I quit because the doctor told me I wasn't in shape for it. I had a small touch of rheumatic fever, and I didn't feel very good—and they weren't paying me very much money anyway."

Rosey Brown

There have always been "sleepers," as they are called, in the NFL draft—those players taken in the late rounds whose chances of making the team are at best remote but who do and go on to become substantial contributors. Of this group, Roosevelt "Rosey" Brown has to be the Rip Van Winkle.

Drafted by the New York Giants in the twenty-seventh round of the 1953 draft (there were thirty choices per team that year), he not only made the team but was a starter at offensive tackle from game one of his rookie year. Then he went on to win All-Pro honors eight times in his thirteen-year career with the Giants—only Lawrence Taylor, a ten-time All-Pro, has exceeded that in club annals, and only Hall of Fame center Mel Hein has equaled Brown's eight. In addition, Brown was invited to ten Pro Bowls and played in nine. Of the twenty-six players drafted ahead of him in 1953, only three made the team and none of them ever made the New York starting lineup.

Rosey Brown came to the Giants from Morgan State, a small college in Baltimore that played in an obscure all-black conference in Maryland, Virginia, and the near environs. Wellington Mara, always the Giants' talent watchdog, had heard good reports about him and had noted that Brown was named to the Black All-America team, selected by the *Pittsburgh Courier*, a weekly newspaper. He was worth a look-see, according to Mara and head coach Steve Owen.

Brown was 6'3" and 255 pounds when he reported to his first Giants' training camp in the summer of 1953—and he had a twenty-nine-inch waistline. He was fast and strong—that was immediately apparent—but he lacked the basic skills to play in the pros. Line coach Ed Kolman and head coach Owen set about rectifying that, down to such basic elements as teaching him the proper three-point stance. Brown proved to be a quick learner.

It took but a few years before he virtually redefined the position of offensive tackle in the NFL. According to an assessment by George Allen, who molded state-of-the-art defenses with the Chicago Bears, Los Angeles Rams, and Washington Redskins, "Rosey Brown wasn't big per se, but he was big enough. He was tall and had wide shoulders and good upper-body development, but narrow hips and legs. He was very fast. He had terrific quickness and excellent straightaway speed. He was one of the best in the pit. But he was actually at his best pulling out and blocking downfield, something only guards did before Rosey came along. He was spectacular and attracted attention in a way that offensive linemen usually do not."

The Giants made excellent use of Brown's speed by designing special plays that used him as a pulling blocker from his tackle position. He was also used on defense in goal-line situations.

Rosey Brown received the ultimate pro football accolade when he was inducted into the Pro Football Hall of Fame in 1975, joining a very select group of New York Giants, including his former roommate and good friend Emlen Tunnell. He was only the second player, after Jim Parker of the Baltimore Colts, to be enshrined based solely on his accomplishments as an offensive lineman.

After retiring from active play just before the 1966 season, Brown stayed on with the Giants—first as an assistant coach, handling the line, and later as a scout. He lives in Teaneck, New Jersey, not far from the Giants' homeland in East Rutherford, and still ranges far and wide, as he did in his playing days—but nowadays in search of players to bring into the Giants' camp instead of opponents to knock on their NFL butts.

I was born in Charlottesville, Virginia, and that's where I went to school. I played football in high school— offensive and defensive tackle—and after my senior year the coach from Morgan State College in Baltimore came down and offered a scholarship. My mother thought that was a fine thing, and she said that's where I would be going. In those days, the mothers made the decisions; nowadays it's more the kids who make the decisions.

So I went on up to Morgan State in 1949. I actually started college when I was fifteen, and I graduated when I was nineteen.

In those days, Morgan was an all-black school. And they had a very good football team then—I believe they had won something like fifty-two straight games by the time I arrived. We played against other all-black schools, like Virginia State College; Virginia Union; Hampton College, which was also in Virginia; Howard University, in Washington, D.C., and schools like that—mostly from that area.

One game I particularly remember from that time was against Central State College, which was in Wilberforce, Ohio. We both traveled to New York to play each other at the Polo Grounds. We were the first two black schools to play outside of our conference. That was my very first trip to New York.

Coming from Virginia to Baltimore was something, but nothing like coming to New York for the first time. The only way I can explain it is like I was starry-eyed, taking in something I'd never seen the likes of before.

I never even thought about playing professional football there. In those days, if you were black, you didn't do much thinking about playing for the pros at all. There were only a few in the league. Some teams didn't have any. The Redskins didn't sign a black until the 1960s. There were a few around that time: Marion Motley, Bill Willis, Tank Younger, Deacon Dan Towler, Len Ford, and, of course, Emlen Tunnell, who was with the Giants—he'd joined them in 1948, the first black they ever hired. He was a walk-on—came to see Wellington Mara and got himself a job.

So I was very surprised when I learned I was drafted by the Giants. In fact, I didn't even know anything about the Giants then. I got a letter from the Giants and then Em Tunnell came down and told me about being drafted, what it meant and everything. The way I saw it, I was chosen to play for the Giants, just like I was chosen to play for Morgan State. I had no idea they could cut you.

They sent me a contract for—I think it was—$2,700 a year [$225 per regular season game]. I showed it to my coach at Morgan, Eddie Hurt, and he said, "Sign it. That's more than I got when I started teaching and coaching." Then I just signed it and sent it back.

I went back to Charlottesville then, and in the summer the Giants sent me a train ticket. It was from Charlottesville to St. Peter, Minnesota, where they held their training camp. When I got there the only other black persons I saw were Em Tunnell and a fellow named Leo Miles from Virginia State. Like Em, Leo was a defensive back, but, unlike Em, he only lasted one year.

I was treated very well when I got there. Some of the players went out of their way to be helpful—veterans like Arnie Weinmeister and Al DeRogatis and Jack Stroud—he was a rookie like me. It was the first time that I had ever played football with any white boys.

I had a very different outlook on football then because my coach at Morgan had always told me there was nobody bigger, faster, or stronger than I. I kind of believed him until I got down to scrimmaging in Minnesota with the Giants. They lined me up across from Arnie Weinmeister and Al DeRogatis right off, and they went two-on-one on me. And, boy, did they hit me—they damn near killed me. I'd never been hit like that before. Afterwards, I took my pads off and said, heck, I'm goin' home. But I didn't. That was my introduction to the Giants and pro football. It was rough, no doubt about that, but all the players and coaches were fair, and I had no problems at all.

I was still only nineteen when I joined the Giants—I

wouldn't be twenty until late in October—and all the others there were a good deal older. I hung around mostly with Em Tunnell, and he was thirty-one years old that year. He really kind of guided me around in the beginning. I was just a kid pretty far away from my home and with very little money in my pocket. He became a very good friend.

We were roommates in New York. We lived in the Henry Hudson Hotel, which was on Fifty-Seventh Street over near Ninth Avenue. Some of the other ballplayers stayed over there too. But it was different on the road.

We had it great, though, Em and I. When we traveled around, we couldn't stay with the white boys. So the Giants would make arrangements for us to stay with a black family. Wellington Mara took care of all that. He would check out the people who we were going to stay with, and they were always fine people and had very nice homes. And we loved it! Hell, we didn't have any curfew like the others had. We could do just about anything we wanted to do and didn't have any coaches to check on us. We could drink beer in our rooms, have people in, party it up. We had the best deal. It made me kind of angry when segregation ended and we had to stay with the white boys. It made our lives more difficult.

Frank Gifford and Charlie Conerly and Alex Webster used to come over sometimes to where we were staying. I remember Frank saying, "Hell, you guys got the best of two worlds."

When I got there, I didn't know the players at all. I didn't know who was supposed to be good or who wasn't. So I just went out there and tried to do the best I could, regardless of who I was up against or who I was competing with for the job. I guess the coaches liked what they saw because at the end of the first camp, I remember Steve Owen coming over to me and saying, "Okay, you and Dick Yelvington are going to be the starting tackles."

Steve Owen was the head coach the first year, and he kind of controlled the whole operation. The line coach was Ed Kolman, and he taught me everything that first year;

Rosey Brown (79) gets a breather. One of the game's all-time great offensive linemen, Brown played tackle for the Giants for thirteen years (1953–65). He earned All-Pro honors eight times and was invited to ten Pro Bowls. He was enshrined in the Pro Football Hall of Fame in 1975.

Steve worked more on the defense than with us. The next year Vince Lombardi came on board to coordinate the offense. He was great.

But you know it's interesting—Ed Kolman and Ken Kavanaugh, who was our end coach and had been quite an end himself with the Chicago Bears, those were the ones who invented the sweep that later was known as the Green Bay sweep. We used it in New York. Vince got the credit for it after he used it so much in Green Bay, but it was Kolman and Kavanaugh who really designed it at the Giants.

After Lombardi got there, they began to have me pull out, which is something tackles did not do. But they had me doing it like the guards. The reason, I guess, is that my forte was speed and quickness and they wanted to take advantage of that. They actually didn't design the pull. I did it on my own because on the sweep I had to cut off the inside man, and I would move out in order to cut him off. But as it often turned out, I was quicker than the inside man—and often he wasn't there, so I just kept on running. A lot of times I was passing the guards, so Lombardi put it in and said, "Okay, Rosey, you pull, and if you can get around the corner, just keep going." I was the first one to do it, and I did it, I guess you could say, by accident. It just worked for me.

With some you couldn't get away with that, however. With one of my own teammates, Arnie Weinmeister, it was impossible. He was very, very fast himself and one of the toughest to go up against. Fortunately, I only had to do that in practice. Another really good one was Len Ford of the Browns—he was so big and quick, a great athlete; he had the whole package. Ernie Stautner of Pittsburgh was also a brutal one—he just kept coming after you, and he never quit, never slowed down, just kept coming. We really had some battles, Stautner and I, because he never would give up. We might be twenty, twenty-five points ahead, but it didn't matter, didn't change things one bit as far as Ernie was concerned.

They all had their tactics, some of them pretty strange.

I remember this guy Don Colo, who played defensive tackle for the Cleveland Browns. He liked to chew tobacco. He was a big guy too, maybe 260 pounds, about 6'3". The first time I went up against him in 1953 he spit tobacco at me. And in those days we didn't wear face masks—but I guess a face mask wouldn't have helped anyway. He did it later too. You'd get down and get in your stance and he'd spit his tobacco across the line of scrimmage at you. He did it, I guess, to throw your rhythm off. I finally said, Okay, I'm gonna fix him—by the time they come to New York, I'm gonna know how to chew tobacco myself. And I learned how. When he lined up opposite me that day he spit, and I spit a hunk of tobacco right back at him. The ball was snapped and we didn't even pay any attention to it. Everybody else was running around out there and we were still in our stances spitting tobacco at each other.

The only championship team I played on was the one in 1956, but we got to a lot of other ones—five other title games, in fact—but we came up short in those contests. In '56, though, we beat the Bears, really beat them, 47–7. Our offense did everything right that day. It wasn't that the Bears didn't have a good defense. They always seemed to have had a good defense—every time I played them. But that day they were way off. They had some big fellas out there that day that we had to keep out of our backfield, keep away from Charlie [Conerly]. I especially remember Doug Atkins and Fred Williams; they don't come much tougher than those guys. But we handled them—that day anyway—and our defense handled their offense.

One of the things I think made us successful was that we were a very close team. Everybody cared about everybody else. I had some real good friends. Besides Em Tunnell, there were guys like Jack Stroud, Darrell Dess—he didn't come until 1959—Andy Robustelli, Dick Lynch, Sam Huff. I hate to name names because I know I'll leave some out. We were just a closely knit team.

In the off-season, we'd all go home and not see each

other until the next year's training camp. I went back to Virginia and taught school some years and did all kinds of other things if there wasn't a teaching job open—just whatever kind of job you could find that would keep you busy and let you earn a little extra money. You couldn't really live very well on what they were paying you to play football in those days. I think most everybody had to work in the off-season in the 1950s.

I always enjoyed going to the Pro Bowl in those years. I went nine times. The Pro Bowl games were played out in Los Angeles in those days. We never got to go to Hawaii like they do these days. You had a lot of fun at them, getting together with a lot of guys you'd played against during the year. But they didn't pay you very much either. I think the players on the winning team got something like $500 and the losers got $300—in the '50s, anyway.

When I played in the Pro Bowls it was always East versus West, the Eastern Conference All-Stars against the Western Conference All-Stars—the American Football League wasn't in it, even in [January] 1966, the last year I went to the game. There were always a lot of Giants invited to those games. Some of the guys seemed to be out there every year—Gifford, Robustelli, Huff, Jimmy Patton. And there were some great ballplayers from other teams who were on our teams, fellas like Jim Brown and Bobby Mitchell, Ernie Stautner and Norm Van Brocklin and Chuck Bednarik. The Packers and the Colts and the Bears used to send the most guys on the other teams, like Hornung and Unitas and Marchetti and Atkins and Ditka. We all had a great time out there.

I had the opportunity to play against some of the greatest football teams ever in the NFL—Baltimore in the 1950s and Green Bay in the 1960s. We played each twice in world championship games [the Colts in 1958 and 1959 and the Packers in 1961 and 1962], but we lost all four. And we played the Bears in another two and split with them, winning in 1956 and losing in 1963. We only had two years in the thirteen I played for New York where we didn't have a winning season. I don't know what our overall record was [regular season it was 98 wins, 61 losses, 7 ties], but it had to be a good one, and playing in six NFL championship games tells you something about the kind of teams we had.

After the 1965 season I had to retire from playing. I developed a case of phlebitis, which is an inflammation of a vein, and that prevented me from playing. I was only thirty-two at the time, 1966, and thought if it weren't for the phlebitis, maybe I could get in a few more years. But it wasn't to be.

I stayed with the Giants, though, as an assistant coach until 1971, coaching under Allie Sherman and Alex Webster. That year, 1971, I started as a full-time scout for the team. As a scout, I worked for Jim Lee Howell, who had coached me for a good part of my career [1954–60]. And I'm still scouting around for the Giants.

◨

Dealing with Looney

Frank Gifford, in his book *Gifford on Courage*, wrote of what it was like dealing with Joe Don Looney, the unorthodox (to put it mildly) running back out of Oklahoma who was the first-round draft choice of the Giants in 1964.

> He had the potential to be an extraordinary player. But—there were problems.
>
> He injured his leg early in training camp. So [coach Allie] Sherman told him to see the trainer about it. To Allie's amazement, Looney refused.
>
> His reason? "It's my leg. I know more about it than the trainer."
>
> He wouldn't go to Detroit for an exhibition game. "I can't play; why should I go?" he asked me.
>
> "You're part of the team," I said.
>
> "I'm not part of the team if I can't play," he replied.
>
> Joe Don came in an hour after curfew one night and was fined. "Not fair," he said. "I was in bed an hour early last night, so we should be even up."
>
> He wouldn't throw his used socks into a marked bin because "I'm not going to do what any sign tells me to do."
>
> Although I didn't see it, I understand that in scrimmages he often ran one way when the play called for him to go another. His reason: "Anybody can run where the blockers are. A good football player makes his own holes."
>
> As a last-ditch measure, Wellington Mara and Allie Sherman asked Y.A. [Tittle] and me to try to talk to the young man. Joe Don was 6'1", 224 pounds and ran the 100 in something like 9.7. They wanted to keep him.
>
> We were still in training camp at Fairfield [Connecticut] University. Joe Don was lying down in his room listening to music when we found him.
>
> Y.A. flopped on the other bed and started to tell

Joe Don about his trade to New York from San Francisco, which somehow Y.A. equated with Looney's problems: how difficult it was leaving the team where he had spent most of his career, his family, his business; being traded for a rookie lineman; coming to a team in a strange city with a popular quarterback [Charlie Conerly] ahead of him; and how "alone" Y.A. had felt.

Clearly talking from his heart and, perhaps for the first time outside of his family, discussing his gut feeling about the trade, Tittle went on for about twenty minutes with Joe Don and me listening intently.

Finally, Y.A. finished and stopped—serious, sad, thinking of what had happened just three years earlier.

Joe Don broke an embarrassing silence. He sat up, completely caught up in Tittle's reverie, and said sympathetically, "It must have been *really* tough, Y.A. Anything I can do for you?"

(The counsel of Tittle and Gifford evidently failed, because Joe Don Looney was traded to the Baltimore Colts before the opening game of the 1964 regular season.)

Alex Webster

Alex Webster, after a fine collegiate career at North Carolina State as a tailback, was a castaway from the NFL in 1953. Cut by the Washington Redskins and unclaimed elsewhere in the National Football League, he was gobbled up by the Canadian Football League. As a running back for two years for the Montreal franchise, Webster tore the league apart and ended up the recipient of the CFL Most Valuable Player award in 1954.

The Giants wooed him back to the United States the following year to begin a ten-year career carrying the ball for the Mara family, first as a halfback and later as a fullback. He was a key counterpoint to the passing games of Charlie Conerly and Y. A. Tittle, throwing to the likes of Frank Gifford, Kyle Rote, and Del Shofner. Webster gained the inches, feet, and yards that were needed on the ground and was a feared force to all opposing defenses when he grabbed a little screen pass—one of his specialties—and motored up the field, gaining momentum with each step.

Alex led the team in rushing his rookie year, 1955, and also in 1961 and 1962. In Giants history, he ranks third in touchdowns scored, his 56 trailing only Frank Gifford's 78 and Joe Morrison's 65.

"He was one of the hardest-hitting running backs you ever

wanted to see," his former coach, Jim Lee Howell, said. "And there were a lot of defensive players who did not want to see him across the line of scrimmage from them."

When Webster retired after the 1964 season, he left with several club records. No one had carried the ball more times for the Giants than his 1,196, nor gained more yards than his 4,638, nor scored more rushing touchdowns than his 39. Those standards were eventually topped by Joe Morris in the 1980s, but Webster had indelibly inscribed his marks in the Giants' book of legends, where they remain to this day.

A few years down the path from the playing field, Webster was handed the head-coaching reins of the Giants by Wellington Mara in 1969. The five years he held those reins were less illustrious than those when he was playing for the Giants. Still, in 1970, he turned in a record of 9–5–0 and was named UPI's Coach of the Year.

Today, Alex Webster tends to business interests down in southern Florida and manages a restaurant that carries his name.

I had the somewhat unique advantage of both playing for the Giants and coaching them. That was not uncommon in the earlier days when people like Steve Owen of the Giants or George Halas of the Bears were around, but coaching the team you played for in the modern era of the National Football League is kind of a rarity. It certainly did give you views from different perspectives.

My first encounter with organized football, however, was back in Kearny, New Jersey—which is just north of Newark—where I was born and raised. That's where I started playing the game in junior high school and then, of course, high school.

I was lucky to have gotten a whole bunch of scholarship offers after finishing school in Kearny. I took a couple of trips to see the colleges. I went over to Tennessee in Knoxville and down to University of Miami and a couple of other schools. Then I went to take a look at North Carolina

State, which is in Raleigh—there's that whole complex of universities in the area there with North Carolina in Chapel Hill and Duke in Durham, all neighbors.

Well, I really liked that area of the country, and the university was very appealing. The coach there was Beattie Feathers, who had gone to Tennessee and later was a fine running back for the Chicago Bears. In fact, he was the first running back in the NFL to gain more than 1,000 yards rushing in a single season [1,004 in the thirteen-game season of 1934]. Of course, he had Bronko Nagurski blocking for him that year, which helped considerably.

There was a fellow by the name of Al Rotella, who was originally from New Jersey but had gone to Tennessee and was now an assistant coach under Beattie at North Carolina State. In fact, all of Beattie's staff were former Tennessee ballplayers. It was Al Rotella who recruited me, got me to go down to the school, and introduced me to Beattie Feathers.

Well, Beattie had a wonderful heart, and he made me feel I had a good deal of potential in his system at North Carolina State. So I took their offer, and it was a good decision. My father had died when I was nine years old, and Beattie became just like a father to me. He and the whole coaching staff there were great.

North Carolina State was not a big school in those days, back in the early 1950s. It was basically an engineering and agricultural school. And it was a place where I felt I would really have a chance to play. They were still playing the single wing and that's what I had played in high school back in New Jersey. I'd been the tailback, and I also played free safety on defense. State was playing the old Tennessee system with the balanced line that General [Bob] Neyland had developed. It focused on running out of the single wing, and that was good for me because as a senior in high school I had suffered a shoulder separation and I wasn't throwing the football very well. Running was what I wanted to do and what I did best.

I had a good four years down there in North Carolina. I played tailback and free safety, just like high school, and we did pretty well. That's where I got the nickname Big Red. I had red hair back then and my face was always red because of the simple fact that I was fair-skinned and was out in the sun so much down there. I think my head looked like a big red apple most of the time. Anyway, that old nickname has stuck through all the years.

After college, I was drafted by the Washington Redskins in 1953, in the eleventh round. Well, it was not easy making the team when you were drafted that low. You were just somebody they considered a remote possibility. Curly Lambeau was their coach that year—he came there after all those years in Green Bay after they had kind of rousted him out of the town.

I was tried out both ways at Washington, but more as a defensive back than a running back. I had some good intrasquad games there, but it was real hard to break in. They had some pretty well-known veterans in their offensive backfield: Bullet Bill Dudley and Choo Choo Justice and Leon Heath. And there was only about one spot seemingly open in the defensive backfield. But when they had to cut the squad to thirty-three, which was the limit in those days, I basically had made the team. I thought so, anyway. But Don Doll, a pretty proven veteran, a defensive back, had been cut by the Detroit Lions, and Washington decided to pick him up. So I—as they say—got the gate. That was about four days before the opening game of the regular season. I remember the moment vividly. After they told me, they gave me a $10 bill to get home on and, I remember, the train ticket from Washington to Newark was $9.45.

I was married at the time and my wife was expecting a baby, so I went back to Kearny to start looking for work. One night I was in this saloon playing darts and in walked a writer I knew, Paul Durkin, who then was with the *Newark Star-Ledger* and later would become sports editor for the *New York Daily News*. He asked me what the hell I was doing back home, and I told him I'd been cut. He said, hell, you gotta try something else. Then he mentioned the Canadian League. He said he knew somebody up there.

We composed an overnight telegram and sent it to Douglas Clyde "Peahead" Walker. He was the head coach of Montreal at the time. Peahead had been the head coach at Wake Forest for many years [1936–50] before going up to Canada. The next morning Peahead called and told me I had to get up there that afternoon if I wanted to play in Canada because this was the last day for the importing of American players. They had a deadline of October 1 in those days.

So I flew up to Montreal and had the good fortune of making the team. There were two fellows I was competing against—one was Jimmy Joe Robinson, who had played at Pittsburgh, and the other was Nub Smith of Wake Forest. Between them they had an assortment of injuries, and so Peahead took me. The day after I got the job, the newspaper up there had a sports headline:

WALKER PULLS BONER OF THE YEAR!

It went on to say that he released Robinson and Smith and signed a newcomer.

I only had about six or seven days before the first game of the season. We played at Ottawa and I had a helluva good day. That was on a Saturday; then we played them again the next day. I carried the ball about fifty times, returned kickoffs, and played defensive back as well. It was one of the most rugged weekends of my life, and I came out of it with a sprained ankle and I'd gotten my nose busted.

We had a good year and got in the playoffs, but we lost to Hamilton. It was different from an NFL playoff game in that they played a two-game, total-points deal. I forget the exact score, but we played the first game in Hamilton and they won something like 30–7. The next week they came to Montreal, and the game started with that score. We beat them that day maybe 21–10, but the final score was 40 to

28 when you added the scores together. The next year we got to the Grey Cup, Canada's equivalent of the Super Bowl, but we got beat there by Edmonton, 26–25. The game had a kind of strange ending. We were winning and killing the clock with less than a minute left. We had this halfback, Chuck Hunsinger, who had played for the Chicago Bears for a couple of years before coming to Canada. For some reason he threw the ball, and it hit one of our guards in the back and bounced up in the air. A kid by the name of Jackie Parker of Edmonton grabbed it and ran about 80 yards for a touchdown, and they kicked the extra point and beat us by one point. From what I heard later, the owners of our team lost so much betting on the game they had to sell the team.

After that season, which had been a very good one for me, I came back to the States and got offers from the Redskins, who now were being coached by Joe Kuharich, as well as the Detroit Lions and the Giants.

Al DeRogatis, who at one time had been an outstanding defensive tackle for the Giants and was now a scout for the team, had come up to watch us in 1954. He was looking basically at Sam Etcheverry, a quarterback, and he came back to New York with my name. Wellington Mara then offered me a contract, and I took it. It was for $10,000 with a $2,500 signing bonus. Up in Canada, even though I'd gotten the MVP award the year before, the offer was only $5,500. So I became a Giant.

After I signed with the Giants, Montreal came back and offered me more than the Giants were going to pay me, but I told them I wouldn't do it.

New York certainly offered one advantage: I could commute during the season from New Jersey, where my family was living, to the Polo Grounds, where we were practicing and playing. We were just across the Hudson River from Manhattan. In Canada, I didn't earn enough to bring my family up there, and that made life less than pleasant.

The Giants in 1955, when I arrived, were just coming into their own. Jim Lee Howell had taken over from Steve Owen and instituted a more modern game. He had Lombardi and Landry on his coaching staff; he had a lot of very good ballplayers who were coming into their own.

In that first training camp, I learned it was going to be more difficult in the NFL. Lombardi really put you through a workout. I thought I was going to die. I was a lazy player to begin with—I hated to practice. But you had to work if you were going to play for him.

I was moving into a backfield that already had stars like Frank Gifford and Kyle Rote and Eddie Price. I knew it wasn't going to be easy. I was playing behind Rote at right halfback. The way it would work when I was in was like this: when we went into a left formation, I was the halfback, Mel Triplett—a rookie that year—was the fullback, and Frank Gifford would be out in the flank as a wide receiver. When we lined up in a right formation, Gifford would be the halfback and I would be the flanker back. As I said, I was lazy, and it was especially noticeable when I was out in the flanker position. I understand they were just about to let me go. But just before the first preseason game against the 49ers, Kyle slipped and turned his bad knee and couldn't play. So they had to play me and, as it turned out, I did pretty well—scored a couple of touchdowns, caught a few passes. Lombardi and Jim Lee Howell decided then they were going to keep me. That's when Lombardi really started to work me, yelling and screaming at me in practice. He knew I could do it, but he had to make me shed the laziness—which he did. And that was really a turning point in my pro football career.

I got off to a good start in the regular season and was playing a lot. One game really helped my position with the team. It was against the Chicago Cardinals, the second game of the season. I gained 139 yards rushing that day—as it turned out that was the most I ever gained in the ten years I ran the ball for the Giants. We ended up losing the game that day, which was a big disappointment, but we all had the feeling I could run the ball for the Giants, and I think that was a milestone in my career.

I was not the fastest of ball carriers. Long yardage was not my plan. Hell, if I could get ten yards on a play I was ecstatic—everything else was a bonus. I think I probably hold the record as a running back for getting caught from behind. The open field was not my country, and if I managed to get into it I thought, Hallelujah!

I did have a pretty good year in 1955. Eddie Price and Kyle Rote were banged up and didn't carry the ball much. I carried it the most that year [128 times for 634 yards, an average of 5 yards a carry]. After the season I signed a two-year contract.

The next year was a good one too. That was the year we moved to Yankee Stadium, 1956, and it was the year we won the championship. We had played the Bears to a tie in the regular season [17–17]. But we were really up for them in the championship game, and we just walked all over them that day [47–7].

The next year was a bit of a letdown. The Browns beat us twice that year—in fact, we lost the last three games of the season and ended up in second place in our conference. But in 1958 we came back and made it to the championship game again. That, of course, was the sudden-death overtime game with the Colts. I believe that game, with its national television coverage, turned the whole thing around in pro football. The popularity of the game throughout the country took an enormous leap after that.

We got there because of Pat Summerall's famous field goal against the Browns two weeks earlier. Pat owes me for that. If it weren't for me he wouldn't have got the chance to kick a 50-yard field goal [actually, 49-yard] to win the game. Hell, two plays earlier I dropped a pass on about the 5-yard line. It came out of the snow and I misjudged the damn thing and dropped it. I could have been the hero. I could also have been the goat had Pat not made that field goal. There was nobody who wanted him to make that field goal more than me. Once he did, everybody forgot about my dropping the pass. Pat won a lot of games for us during those times with last-minute field goals.

We used to use a lot of pick plays in those days that are illegal now. Sometimes I'd line up in a wingback position. The tight end would go down and cut out, and I'd cut right underneath him. This worked pretty well for us. We didn't use a lot of trick plays. Some of the other teams did, though. I remember one when we were playing the Pittsburgh Steelers in the 1960s. Bobby Layne was their quarterback then. He had Tom Tracy at fullback. And they had to win this particular game against us to get into the playoffs. Layne came up to the line and started to call the signals; then he turned around and said something to Tracy and started to call the signals again. Finally he turned around again to Tracy and shouted, "Goddammit, don't you understand?" and started to walk back toward Tracy. Our defense stood up, and as soon as they did the center snapped the ball to Tracy, and he tore right up the middle and gained something like 20 or 25 yards. Only Bobby Layne could get away with something like that.

Layne was great—a true and colorful character. He wouldn't take any guff from anybody, and he was a wild man. I remember when I went to talk to the Lions before I signed with the Giants. It was the last game of the 1954 [NFL] season. They were playing in Cleveland and I went there. I met with their general manager, and after the game I went out to the airport with the team. They were going back to Detroit, and I was going to Newark. Well, I'd never seen anything like it. There was Layne walking through the airport with a case of beer under his arm. With him was Les Bingaman, one of their defensive linemen who weighed about 320 pounds. He said to me, "C'mon with us, kid, and we'll make something out of you. Maybe we won't make you play any better, but we'll sure be able to teach you to drink with us." They were quite a group of characters, and Bobby was their ringleader.

Another story about Bobby was when he was with

Pittsburgh—this was somewhere around 1960. They were in town to play us and their coach, Buddy Parker, cornered Bobby and his roommate, Ernie Stautner, on Saturday. "We really need to win this game tomorrow," he told them, "so I want you two guys to be sure to get in early tonight, to make curfew."

So Bobby said to him, "Don't worry about it." Well, that night they got back at about ten-thirty—eleven was curfew—and went to their room. They put the television on and Ernie went to bed. About eleven-thirty, Bobby sat down and wrote a note that said something like this:

Buddy,
    Ernie and I got home at 10:30. It's now 11:30 and Ernie's asleep and I'm going out of my goddamn mind. Don't worry, I'll play good tomorrow.

Bobby

P.S. Here's my fine money.

He put the note and the money in an envelope and on his way out slipped it under the door to Buddy Parker's room. Word was that he closed P. J. Clarke's at four in the morning. And then he came out and threw three touchdown passes against us that afternoon.

In 1961, I was switched to fullback. That was when Jim Lee Howell retired and Lombardi had gone on to Green Bay two years earlier. Allie Sherman was our new head coach. I had been out for most of the 1960 season with a bad knee. We had Phil King and Joe Morrison and Bob Gaiters as halfbacks. Gifford was out that year because of the concussion he got in 1960. So Allie moved me to fullback. I kind of liked it because I was too damn slow to be a receiver and I was weighing around 225 pounds, so fullback seemed like the natural place to switch me to. As it turned out, it was the best year I ever had rushing. I gained

Alex Webster was the Giants' premier running back from 1955 through 1964. He ended up with most of the team's rushing records before he retired after the 1964 season. Then he came back to coach the Giants in 1969 and guided the team through the 1973 season.

928 yards. At that time the only player with the Giants who had ever gained more in a single season was Eddie Price [971 in 1951].

I had a good year in 1962 as well; that year I gained 743 yards. Y. A. Tittle had been our quarterback in '61 and '62, and one of his favorite plays was to backpedal into the pocket and then toss a little screen pass to me. I was the second-leading receiver on the team in '62 after Del Shofner—I caught 47 passes.

In 1963 we won our conference again but got beat by the Bears [14–10] in the championship game. By 1964, I was 33 years old and pretty much over the hill; so was most everybody else who was left. Sherman had traded away a lot of ballplayers after the 1963 season, like Sam Huff and Dick Modzelewski. We had a terrible year—we won only two games and for the first time in history ended up in last place. I hung it up as a player after that year.

I had the opportunity to play on a lot of outstanding Giants teams in the ten years I was with the club. And I played against a lot of the great ones. We went out and beat the hell out of each other but at the same time we could still be good friends. You knew if you played a team like the Eagles or the Steelers or the Bears you were going to wake up on Monday morning and know you had been in one helluva game. You'd feel it from head to toe and then some—you were downright physically beat up.

After 1964, I stayed on with the Giants to a degree by doing a little scouting for them. I also had a radio show, talking about football and the Giants. Then in 1967 Well Mara asked me to sign on as the backfield coach. So I went in and talked with Allie Sherman; we agreed on things, and I became a member of the coaching staff.

They let Allie go after the last preseason game of the 1969 season—we had lost all our preseason games that year—and they offered his job to me. We were up in Montreal, where we had just played the Steelers. It was a Friday night game. Allie gave the players and the coaching staff Saturday and Saturday night off. I went home after the game that night, and on Saturday morning I got a telephone call to report in to the Giants' front office right away. I didn't know what the hell was going on. I wondered if I was being fired. When I walked in and sat down with Well Mara, he told me he had let Allie go and he wanted me to replace him. The head coaching job was not something I really wanted—something I didn't feel I was prepared for. I'd only spent two years as an assistant—I felt it was like going from a salesperson one day to the president of the company the next. We talked for a while and he offered me a two-year contract at $55,000 a year—and I was only making $18,000 as an assistant—which cleared away a lot of doubts I was having. So I took the job.

It was a tough five years, though. I'd enjoyed the hell out of coaching as an assistant, but head coaching was another thing. We didn't have a whole lot of talent around at that time, and I was really a rookie at running a team. We never did really get on track. We did have one good year— 1970. We'd gotten Ron Johnson, a fine running back from Cleveland, and he became the first Giant to gain more than 1,000 yards rushing in a season [1,027]. And Fran Tarkenton, who was quarterbacking for us, had a good year too. We ended up 9-5-0 but were still a game behind the Dallas Cowboys in the NFC East. They went on to the Super Bowl that year—beat the 49ers for the NFC title but then lost to the Baltimore Colts in Super Bowl V.

We had another decent year in 1972 when we turned over the quarterbacking to Norm Snead. That was also the year Ron Johnson broke his own rushing record by gaining 1,182 yards. We ended up 8-6-0, but that was only good enough for third place in the NFC East [the Redskins, under George Allen, were 11-3-0 and Tom Landry's Cowboys were 10-4-0].

There were some very good ballplayers on the team I coached there. Besides Ron Johnson, there was—of course—Tarkenton, but he was not the easiest to deal with. He knew a lot about the game himself, but you ended up constantly arguing with him. He would often ignore plays sent in for one reason or another, and he'd call plays he thought were better. It did not make for a good relationship. He was never happy. He got to the point where he made it clear he wanted to be traded. In fact, he walked out on us—he was having some differences about money with management—at a preseason game in Houston. We were playing the Oilers, and before the game he came up to me at the end of the warm-ups and said he was sorry but he had to do what he thought was best for his family. Quite frankly, I didn't know what the hell he was talking about because I was working with the punters at the time. By the time I got in the locker room he was gone—walked out. Well, he came back a few days later, but we gave him his wish and traded him at the end of the season.

There were some others who were really very good. Bob Tucker, a tight end who came to us in 1970, was great. He led the league in receiving in 1971—caught 59 passes. Spider Lockhart was excellent in our defensive backfield. And we had Fred Dryer—he was a helluva defensive end, but he became much more famous later on the television show "Hunter."

We didn't have the defensive team we had had when I was playing. We could put points on the board but the opponents seemed to be able to put more on—at least most of the time. We could sure have used a Robustelli or Huff or Tunnell or Modzelewski. I guess I'd been spoiled.

I left the Giants as head coach after the 1973 season. The next year I did the wrap-up of the Giants' games on television. After that I got into the printing business, mostly in the sales end. I went to work for a printing company that was run by Ralph Guglielmi, who had been a great quarterback at Notre Dame and came up with the Redskins the same year I joined the Giants, 1955. He later played with the Giants [1962–63] and a bunch of other NFL teams.

After that I went to work with a food company, Standard Brands, in public relations; they were bought out by Nabisco, and then the whole thing was bought out by R. J. Reynolds, the tobacco company. We had a lot of sports people affiliated with the company—Frank Gifford, Jack Nicklaus, me. . . .

Today I'm out of all that. I live down in Florida in a town called Tequesta, near Jupiter, just north of Palm Beach, and have a restaurant there called Alex Webster's, and I spend a lot of time tending to things around the place.

There are a lot of us down here in Florida—Pat Summerall, Joe Namath, Bill Parcells, Phil Simms—almost NFL south. We're all still very much in touch with the NFL.

Rice on Owen

Dean of sportswriters Grantland Rice used his poetic pen to describe Steve Owen in the mid-1940s.

"Stout Steve" is the name you've got—the moniker that you've earned—
Stout in body and stout in heart, wherever the tide has turned,
One of the best who has come along in this morbid vale of tears,
A massive fellow who rides the storm in the march of the passing years.
Never a boast and never a brag and never an alibi,
But the breed we label in any sport as a typical four-square guy,
A mighty hunk of the human mold, blown from the rugged West,
Whatever the odds from the off-side gods—a fellow who gives his best.

Red Badgro

Morris "Red" Badgro was an exceptional athlete, lettering in football, baseball, and basketball in each of his four years at the University of Southern California. He was an All-Pacific Coast Conference selection in both football and basketball his senior year. Badgro signed contracts in 1927 with both the New York Yankees football team, which had just been absorbed into the NFL from the defunct American Football League, and the St. Louis Browns baseball team of the American League.

Football, however, is where he made his professional mark. Red Badgro was the perfectly balanced end in that age when a player was required to do more than one thing on a football field. "He could block, tackle, and catch passes equally well," Steve Owen, his coach during his years with the Giants, said. "And he could do each with the best of them."

The bulk of his NFL career, six of nine years (1930–35), was spent with the Giants, and he played on teams that earned their way into the first three official NFL championship games (1933–35). He has the distinction of scoring the first touchdown in an official NFL title game, when he took in a 29-yard pass from Harry Newman in the second quarter of the title tilt against the Chicago Bears in 1933.

With Badgro and Ray Flaherty at ends and Benny Friedman
and later Harry Newman passing the ball to them, the Giants
had one of the first truly effective passing games in NFL history.
Red was named to three of the first four All-Pro teams (1931,
1933, and 1934) and his 16 receptions in 1934 were the league
high.

Another Red, this one with the last name of Grange, said
of Badgro, "Playing offense and defense equally well, he was
one of the best half-dozen ends I ever saw." And Johnny
Blood McNally remembered him as "a tireless competitor, big,
strong, fast, and injury-proof."

In 1981, at the age of seventy-eight, Red Badgro was for-
mally inducted into the Pro Football Hall of Fame, the oldest
person ever elected to it. A decade later, in 1991, at age eighty-
eight, he drove from his home in the Seattle area to Canton,
Ohio, to attend the ten-year anniversary celebration of his
induction.

Howard Jones was the [football] coach of the USC
Trojans [when I was there], and they had a wonderful football program. At the time, they and Notre Dame were two of the greatest teams in the country.
This was in the mid-1920s. We played some very good
football out there on the coast. Besides us, California had
a good team. So did Stanford. They had Ernie Nevers then,
and he was one of the all-time greats, and the famous Pop
Warner was their coach.

I have a particular memory of [Nevers] out there. One
year we would have gone to the Rose Bowl if it weren't for
him. Nevers was punting out of his own end zone. We were
losing, 13–12, late in the game, and a safety would win it
for us. Well, we put on quite a rush, and Jeff Cravath, our
center, blocked Ernie's kick. I was right alongside him, and,
crazily, the ball bounced back up into Nevers's hands. If
either Jeff or I had come up with the ball we would have
gone to the Rose Bowl. But Ernie had it and ran the ball out
for a first down.

Another wonderful player out there at that time was Mort Kaer, who was the first All-American from Southern Cal. He was our quarterback and I was at end. We got some attention because we had such a good team my senior year [1926]. Kaer was the best known of our players, and as a result a number of pro scouts came out to talk with us.

I was thinking mostly about playing professional baseball when my college days would be over. And I had a couple of offers. I still had a couple of units to go at USC when one day I bumped into a fraternity brother who had also been a starter on our football team. He was leaving the frat house with a suitcase and told me he was going out east to join Red Grange's New York Yankees. He asked me if I wanted to play pro football. I told him I hadn't really thought about it but baseball was what I had in mind. I said I probably wouldn't mind playing it, however.

Well, he said when he got to New York he would make a pitch for me. "You'll hear from me in a couple of days," he said. "That is, if they haven't signed up all their ends yet." And I got a call in a couple of days, and pretty soon I was on the train going from L.A. to New York.

The Yankees were owned by C. C. Pyle [the entrepreneur who arranged the famous Red Grange/Chicago Bears barnstorming tour of the nation in 1925], and I think Grange had part of it as well. They had been in the league Pyle started, the first American Football League, the year before, 1926. When that league went broke and folded up, the Yankees were brought into the NFL. We were a road team for the most part [they played only three of their sixteen games in Yankee Stadium]. The Giants were there, already well established and playing at the Polo Grounds. We had a pretty good team. We had Grange, of course, but he got his knee pretty badly hurt after about four games. We also had Eddie Tryon, who was a good running back. He had been an All-American at Colgate. I got to start at one end and Ray Flaherty was at the other. We also had Mike Michalske, a great lineman, and Wild Bill Kelly, who was our passer.

The Yankees broke up after the 1928 season. When they did, many of the fellows went to Green Bay, some went to the Bears, and a few to the Giants. I was playing baseball at the time too, with the St. Louis Browns, and I thought maybe I'd just concentrate on that. I felt if I could hit pretty well and really make it in baseball—well, that would take care of it. But I didn't hit the ball as well as I thought I would; I wasn't in the starting lineup. So after two years I decided I'd go back to football.

I qualified as a free agent. Steve Owen came down to Houston, where I was playing in the Texas League at the time, and asked if I'd like to come to the Giants. I said sure. And so I spent the next six years in New York with the Giants.

Tim Mara signed me to my first contract with the Giants. He was a good owner. I never had any trouble with him—or any owner, for that matter. I signed up to play for just so much and that was it. At that time, we didn't consider what the other fellow got. If he made $500 a game or $1,000 or only $2, we didn't care. But the money sure wasn't very good in those days. I got $150 a game when I first signed with the Giants. I didn't exactly get rich on that salary.

In that time of the Depression, a player needed to work in the off-season too, and I did as much as I could; but it was hard to pick up a job. Times were tough for everybody.

Dr. Harry March, a grand old fellow, was running the Giants for Tim Mara when I came to them in 1930. One thing I'll never forget about him: I got my chin cut open in practice one day, and I needed eleven stitches to close it up. I just went by his office, and he didn't have any of his medical equipment with him, so he got a plain needle and sewing thread out of his drawer and sewed up my chin. He liked football more than the practice of medicine, I believe.

We only had about twenty or twenty-two players on the team in those days. You had to play offense and defense, and the schedule wasn't always like it is today. Sometimes we would play as many as four games in eight days, what with the barnstorming and exhibitions and that sort of thing.

I was fortunate to latch onto a very good team. In 1930, we had Benny Friedman at tailback. We also had Steve Owen in the line; he didn't take over full duties as head coach until the following year. We ran second to the Green Bay Packers, as I recall. They had Johnny Blood McNally in his prime and Red Dunn and Cal Hubbard and Lavie Dilweg.

That was also the year we played the special exhibition game at the end of the season against Knute Rockne's all-star team of former Notre Dame players at the Polo Grounds. Tim Mara had arranged it, and the receipts were to go for the benefit of the unemployed in New York City. Rockne had the Four Horsemen there [Harry Stuhldreyer, Elmer Layden, Don Miller, and Jim Crowley] and Hunk Anderson, quite a lineman in his day, and a raft of others. We walloped them pretty good, though [22–0]. There was a huge crowd for it. Mayor [Jimmy] Walker was there and so was Governor Al Smith. And the game earned over $100,000 for the charity.

We played in the first NFL championship game in 1933. That year we had Ken Strong, probably one of the best fullbacks and kickers ever to play the game. And there was Harry Newman, a fine passer. Ray Flaherty and I were at the ends, and in the line we had Mel Hein and the Owens, Steve and Bill, although Steve was pretty well along in years as a player by then. I thought we were going to win that game. We were really up for the Bears. I caught a touchdown pass from Newman kind of early, and in the fourth quarter we were ahead by four or five points. But then Bronko Nagurski threw a pass to Bill Hewitt and he lateralled off to their other end, Bill Karr, who ran it in for a touchdown.

Even after that we still had a shot at it. On the last play of the game I caught a pass, and the only person between me and the goal line was Red Grange. I planned to lateral

to a teammate who was running along just behind me—it
was Hein or Dale Burnett—but Grange grabbed me around
the arms and upper body and I couldn't. Had I been able
to, we would have won the championship. It was the perfect tackle, and that's why Grange is heralded as one of the
great defensive backs of that era. So we lost it [23-21].

We got to the championship again the next year and
again against the Bears, but I didn't play in it because of an
injury. Neither did Harry Newman. But we won it anyway.
That was the game where our fellows wore sneakers in the
second half. We were able to run much better on the frozen
field as a result, and so this time we won [30-13].

The Bears were a real rival. We had some good games
against the Packers in those years too. I remember a couple
of incidents. One involved Clarke Hinkle, their fullback, a
great runner. Well, we were playing at Green Bay and
leading 10-7. It was late in the game, and we had kicked off
to them. Hinkle got the ball, broke out to the side with it,
and had a blocker in front of him. I don't know where the
rest of our team was, but suddenly there was only me
between him and his blocker and the end zone. I figured I
had to get him some way or they would win the ball game.
The odds sure weren't with me because Hinkle was such a
powerful runner. He didn't even need that blocker, probably. And he had the goal line in his eyes. I don't know
exactly how it happened, but I held off the blocker and
Hinkle ran right into him, bounced off, and hurtled into my
arms. We both went down and the blocker ended up on top
of us. I know Clarke would love to have that play over,
because probably ninety-nine times out of a hundred he
would have scored. He was more surprised than I was
when he found himself on the ground. Afterward he told
me he thought his blocker had tackled him.

Another situation involved Johnny Blood [McNally].
This time we were playing Green Bay in New York and we
were leading 13-7. They were down on our goal line and
they ran the ball three times but didn't make it. There were
just seconds left, and I sensed they wouldn't run at us on

Morris "Red" Badgro played end for the Giants from 1928 through 1935 and was named to three of the first four NFL All-Pro teams. In the words of another redhead, the immortal Red Grange, "Red was one of the best half-dozen ends I ever saw." He was inducted into the Pro Football Hall of Fame in 1981.

fourth down, the last play of the game for them. They had a play they relied on a lot in those days. It was a quick pass to Johnny Blood out in the flat—a fake to the fullback first and then out to Johnny. It would work in this instance, they thought, because there was only a yard to go and we'd be bunched up to stop Hinkle if he tried to bull it in. I still didn't think they would run it, and so I kept my eye on Blood—and sure enough I saw him take off for the flat. I said, to hell with it, and I just ran across the line of scrimmage and tackled him in the backfield. When the quarterback looked up from his fake to throw the ball, all he saw was Johnny and me on the ground. He was standing there with the ball and no one to throw it to. Then our fellows smothered him. The referee didn't call anything, and we won the game. Things like that you remember.

The Giants were a fine team all the years I was with them. The team I was with my last year, the Brooklyn Dodgers, wasn't much of a team, however. What happened was that when I quit after the 1935 season the Giants' management didn't think I'd ever play again, so they didn't keep their ownership of me. I'd left them to go up and coach and play for a team in Rochester, New York, in what was the second American Football League, destined to go the same way as the first one. I got up there and played in two games, and then the guy who owned it went broke and couldn't even pay me a week's salary. So I said to heck with it and left and went back to New York City.

I found out that the Brooklyn Dodgers, Dan Topping's team [bought a few years earlier from pal and former Giant Shipwreck Kelly], had picked up my option, and so I went over there and played one more year in the NFL.

After Brooklyn, I went back to Southern Cal to get the couple of units I still needed to graduate. After that I went to Ventura Junior College in California and coached football, baseball, and basketball. While I was there, I was contacted by Lou Little, the great coach at Columbia. He used to come over from Columbia to watch the pro games when I was with the Giants. He wanted to know if I would like to come back east to Columbia and be his assistant football coach. I went back there and stayed in that capacity for five years.

After that, it was back across the country to the West Coast, where I coached football at the University of Washington as an assistant for eight years. Then I went to work for the Department of Agriculture in the state of Washington until I retired.

Between playing and coaching, I guess I spent about twenty-five years in football. I hold a lot of fine memories from it.

Blocks, Tackles, and Umbrellas

The great triple-threat back of the 1930s, Ken Strong, always liked to tell this story of a personal encounter with the Giants before he joined the team. At the time, he was the star attraction of the NFL franchise known as the Staten Island Stapletons, who played a borough away from the Giants.

> During those years [1929–32] I developed a rivalry with [end] Ray Flaherty, the Giants' captain. One day when we were playing at Thompson Field over on Staten Island, I went around his end and he grabbed me in a headlock.
>
> Right near one side of the field we had a small wire fence that was right against the sideline. Now Flaherty started to force me toward the wire fence. And something was getting him real mad. When the whistle blew, he looked up and saw this little old lady leaning over the fence waving an umbrella. She'd been hitting him on the head while he was pulling me toward the sideline, and he thought that I had been reaching up and punching him on the head.

Kyle Rote

While still a junior at Southern Methodist University, Kyle Rote filled in for the injured Doak Walker in the last game of the 1949 college football season and almost single-handedly upset top-ranked Notre Dame. After the game, Frank Leahy, the coach of the Fighting Irish, said, "That Rote boy is the most underrated back in football."

The following year, with Walker graduated and gone to the NFL, Rote got the rating: a consensus All-American halfback and runner-up to Vic Janowicz of Ohio State for the Heisman Trophy. He started at right halfback for the College All-Stars in their traditional meeting at Soldier Field in Chicago with the previous year's NFL champion. Unfortunately for the collegians of 1951, it was against the ultra-imposing Cleveland Browns, coached by Paul Brown and with a roster rife with future Pro Football Hall of Famers (the All-Stars lost 33–0).

Rote was the number-one selection in the 1951 NFL draft, chosen by the New York Giants with that year's bonus pick. He became a starter immediately at halfback in a backfield that also included quarterback Charlie Conerly and fullback Eddie Price; but almost as immediately he was plagued by knee injuries that would curtail the speed and special moves he had exhibited at SMU.

197

After the arrival of such distinguished backs as Frank Gifford and Alex Webster in the Giants' camp, Rote was switched by head coach Jim Lee Howell to flanker, a move that Kyle says added six or seven years to his pro football career. As a flanker, he became one of New York's most effective and dependable pass receivers.

A favorite target of both Charlie Conerly and Y. A. Tittle, Rote ranks fourth in career pass receptions for the Giants, with a total of 300 for 4,797 yards. His 48 touchdown catches remain today the most in Giants' history, and the seven consecutive games in which he caught a touchdown pass (1959–60) is another still-standing Giants' record. Between 1956 and 1958, he notched a club record by catching passes in 23 consecutive games, a mark that was not eclipsed until ten years later.

Rote played in four NFL title games (1956, 1958, 1959, and 1961) and was invited to the Pro Bowl four times (1954–57).

As his playing career was coming to an end in 1961, New York fans and his friends from Texas held a Kyle Rote Day before one of his last home games, at which he was not merely honored for his eleven years as a Giant but also received gifts ranging from a 1962 Ford Thunderbird to a genuine Texas champion Hereford steer to assorted toys for his children. As teammate Alex Webster said later, "He was so well liked by his fellow ballplayers that about six or eight of them named their kids Kyle."

Kyle Rote forged a radio broadcasting career in New York City after football, handling sports news as well as color commentary for the Giants' games. Today he is in private business in New York.

I t was in San Antonio, Texas, where I grew up, that I started playing football. I attended Thomas Jefferson High School and played football and basketball; we went to the state championships in both my senior year.

Then I went to Vanderbilt University in Tennessee, where I thought I might play football. They had a summer program there, which enabled freshmen to become eligible for the varsity. And I thought that was a pretty good idea.

We had to be enrolled before September, however. Well, I got up there in Nashville and my first thoughts were that I didn't see myself living in that part of the country after college.

Red Sanders was the head coach at Vanderbilt then, and he was a great recruiter. He'd been there since like 1940, and this was 1947. Later, of course, he would go on to make quite a name for himself coaching at UCLA. I went in one night to talk to him and explained that I was going to head back to San Antonio and that I had appreciated what he'd done for me, but I thought Texas was really the place for me.

It wasn't your classic case of being homesick; I was just concerned about the four years I would be spending up there and then going back to my friends and former teammates in Texas. He asked me to give it some thought, which I did. And then I booked myself on a train back to Texas. Ironically enough, as I was going back by train to Texas, four of my closest teammates were driving up to Vanderbilt. They had been invited by Coach Sanders. Anyway, they arrived and were looking all over for me, but I was headed back to Texas. When I got to San Antonio, they were in Nashville.

But it was a good decision on my part. I had a kind of standing offer at Southern Methodist—for basketball as well as football. So I went up to Dallas and talked to the football coach, Matty Bell; I asked him if the offer was still on the table, and he said the scholarship was still open. Between that and the fact that my girlfriend, who was to become my wife, was also planning to go there, the decision was not a very difficult one.

Doak Walker was already there at SMU—he was a year ahead of me—and he had already been in the military service too. Doak was a fabulous ballplayer. He won the Heisman Trophy when he was a junior [1948]. Doak had made All-American three years in a row—as a sophomore, junior, and senior. He was a tough act to follow.

We had been playing our games at a little stadium on

the SMU campus back then, but with all the publicity Doak was getting it wasn't big enough. So they moved our home games into the Cotton Bowl down there in Dallas. We went from a campus-type sport to the major leagues, so to speak. Like they called Yankee Stadium The House That Ruth Built, they got to calling the Cotton Bowl The House That Walker Built.

After freshman ball, I played two years with Doak [1948 and 1949]. We went to the Cotton Bowl after the 1948 season and beat Oregon [21–13], whose quarterback that year was Norm Van Brocklin. Both Doak and I scored a touchdown in that game.

There was also a very memorable game the next year when we played Notre Dame at the Cotton Bowl, the last game of the 1949 regular season. They were ranked number one in the nation at the time—in fact, Notre Dame hadn't lost a game since the last one of the 1945 season—and they had a bunch of All-Americans on the team: Bob Williams at quarterback, Emil Sitko at halfback, and Leon Hart and Jim Martin were their ends.

We had lost three games in the Southwest Conference, and on top of that Doak was injured and wouldn't be able to play at all. We were a definite underdog [the spread was 28 points]. Their coach, Frank Leahy, said when the team arrived in Dallas, "We come here to round off a perfect season."

There was really a lot of money floating around Texas at that time—the oil business was booming. And the SMU backers had a lot of it. The game was played on December 3, a week after most all the other college teams had ended their seasons. And it was on national television and on armed-forces radio overseas. The SMU supporters took one look at that 28-point spread, and a lot of money went down on us. Word was they were betting the farm on SMU, or maybe the oil patch.

I filled in for Doak at tailback and it turned into a great game. We shook their confidence. We were losing 13–0 at the half, but we came back very strong. In the fourth quarter we tied it up at 20 apiece. They got another touchdown to take the lead. I got hurt and had to come out but came back in a little later and got us down to their 4-yard line. They were thinking I was going to run the ball and keyed for it, but I was really beat up by that time. I tried a little jump pass and Jerry Groom intercepted it, and that was the game [27–20, Notre Dame]; but we gave them a heckuva scare. [Rote scored all three of the Mustangs' touchdowns that day.] The *Dallas Morning News* the next day had a headline: SMU Wins 20–27. And even if we didn't win, all those guys in Dallas who bet on us made a killing.

In 1950 Doak went on to the Detroit Lions, and I took over full-time as tailback. We didn't have any games my senior year quite as exciting as the '49 Notre Dame game, but we had some good ones. We went up to Ohio State— they had Vic Janowicz at tailback, and he won the Heisman Trophy that year—and they were highly ranked. But we won up there in Columbus [32–27]. We won six of our ten games that year but didn't do too well in our conference.

I really didn't know much about pro football while I was in college. The only team I ever followed—and that was only on occasion—was the Detroit Lions, because Doak and his buddy Bobby Layne played for them. I didn't really even know how the draft worked. In those days they had a bonus pick—each team would draw from a hat and one would get the bonus, the first pick, regardless of where the team had ended up in the previous year's standings. Then it would go in order like today—the team with the worst record picking, then the next worst, and so on.

In February or March of 1951, they held the draft and Steve Owen picked the bonus out of the hat. It was quite a bonus for the Giants because they had a 10–2–0 record the year before and otherwise would have picked way down the line. Well, they selected me with it.

They called after the pick and wanted to know if I'd be amenable to talking to them. Then Wellington Mara came down to Dallas, and we agreed to the terms of a contract. A while later I went up to New York for the formal signing, which was done at Toots Shor's restaurant.

I'd been to New York City once before, but I was still overwhelmed with it. Even today, and I've been here a long time now, I'm still amazed with it. It's the most complex, dynamic city in the United States—maybe even the world.

When I first arrived I stayed in the Concourse Plaza Hotel, which was up in the Bronx about two blocks up the hill from Yankee Stadium. I was married, and my wife and my oldest son, who had been born on Christmas Day 1950, came up to New York with me. We stayed in the Concourse Plaza during the football season for several years, but in the off-season we would always go back to San Antonio. It wasn't until 1958 that we stayed permanently in New York.

I'd met a couple of the Giants before going to that first training camp; but when you go there, you know, every rookie is scared to death. Most were pretty nice—guys like Charlie Conerly and Al DeRogatis, I remember, went out of their way. Charlie and I were a little closer in that he and his wife were also living in the Concourse Plaza. Tom Landry and his wife were living there too. Most of the single guys lived in other hotels down closer to the action.

Steve Owen was the coach when I got there, near the end of his career. He was a real character. He was of the old school of coaching—he would get us out on the field, and before you knew it you'd been out there three hours. The offense ran all of the Giants' offensive plays, and then the offense would run all of the other team's plays against our defense.

Paul Brown over at Cleveland was the one who stream-lined practice sessions—he was the first of the modern coaching era—so you were out there for maybe an hour and a half and actually got more done. When Jim Lee Howell took over [1954] after Steve retired, he brought that kind of thinking into the Giants' camp.

They had me starting in training camp, and everything looked great. But we were going through these three-hour practice sessions with contact, and one day my left knee just went out. I made a cut upfield and I felt it go. I tried to get back into the game four or five weeks later, after we were into the season, but this was before arthroscopy. I played a couple of games and it went out again; so I waited out a few games and then came back, and it went out again. Finally, when the season was over, I had an operation on it.

In 1952 I was playing, but I was still hobbling around there in the backfield. I was second in rushing to Eddie Price that year, but I was hurting most of the season.

Then in 1953, in an exhibition game we played at Hershey, Pennsylvania, I made the mistake of standing there admiring one of the kicks I'd made, and one of the Steelers' linemen came and hit me—and there went the right knee. For the balance of 1953, I was gimping around again, but I played pretty much. I was our leading receiver, but we didn't have a very good year. We had some really fine ballplayers, though—Arnie Weinmeister, Emlen Tunnell, Charlie Conerly, Frank Gifford, Rosey Brown, Tom Landry, Jack Stroud, Ray Wietecha—but we won only three of our twelve games, and after that Steve Owen was gone.

In 1954, with Jim Lee Howell as our head coach, they were thinking of switching me to flanker. As a result, I would run pass patterns in practice against Tom Landry, who was an excellent defensive back. Well, before long Howell made Landry a player-coach and put him in charge of the defense. Then he brought in Vince Lombardi, who had been coaching at Army under Red Blaik, to run the offense. Landry lobbied for switching me permanently to flanker. After all, we now had Frank Gifford as a halfback and Eddie Price as a fullback. And then it was guaranteed forever in 1955 that my halfback days were over, because that year we acquired Alex Webster, who would go on to become one of the greatest running backs the Giants ever had. As it turned out, the switch to flanker gave me maybe six or seven more years in the league—ones which, because of my banged-up knees, I'm sure I wouldn't have had if I'd stayed at halfback.

Speaking of Gifford, I remember in one game against

the Chicago Cardinals somebody split his lip. It was in the latter part of the second quarter. We were playing at Comiskey Park in Chicago, which was a baseball stadium where the White Sox played. Anyway, to get to the locker room at halftime, we had to go through the dugout and climb these stairs up into this antiquated locker room. When I got there, I saw Frank sitting on the training table and Doc Sweeney, our trainer, who was not averse to having a nip or two in cold weather—and it was cold up in Chicago that day—was mucking around getting ready to stitch up Frank's lip. Finally he got to it and started to stitch the lip, but the problem was he hadn't gotten around to threading the needle. When he realized that, he went off to get some thread and Frank was sitting there with the needle stuck through his lip. Finally the doc got some thread and sewed it up, but I recall Frank wasn't all that happy about the situation.

The year 1956 was an especially memorable one. We had moved from the Polo Grounds, and this was our first year playing in Yankee Stadium. The facilities were so much better—the stadium, the locker rooms. It was really first-class, from what we had just come from. At the Polo Grounds, there hadn't been any carpets and there were splinters coming out of the wood floors. The best word to describe the whole place was "rickety." At Yankee Stadium there were tile floors, rugs—everything was first-class, and I think that gave us all a lift.

We also knew we were now a pretty good ball club. That year we got some really fine newcomers. Andy Robustelli and Dick Modzelewski came by trades, and we drafted Sam Huff and Jim Katcavage. All of them became instant starters and major contributors. It was Wellington Mara who put this all together, the trades and the good draft— that was his specialty.

At this point then [assistant coaches] Landry and Lombardi really started molding their units as they wanted to. Our defensive team especially developed with the new players, and it became very obvious in the league.

We got to the championship game that year and we won it. We scored 47 points, and our defense was exceptional. The Bears only scored 7 points. The one thing I kept thinking in that game was that we had to be careful. So often you get up by, say, 17 points early and then relax, or the other team gets fired up and suddenly they come back with a roar. More times than not it will go for the team that is losing, and I was afraid of that happening as we were running up the score in the first half. It's so easy to get complacent. Well, fortunately, it didn't happen.

Lombardi was instrumental in getting the offense up that day. He was just so dynamic, so very intense. I remember him at the blackboard. He would talk and at the same time be drawing the zeros and X's up there and everything was emphasized so strongly—you thought he was going to break the chalk, maybe even knock the chalkboard over.

He was an inspiring man. Players have said a lot of different things about him. The guy in Green Bay, [tackle] Henry Jordan, he said, "Lombardi treats us all the same—like dogs." And Max McGee, their fine end, said, "When coach Lombardi says sit down, I don't even bother to look for a chair." There is no question that he demanded a lot from his players—he got it in New York, and he got it in Green Bay. But he also had the respect of all his players in both those cities too.

Nineteen fifty-eight was another great year for us. I was on the sideline when Pat Summerall kicked that incredible field goal in the snowstorm against the Browns. I forget what they credited him for [it was for 49 yards], and I don't know how they were able to—you couldn't see the yard markings for all the snow on the field. I think I was standing at about the 50-yard line, and he kicked it from farther away than I was. Nobody thought he had a chance, but Pat proved them all wrong. And, of course, we went on then to win the conference.

We had a lot of great characters on those teams. One, Cliff Livingston, a linebacker of ours, was very funny. I

remember once out at training camp in Salem, Oregon, it was after eleven, which was our curfew. The coaches would come around to check if we were in our rooms, and then they'd go downstairs to a kind of lounge and have coffee and talk. Well, this particular night Cliff had made arrangements to go out. Someone had loaned him a car, and so after the bedcheck he was tiptoeing downstairs with his shoes in his hand. He was just about out the front door when Jim Lee Howell, our head coach, saw him and said, "Cliff, where the hell are you going?"

"Coach," he said, "I was out earlier and I lost my wallet somewhere, and I was just going back to the café to see if I could find it."

Howell looked at him and then at the shoes in his hand and said, "What the hell you plannin' to do, Cliff—sneak up on it?"

In that same dormitory were Harland Svare, another linebacker, who came to us from the Rams, and Don Heinrich, a quarterback, who we drafted that year [1954]—both West Coast boys. Well, Jim Lee Howell, who was from Arkansas, had great—what would you call it?—distrust of the guys from California and the West Coast. He used to talk about them always playing with their sleeves rolled up to show off their suntans. One night he was going around after eleven o'clock. It was really a hot, boiling night too, and, of course, there was no air-conditioning in the dormitory. Well, Svare and Heinrich, who were rooming together, were lying in their beds buck-ass naked. We had had a scrimmage that day, a hard one, and Svare had hurt his back in it. Well, Svare was moaning and groaning about it so much that Heinrich couldn't get to sleep and finally said,

◄ Kyle Rote takes off around end in a 1953 game at the Polo Grounds. Rote (1951–61) started out as halfback with the Giants, but banged-up knees forced him to switch to flanker in 1955, a position from which he became one of the Giants' best pass receivers. Number 31 is New York fullback Eddie Price.

"Damn it, Harlan, get up. I'm gonna pop your back so we can both get some sleep around here."

So they both got up and Heinrich's there close behind Svare with his knee up in Harlan's back and his hands on his shoulders, and here comes Jim Lee Howell with his flashlight. He opens the door, takes one look, and closes it and goes back downstairs. He goes up to where the other coaches were sitting, shaking his head and mumbling, "West Coasters, West Coasters—I don't know what, but we gotta do something about those West Coast boys."

I had the good fortune to play with two of the best quarterbacks that ever passed through the NFL—Charlie Conerly and Y. A. Tittle. Conerly was there when I arrived [1951], and he was our starter for ten years; then Tittle took over my last two years with the Giants [1961-62].

Conerly was quite a guy. He had left college to join the marines in World War II and fought in a number of battles in the Pacific. He was a laid-back kind of player, almost casual about the game. He showed little excitement on the outside, but there was a lot of it, I know, on the inside. He just never exhibited his emotions. But Charlie had an incredibly good touch when he threw the football, and he was especially effective on the shorter passes.

Tittle, on the other hand, was much more vocal, more emotional outwardly on the field. It was tough for him to come to New York, however. We had had a good amount of success with Conerly quarterbacking—won the world championship in 1956, played in championship games in '58 and '59—heck, we had had only one losing season since I got there in '51. And Charlie was very well liked by all the other players.

But Charlie was old and wearing down. Tittle wasn't any bird of youth by any means, but he was still quite explosive. He could really throw for distance—as good as Norm Van Brocklin, who was one of the all-time greatest throwing long. And this helped when we got Del Shofner because he was a real speedster who could get open deep.

Before that we didn't have any real deep threats. I wasn't fast because of my knees. So we had been settling for the shorter passes with Conerly. Now we had another piece of ammunition.

I had one play with Conerly that worked quite well. I would run from the inside slot position and do a zee-in: the right end would take care of the off safety and I would work our wide side, where our left split end would go down and fake like he was cutting in and then cut out. That left the other safety on me, and I would fake in, start out, and then cut back in. I got a good number of my touchdown catches on that particular play. Conerly really had the timing on that one down right.

We used that play too when Tittle took over. We also used about a 14-yard hook play with a lot of success with Y.A. He would fire that ball in there like a cannon shot, and a receiver really loved that because the longer that ball is in the air the more time the defensive back has to size you up and cut you in two. It's where Tittle's strong arm came in very handy.

My last game was the championship game of 1961. We played [Vince] Lombardi's Packers with all those great players they had at the time: Hornung, Taylor, Starr, Nitschke, Willie Davis. I knew it was going to be my last game because I had already decided to retire after the season. You kind of dread the retirement because of all the friends you have on the team and just giving up the game, but I knew it was time—I certainly wasn't going to be getting any faster, and the injuries catch up to you. You know it—the player is the first to know it.

It wasn't the best of games to go out on. We got beat up pretty bad that day [37–0]. I caught a couple of passes [3 for 54 yards], and that was it.

After I retired from playing, I coached the backfield for the Giants in 1962 and 1963. I liked that a lot. There were some moments when you would be watching the backs and flankers and you would wish that you could still be doing the kinds of things they could. But overall at that point I did not miss playing.

I had been doing some radio work while I was still playing, an after-game show for WNEW in New York, the station that broadcast our games. And that enabled me to segue from football into broadcasting full-time. I would do the nightly news on radio and the color for the Giants' games. I continued to do that for a number of years after I retired from the Giants. In 1967, I went to NBC.

Later, my wife and I formed our own business, Ronina Chemical Company—we specialize in the processes of breaking precious metals out of ores. That business occupies most of my time these days.

But, I must say, football with the Giants was a great eleven-year ride, and I'm certainly glad I had the opportunity to be along for it.

Benny Friedman Remembers . . .

From *Pro Football's Rag Days* by Bob Curran:

I think one of the highlights along the charity trail was when we played the Notre Dame alumni [1930] for Mayor Jimmy Walker's unemployment fund in the depths of the Depression. . . .

There were a couple of funny things that came out of it. Just before the game [Knute] Rockne walked into our dressing room with a cane—he wasn't well at the time. I was getting my ankles taped . . . I looked up at him—he was one of my idols—and said, "Hi, coach," and he said, "Hello, Benny."

He asked how I was. I said, "Fine."

He said, "That's too bad."

I asked, "What can I do for you?"

He started giving me a story about some of these old men that he had [on his team], and he told me that one of these guys had taken a big step off a Pullman and got a charley horse. He said, "I think we ought to have free substitution."

I said, "Okay, coach, anything else?"

He said, "Yes, I think we ought to cut the quarters down to ten minutes—from fifteen."

I said, "Oh, Lord, we can't do that. There are 45,000 people out there who have paid five bucks apiece to see this game. I'll tell you what we'll do—we'll cut it down to twelve minutes and a half, and if it gets bad we'll cut it down some more in the second half." I then said, "Anything else?"

He said, "Yes, for Pete's sake, take it easy."

(The Giants won 22–0, with Friedman scoring two touchdowns and passing for another.)

Arnie Weinmeister

Although he was born in western Canada, raised in the state of Oregon, and played his college football at the University of Washington, Arnie Weinmeister spent his entire U.S. pro football career on the opposite coast, playing six years in New York City.

The first two years (1948–49) were spent with the New York Yankees of the All-America Football Conference, a team that showcased such football talents as tailback Spec Sanders, halfback Buddy Young, and defensive back Tom Landry. In the AAFC, Weinmeister played both offensive and defensive tackle and was named All-AAFC in 1949.

When the AAFC merged with the NFL in 1950, Weinmeister signed with the New York Giants, where his star would shine brightly for the next four years. From 1950 through 1953, the 6'4", 235-pounder earned All-Pro honors each year as a defensive tackle and started in each of the first four Pro Bowls.

Weinmeister was recognized as the fastest lineman in pro football, and he was such a dominating force on the field that he became the first defensive player to capture the same amount of attention as those players in the glamour positions like quarterback or running back.

He was known for his keen football instinct and uncanny ability to diagnose plays. As Tom Landry later said of him, "If you wanted to know where the opponent's ball was, all you had to do was look for Arnie's jersey number."

After the 1953 season, Weinmeister played two more years in the Canadian Football League for the Vancouver, British Columbia, franchise. After that, he started a thirty-six-year career as an official of the Teamsters union, from which he retired in 1992.

Arnie Weinmeister was elected to the Pro Football Hall of Fame in 1984.

I was born in Canada, in a little town named Rhein, about forty miles from Regina, Saskatchewan, but we moved to the United States when I was six months old. I was raised in Portland, Oregon.

When I was finishing up high school we moved to Seattle. There were several colleges that offered me scholarships; University of Oregon was the only one I considered besides Washington, which was my first choice. But I guess I had really predetermined that I was going to go to the U. of Washington right there in Seattle.

I started out playing end there as a sophomore in 1942 and then went into the service. When I got out in 1946, I came back and started as a fullback but got my knee wrecked. As a senior I switched to tackle and, of course, we played both ways in those days.

While I was still playing fullback, the New York Yankees of the All-America Football Conference sent a man over to talk to me. They were training over in Spokane then. They told me they had me as their first choice in their draft. So they sent me a contract right off, apparently to prevent anyone else from signing me. They offered me what was at that time a pretty good salary. I didn't talk with anyone from the NFL. So I signed with the Yankees.

The Yankees coach, Ray Flaherty, invited me to come over to Gonzaga, a college in Spokane, where the Yankees were training. They were having an exhibition game that evening, and I saw the players sitting out in front of the gym there at Gonzaga before they went into the locker room to get dressed. I thought, Gee, these guys are really fat. But the most amazing thing to me in watching the game that night was to see how quick and fast they were. That was an eye-opener for me.

After that, I got to play in the College All-Star Game, which they held every year before the opening of the pro season. It was always played at Soldier Field in Chicago, and they used to draw more than 100,000 for the game. It was quite an event and an honor to be selected to play in it.

The coach of the All-Stars that year [1948] was Frank Leahy of Notre Dame. Well, he picked his own two tackles to start, George Connor and Ziggy Czarobski. But he said to me, "You've impressed me as a football player, young man, and even though you're a tackle I'm going to start you as a guard." So I got to be one of the starting lineup who runs out in the spotlight just before the game—it was always played under the lights at night then.

We had a great team: Johnny Lujack at quarterback, and Charlie Conerly from Ole Miss and Bob Chappius and Bump Elliot from Michigan in the backfield; and also Len Ford from Michigan at end. But we got trimmed and learned what pro football was going to be like. We played the Chicago Cardinals, and they were just too much—they whipped us 28–0.

When I got to the Yankees that first year, Ray Flaherty, who'd been a great end for the Giants in the 1930s and is in the Hall of Fame, was the coach. But we got off to a disastrous start and after a few games he was replaced by Red Strader. Mel Hein, another former Giant and also a Hall of Famer, was the line coach.

New York City was not all that new to me when we went back east. I'd been stationed there for ten months at an army engineering college.

I remember my first impression of working out with the pros—it was the beating you took playing both ways. It was bad enough in practice or an intrasquad scrimmage, but it was worse in a game. Most of the other teams had already started two-platooning it; but we hadn't, and so I ended up facing two, three, four different guys in a game. After a game I used to spend the next two days down at the stadium in the whirlpool in order to get the bruises and muscle strains out before I could really start preparing for the next week.

What helped me a lot was the speed I had. I've been asked if I trained in any special way to develop it, but I didn't. I guess I was just naturally endowed with it. I did a lot of running in training, but that didn't develop speed— stamina maybe, but that's about all. In the off-season I would train with exercises; and I played a lot of handball then—and I mean a lot. I'd play maybe half a dozen different guys in a day. Then I'd go out and run around the track for maybe an hour. I would increase the regimen as time drew closer to training camp.

When the All-America Conference folded after the 1949 season, the Giants got a kind of special deal. Apparently to allow Ted Collins to maintain the New York Bulldogs, which was an NFL franchise that had been allowed to come down from Boston the year before [it became the New York Yanks in 1950], to stay in New York, part of the deal was that the Giants got to select six players from the now defunct Brooklyn/New York Yankees of the AAFC.

The Giants took me and a couple of terrific defensive backs—Tom Landry and Otto Schnellbacher. So I joined the NFL in 1950.

When the Giants selected me, they sent me a letter that said something to the effect that they were happy to have me and that they were proud to offer me a contract. Only thing was, the contract offered $6,400 for the year. The year before, with the Yankees, I'd made $10,000. So I wrote back and I told them that I wasn't interested because I wouldn't play for any less than I had the year before. The banter went back and forth over phone calls for some time.

I had gone back to Seattle, and the Giants were in training camp. By this time I'd gone to work for the Aetna Life Insurance Company. They called again and said they really wanted me to come back and talk contract. I said I would if they provided me a first-class, round-trip airline ticket. They did.

The Giants were in training up at Saranac Lake, New York. So I went up there. It was around lunchtime when I arrived, and they suggested I go have lunch with the players and that we would get together afterwards. So I set my bag in the hall of the lodge there, which is called the Eagle's Nest, and had lunch. A couple of former teammates with the Yankees, Tom Landry and Otto Schnellbacher, were sitting with me, and they were telling me that they were badly in need of tackles. That reinforced my resolve for the upcoming meeting.

I met with Wellington Mara and the coach, who was Steve Owen at the time—the only coach they'd had over the previous twenty years. I told them that under no circumstances would I play for any less than $10,000 the first year, $11,000 the second, and a two-year, no-cut contract. A no-cut contract in those days was unheard of.

They said they simply weren't going to do that.

I said, "Well, that's fine. I haven't even unpacked my bag, and so I'll be on my way." And I got up.

They said, reluctantly, "Okay, we'll write up the contract."

Steve Owen said to me then, "Let's get going." Steve was the coach my entire time there—he had played tackle for the Giants for six or seven years himself in the late '20s and early '30s before he became their full-time coach. In fact, Steve and I both retired the same year, after the 1953 season.

Steve was a rotund, fun-type individual. He was a very down-to-earth guy, a great defensive coach. His only problem was that he spent all his time on defense and almost no time on offense. So we wound up having the best defense in the league but we didn't score any points to speak of, and therefore we didn't win as many games as we should have.

Although the Giants were mainly a defensive team—at least that's what was stressed by Owen—I don't want to take anything away from the offense. We had some good offensive players—Charlie Conerly, Eddie Price, Bill Swiacki, Kyle Rote, Frank Gifford—but Steve and the other coaches didn't devote much time at all to the offense.

Tom Landry was in our defensive backfield that first year, and he was an outstanding ballplayer. Even then he was kind of a player-coach—he hadn't been named player-coach yet but he just kind of naturally took over as far as guiding what was then called the umbrella defense. It was just being installed around that time, and Tom was essentially the brains behind that defense. Steve Owen invented it, but Landry really shaped it. It was a 6-1-4 formation—six men on the front line, one linebacker as the stem of the umbrella, and four backs, with the two halfbacks shallow and wide and the two safeties deep and tight:

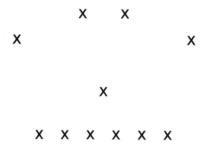

It was certainly a much different sport from what it is today. The basics, of course, were the same—you block, you tackle, you run the ball, you pass it. But the approach was different from the players' end. Today, with the television exposure, the players are almost like movie entertainers, and the salary levels are not even close to being proportionate to the times; so they approach the game differently than we did. I was supposed to be the highest-paid lineman in the league; when I left the NFL I was earning $12,000 a year. There is much more specialization now—the guys are bigger, faster, spend more time refining their skills for each element of the game. It makes for a much better, smoother-flowing football game, technically speaking; but it's difficult sometimes to see one team matched against each other. By that, I mean, the many rotations on different downs—a passing down will bring in different defensive players from those who were in on the first two downs, all kinds of variations. When we played, it was basically one team of players out there against another.

There were a lot of great players out there in the early 1950s. Otto Graham, the quarterback of the Browns, was especially effective. The Browns, of course, were the perennial champions in the All-America Conference and also when they went to the National Football League. Lou Rymkus, an offensive tackle for Cleveland, is another I always considered outstanding—I used to go toe-to-toe with him. And [fullback] Marion Motley was really a horse. They used to have a trap play—called a 32-trap, I believe—where he ran up the middle. One game, Otto Schnellbacher, an All-Pro safety we had then—he was also a professional basketball player at the time for Providence—met Motley head-on, and Motley never even broke stride going for the goal line. Schnellbacher was knocked over backwards by Motley and knocked out cold. From that day forward, Schnellbacher said, "When that guy comes through, all I'm going to do is wait till he goes by and grab onto the back of his shoulder pads and take a ride. I'm never going to meet him head-on again."

All of our games with the Cleveland Browns were memorable. Almost all were decided by a touchdown or less. We were able to defeat them when they were mopping up everybody else. The closest I ever got to a championship game when I was with the Giants was the time in 1950 when we met the Browns in a playoff game. We had both ended the regular season with 10–2–0 records. We had beaten the Browns in Cleveland 6–0 in the second game of the year; then later they took us at the Polo Grounds 17–13.

The playoff game was at Municipal Stadium in Cleveland. It was only about ten degrees above zero that day and there was a raw wind coming off Lake Erie, and, on top of that, the ground was frozen.

Lou Groza kicked a field goal for them in the first quarter—a short one, not much more than an extra point. That was the only score until the fourth quarter. We had the ball on Cleveland's 3-yard line thanks to [halfback] Choo Choo Roberts breaking one for us. Then all kinds of crazy things started happening. We were, of course, going for the touchdown which would put us ahead. And we got it: Charlie [Conerly] threw into the end zone and one of our receivers [end Bob McChesney] grabbed it. But we were called for offsides. We couldn't get it in on the next two downs; then on fourth down we went for it and Charlie threw an interception. This time the Browns were penalized. So we got another chance, but now it was from the 9-yard line because we got a penalty [illegal motion] before the ball was snapped. We settled for a field goal, which tied the game.

Otto Graham and Groza saved the game for them in the last minute or two. Graham broke free on a quarterback draw and got it close enough for Groza to kick a field goal [28-yarder] and they had the game. [There was a safety in the last seconds when Bill Willis tackled Conerly in the end zone to make the final score 8–3, Browns.]

We should have won because we should have scored a touchdown when we were first and goal on their 3. Anyway, that's as near as I ever got to the big game.

Another team we had a strong rivalry with in those days was the Washington Redskins. They didn't have all that good a team in those years—Sammy Baugh was at the end of his career, in his late thirties. But they always gave us trouble, for some reason or another. I guess they really got up for the games against the Giants. They did have some good players, though: [halfback] Bullet Bill Dudley was with them then; Bones Taylor was a terrific end, and Gene Brito was a good one too; and Al DeMao, who played center and linebacker, was a tough one. They beat us at the end of the 1952 season, which knocked us out of the running for the conference title [the Giants ended up a game behind the Browns that year]. And they beat us twice my last year [1953].

Philadelphia was another good team. They, of course, had Steve Van Buren, probably one of the best running backs I ever saw. He was big, strong, fast—great moves. He was also at the end of his career when I played against him. And they had Tommy Thompson at quarterback and Pete Pihos at end. Then there was Chuck Bednarik, I think probably the greatest of all the sixty-minute players, at center and linebacker. And Al Wistert and Bucko Kilroy played on their offensive line—they didn't come any better than those two. They were not the team they'd been in the late 1940s when they won the NFL title [twice, in 1948 and 1949, and they lost it to the Cardinals in the 1947 championship game]. But they beat us in '52 too, like the Redskins, which helped keep us behind the Browns.

Two years after I was there, we got Frank Gifford. He was the Giants' first-round draft choice that year [1952]. And he was a great player—Frank could do anything. It always amazed me, his versatility. He could play quarterback, halfback, tailback; he could punt, pass, catch the football, placekick—a great runner. There wasn't any position they put him in that he didn't produce.

Another player who was especially good but, unlike Gifford, never got the acclaim he should have, was Al DeRogatis from Duke, who played the other defensive tackle. He was a tremendous tackle—played above and beyond the call of duty because he had really bad knees during his entire pro career [1949-52]. He was an awesome tackler.

I left the Giants after the 1953 season. In fact, I had informed them before the season that this was going to be my last season with them.

We had had a terrible year—won only three out of twelve games, which only served to confirm my decision to leave New York. In addition, I had heard about the start-up of a team in Vancouver in the Canadian Football League. I talked to them and they offered me a position as player-coach at quite a bit more money than I was being paid by the Giants.

The Giants had told me they were not going to give me an increase for the 1954 season even if I decided to come back for another year. So I reiterated to them at the end of the 1953 season that that was my last with them.

The Giants took me to court for supposedly breaking my contract under the option clause where they have a perpetual ownership of you. However, a conversation I had had with the owners of the club [Jack and Wellington Mara] before the 1953 season was confirmed by a letter in which I asked earlier what my status with the club was, because at that time I had been offered an assistant coaching job at the University of Washington. I wanted to know if I would be able to accept it or not. They responded with a letter which contained substantive proof that I had informed them 1953 was to be my last season with the Giants—and that I was free to take the other job. When they came to court in Seattle, they lost the case. And I went up to Canada for two more years of football.

After football, I joined the Teamsters union as an organizer in the San Francisco Bay area. I worked my way up to director of the thirteen western states and was second vice president on the executive board. I stayed with the Teamsters for thirty-six years and retired in March 1992.

◀ Arnie Weinmeister merely went through the motions in this publicity shot, but the truth was that you indeed had to double-team Weinmeister if you wanted to keep him out of your backfield. In his four years (1950–53) with the Giants, he was named All-Pro each year and was considered the fastest, most devastating defensive lineman of that era. He was inducted into the Pro Football Hall of Fame in 1984.

◙

Runyon Predicts

The first night football game to be played at the Polo Grounds
pitted the College All-Stars against the New York Giants in the
1936 preseason, a benefit for the *New York Herald Tribune*
Fresh Air Fund. Damon Runyon devoted several of his "Both
Barrels" syndicated column to it.

It's our private opinion, and don't let it get around
any more than you can help as it might affect the
odds, that the College All-Stars will knock the spots
off the New York Giants. . . .

It is to be held at night on a light-flooded field,
which in itself is a tremendous novelty in New York
and may be the beginning of regular night football
and baseball, too, here.

They are presenting against the professionals a
team of college stars that will include some of the
most famous players in the United States, under the
coaching of Bernie Bierman, who is accounted one of
the smartest football generals alive.

Neighbor Caswell Adams reports from Evanston,
Ill., where the College All-Stars are training, the presence of fellows like Wayne Millner and Bill Shake-
speare of Notre Dame, Phil Flanagan of Holy Cross,
Amerino Sarno of Fordham, and Dick Crayne, Sheldon
Beise, Riley Smith, and numerous others whose names
and exploits threaded the football news last fall.

Jay Berwanger, of Chicago, halfback selection on
everybody's All-American team, is there. So is Joe
Maniaci, Dick Pfefferle, and Dale Rennebohm. . . . We
think the collegians are a fair bet to beat the Giants.

The Giants won, 12–2.

◙

Dick Lynch

Dick Lynch came to the Giants in 1959 by way of a trade after spending a year with the Washington Redskins. They had selected him in the sixth round of the 1958 draft. Once with New York, he immediately won the starting job at right cornerback, a position he would maintain with consummate skill over the next eight years.

A tough, talented, brash defensive back who was as intense on the field as he was fun-loving off it, Lynch was an integral part of one of the best defenses ever mustered in the NFL—that of the Giants who went to four championship games in the first five years he was with the team. He was there right along with Andy Robustelli, Sam Huff, Rosie Grier, Jim Katcavage, Dick Modzelewski, Jimmy Patton. . . .

Lynch was a product of Notre Dame, where he played right halfback on offense and right corner on defense. He led the Fighting Irish in pass receptions (13 for 128 yards) his senior year, 1957, and scored the lone touchdown to defeat Oklahoma that same year and snap the Sooners' all-time record 47-game winning streak. In the pros, he eschewed offense for defense, and that is where he left his mark in Giants lore.

Well established with the Giants by 1961, Lynch led the

NFL in pass interceptions with 9. He repeated that feat with the same number of steals in 1963. He remains today the only Giant ever to lead the league twice in pass interceptions. He also led the club in interceptions in both 1964 and 1965. In 1963, a year the Giants won the NFL East crown, Lynch received All-Pro honors and was invited to that year's Pro Bowl.

Overall, Dick Lynch holds or shares several all-time Giants' records. Three times he intercepted 3 passes in a single game, a Giants mark shared with several defensive backs. Another club record he shares (with Hall of Famer Emlen Tunnell) is the single-season mark of 251 yards he gained on interceptions in 1963. Still another club record he and Tunnell claim is a career 4 touchdowns on pass interceptions. And no one has ever scored more on interceptions in a single season than the 3 touchdowns he registered in 1963.

In team history, Lynch ranks fourth in pass interceptions; his 35 are exceeded only by Tunnell (74), Patton (52), and Spider Lockhart (41). But beyond the mere statistics, Dick Lynch was a driving force on and off the field in New York. "Keeping up with him was the major measure—anywhere," confided one of his teammates, who then requested anonymity because he fully admitted he could never keep up with him.

After football, Lynch moved through the corporate world, from the printing business to the world of Wall Street. Today, he is the president of Tri-State Capital Markets Group in Cranford, New Jersey, a company that deals in government and municipal bonds.

I was born in New York, went through my first six grades in Manhasset, out on Long Island, while we were living in the Great Neck–Roslyn area. Then we moved out to Patenburg, New Jersey, and lived on a farm. I went to Phillipsburg Catholic High School, which was in a town right across the river from Easton, Pennsylvania.

I was a halfback at Phillipsburg. Our coach there, Charlie Passini, wrote a letter to Frank Leahy at Notre Dame when I was a senior, which said something to the effect

that I've got a kid here I think can play for your team. Leahy
sent the letter on to a scout whose name was McGinley, a
postman in the area; and he, unbeknownst to me, scouted
me. Then one day he just walked in and said, "We'd like to
offer you a scholarship to Notre Dame."

Aubrey Lewis, who was from Montclair, New Jersey,
and I were invited to come over to meet Frank Leahy in
Newark after that. We shook his hand, and all he said,
essentially, was, "Kid, do you want to come to Notre
Dame?" We said, "Yes, sir," and that was it. We didn't sign
any papers or anything like that. He felt a handshake was
all that was necessary. That was the way he handled
things—his word, your word; you understood the deal,
sealed with a handshake.

I never played for Frank Leahy. The spring before I got
there he resigned, and Terry Brennan took over for the 1954
season. I played halfback on offense and right cornerback
on defense for Brennan. Terry was an excellent coach, and
he had a great staff: Hank Stram, who later won a Super
Bowl; Bill Walsh [not to be confused with the Bill Walsh
who coached the San Francisco 49ers to four Super Bowl
victories], who was one of the best offensive line coaches
ever to coach in college and the NFL; Bill Fischer, an All-
American guard when he played at Notre Dame, who
coached the defensive line; and Jim Finks, who coached
the quarterbacks for a year or two.

The biggest game I was ever in at Notre Dame was in
1957, my senior year. We went down to Norman to play
Oklahoma. They had a 47-game winning streak at the time,
the longest ever in the NCAA—it still is the record, in fact.
They had beat us the year before 40–0 in South Bend. They
were an 18-point favorite. We didn't care. In '57 we were
really prepared for them. We worked our asses off the week
before the game. Terry Brennan kept reminding us that we
were the last team to have defeated Oklahoma, which was
all the way back in 1953 [it was the opening game of the
season at Oklahoma, and Notre Dame prevailed 28–21].

We decided we were going to book-end their win

streak. Our defense was outstanding that day—just shut
them down completely. In the fourth quarter it was 0–0.
Then we marched 80 yards down the field. Bobby Williams
called all the plays from the huddle, and we just surged. We
were at the 3-yard line with a fourth down and a little less
than four minutes to go. We decided to go for the touchdown. They were all scrunched up in the middle, thinking
we were going to give the ball to our fullback, Nick Pietro-
sante, who, after all, was an All-American. Bob Williams
faked the ball to him and Nick hit the line, and then Bob
pitched the ball out to me and I went around right end,
untouched, for the score. Monty Stickles kicked the extra
point and we won 7–0. As we later learned, Oklahoma had
not been shut out in 123 consecutive games. That was a
great day, the highlight of my college football career.

Paul Hornung was the big guy at Notre Dame my sophomore and junior years. He had a buddy down there who
was another halfback, Sherrill Sipes. I used to tell him,
"Paul, Sipes walks on eggs. Don't give him the ball. Give
me the ball." Paul said I was the cockiest ballplayer he ever
met. We never saw much of Paul around school. He must
have graduated from St. Joseph's or someplace else. The
only time we saw him was in the huddle.

The Redskins drafted me in 1958, and I didn't want to
go there. It's a kind of story in itself. While I was at Notre
Dame, to get some pocket money I'd joined the ROTC. And
I got very high grades in ROTC, a lot higher than the 83 or
something I got in regular classes. After graduation you
had to put down your preference; I preferred to serve six
months, so I put that down.

I had no ambition at all to play pro football. I was
going to take a job with Encyclopaedia Britannica in Chicago. After I signed up with EB for the job, I got a letter
from the army saying I was drafted. I was to go in in
January of 1959 for two years. So I had to tell the people at
Encyclopaedia Britannica I couldn't take the job.

At any rate, I was in Chicago to play in the College All-
Star Game and I was interviewed on television. The guy

asked me, "Dick, what are your plans for the future?"

"My plans have been drastically changed. I went to Notre Dame for four years and got a great education, and now I just found out I'm going to be stuck in the army for two years. I applied for six months but they stuck me for two years. I can't take the job I want. So, as long as I don't have to go in until January, maybe I'll try to play pro football until then."

So I went to the Redskins' training camp and I made the team. When we were back in Washington, I told George Preston Marshall, the team owner, about my two-year army commitment. He groused around and then tried to see if there was anything he could do, but there wasn't.

Well, as it turned out, some colonel had heard what I said on television and raised holy hell. He called Notre Dame and ranted about my saying I was going to be "stuck" in the army: "What kind of people are they turning out of ROTC down there? We don't want guys like him for two years!" and on and on. So I ended up getting the six months after all and served it at Fort Monmouth, New Jersey, after the first season with Washington.

I hadn't really been very happy with the Redskins, and I didn't plan to go back when I got out of the army. They sent me a couple of different contracts and I never sent one back. They got upset and finally just traded me to the Giants.

Everything then worked out. I liked the Giants and the Maras. Timmy Mara, whose family owned half the team, was a real good friend, and his uncle Wellington Mara, who owned the other half, was a fine man. And I knew the city real well. Tom Landry, who was coaching the defense then, was sensational to play for. Nobody could analyze an offense like he could. He'd tell you this is what's going to happen, and sure as hell it would. He told me when I got there that they definitely needed help at the right corner spot. They'd gotten beat the year before in the title game with Baltimore. The Colts and especially Raymond Berry had burned them a couple of times at the right corner.

I got the starting job, and we had a heckuva defensive backfield with Jimmy Patton, Dick Nolan, and Lindon Crow, and then Erich Barnes came in 1961—"The Baby," we used to call him. Erich and I, the twin corners they called us, were and are great pals; he is in business with me today.

The team was a very close-knit one when I came in 1959. There were some great ballplayers but no big egos. It was all a matter of working together as a team. Both units were that way—good camaraderie, respect for each other, no bullshit, stick up for each other, and we had a helluva lot of fun at the same time. I roomed with Cliff Livingston—we were both bachelors and lived in the Manhattan Hotel. We used to go over to Downey's all the time where a lot of the young actors in New York hung out, guys like John Cassavetes and Ben Gazzara who were just getting started in the theater.

I didn't do anything in the off-season then until I was getting ready to get married. My wife said she wouldn't marry me if I didn't have a job. I told her I had a job. She said, "That's only a game." I said, "Hey, you got to be kidding. I get paid to play." She said, "It's a game." So I asked our coach, Allie Sherman, to see if he could find me a job. And he got me one in sales in the printing business.

There's a lot to remember from those days. There were some backs that were really tough to tackle—guys like Jimmy Brown, John David Crow, Jim Taylor. There were some receivers really tough to cover. I remember one day I held Sonny Randle of the Cardinals to 16 catches—that was in 1962. I think it was close to an NFL record [at the time only Tom Fears of the Rams had ever caught more passes in a game—18]. He didn't catch all 16 off me, but it was a rough day—what I like to call an astigmatism day.

On the other hand, I had a couple of really good days the year before. We were playing the Cardinals in 1961 down in St. Louis, and I picked off three passes in that game. That was the same team that had Sonny Randle, who was obviously gearing up for the next year. A few weeks later, I did the same thing against the Philadelphia Eagles—

grabbed three of Sonny Jurgensen's passes. We won both of those games. But I would like to point out—because I think it is very important—we won because we were playing as a team. When I was picking off a pass, it was because guys like Robustelli, Katcavage, Grier, Mod [Modzelewski] were all over the passer. Hell, that's what we were—a team: they thought it was great I picked off a pass, I thought it was great they set the damn thing up by getting all over the quarterback.

Then Sonny Randle came back the next year. Why do I keep going back to that disaster?

Back to the Giants. Andy Robustelli was really the leader on the field for our defense. I used to have some fun with him. We called him "The Pope." You'd put your arm around a girl, and he'd be over in a minute next to you, saying, "Quit that—get your hand off her." Sometimes I'd kneel in front of him and ask if I could kiss his ring. I'd play some mind games with him too. One time we were having one helluva tussle out there and he came over to me and said something about you're not covering right, you're not doing this, you're not doing that. I said, "Why don't we just switch positions. I'll play end, you come out here and see what you can do." I'd do it just to get him going. Don't get me wrong—I always thought the world of Andy. He was a great leader and a fine guy, and I'd do anything for him. But we liked to have a little fun too.

Sam Huff was a leader in his own way too. He was one tough son of a bitch out there. He'd make a lot of tackles because he would be keying on a hole, and, of course, he had that great line in front of him—Katcavage, Grier, Modzelewski, Robustelli; they don't come any better than that. He got a lot of the notoriety. I used to say to him things like, "Hey Sam, is it still the rule that we can't get up until you get on the pile?" Just to give him a hard time, keep his feet on the ground; we didn't want him to get carried away with all the publicity. And he didn't. He just played one tough game out there, and every running back knew he was in the game—they could feel it for days after the game.

I thought we should have won one of those two championship games with the Packers in the 1960s. Not the first
one where we got cleaned 37-0 [1961] but the second, the
next year. We outgained them that day by about 50 yards.
But we had a couple of crucial fumbles, one that Phil King
coughed up set up their one and only touchdown. I still
think if a couple of things had been different we would
have won.

The Packers were a great team under Lombardi, there's
no taking that away from them. Cleveland was always good,
especially well coached—they had Paul Brown. And Pittsburgh was always a physical game. We won most of the
time, but you got the shit kicked out of you coming out of
it. I got paralyzed in a game against the Steelers in my last
year [1966]—from the neck down for about ten minutes. I
got whacked in the back. The first thing I thought about
was Roy Campanella, the great Dodgers catcher, and what
happened to him from that auto accident. But I said to the
doc, as I was lying there—supreme optimism, as we all
had stupidly in those days—"Don't worry, it'll come back.
I been here before." Actually, that was the second time I'd
been paralyzed in a game. It happened to me in that Oklahoma game where I scored the touchdown and we stopped
their win streak. That time I was paralyzed for about two
minutes, but it came back and I finished up the game. And
I came out of it in Pittsburgh too. I was just lucky, I guess.

That little incident in Pittsburgh helped me with my
decision to retire after the 1966 season. I was actually ready
without it. I'd been around for nine years, and '66 had been
less than memorable. We only won one game, lost twelve,
and tied one. And I was pretty established in business by
that time.

Still, it's hard to walk away from the game. I remember
Harland Svare, who was one of our linebackers when I first
came to the Giants, asked me to come back and play and
coach for another year. He'd just taken over as the Giants'
defensive coach. At the time I was working for Shorewood

Dick Lynch (22) and Dick Pesonen (25), in this statuesque scene, break up a Sonny Jurgensen pass intended for Joe Hernandez in a 1964 game against the Redskins. Lynch (1959–66) holds a number of defensive-back records for the Giants.

Press in the printing business, and I was making more money there than I was playing football.

I thought about it. I still was tempted. I got up one morning and put on the workout suit. I was halfway out the door when my wife said something like, "What the hell are you doing?" I said I was going out, get a little in shape; maybe I could do one or two more years—might be fun, might be . . . Well, she gave me about five quick reasons why it wasn't a good idea, the last being my neck—the paralysis thing. "But it's your decision, dear," or something like that, is what she left me with.

Well, I started jogging, and they all fell into place—each concern, or suggestion, whatever it was she laid out. Plus, after about three blocks of running I could really feel it—feel what it would be like if I tried to come back for another year.

"And your neck, dear," she'd said as I went out that day. I thought about that and knew it was over. I turned around and went home, and that was it.

We still get together at Giants alumni functions, and I love it. I don't live very far from the Giants, and I do get involved with the organization in a variety of things. It's great to keep in touch with the people I played with and played for, and the organization, which I have a great feeling for—and the game itself, for that matter.

And They Lost?

Phil Simms had his finest day as a Giant on October 13, 1985, and at the time the second most productive passing game of any quarterback in the history of the National Football League. On that day in Cincinnati he threw for 513 yards against the Bengals. The mark stood second only to the 554 yards Norm Van Brocklin of the Los Angeles Rams picked up against the New York Yankees in 1951. (Simms's mark has since been surpassed by Dan Marino of the Miami Dolphins—521 yards, 1988—and Warren Moon of the Houston Oilers—527 yards, 1990.)

Simms completed 40 of 62 passes. His number of completions has been exceeded in NFL history only by the 42 chalked up by Richard Todd of the New York Jets in a 1980 game against the San Francisco 49ers and equalled only by Ken Anderson of the Cincinnati Bengals in 1982 against the San Diego Chargers.

Rookie tight end Mark Bavaro caught 12 of Simms's passes, one more reception than the Giants' record of 11 shared by Frank Gifford, Del Shofner, Doug Kotar, Billy Taylor, and Gary Shirk.

The Giants' offense that day set a team record of 34 first downs and an NFL all-time standard of 29 passing first downs.

New York's defense held the Bengals to a paltry 199 yards of total offense in the game, including minus-3 yards of total offense in the second half.

And still the Giants lost that day to the Bengals, 35–30.

Jim Katcavage

They were the original Fearsome Foursome: Andy Robustelli, Rosie Grier, Dick Modzelewski, and Jim Katcavage. The Giants' front four of the late 1950s and early '60s, before the Los Angeles Rams usurped the title, was the quintessential defensive line in the National Football League. Handling the trench work for the Giants' defense during that epic era, they were an awesome force, enabling the Giants to win six conference championships in an eight-year period.

Katcavage, who played his college football as a defensive end at the University of Dayton, was New York's fourth-round draft choice in 1956, the same draft that brought aboard linebacker Sam Huff and kicker Don Chandler. The Giants, and especially assistant coach Vince Lombardi, had been impressed with Katcavage's showing in the East-West Shrine Game against more highly touted players from schools much bigger on the college football scale than Dayton.

Katcavage got an invitation to the College All-Star Game in Chicago in the summer of 1956, the first player ever from Dayton to be so honored. He answered by turning in a performance that gained him the honor as runner-up for the Most Valuable Player award to All-American center/linebacker Bob Pellegrini of Maryland.

Joining the Giants immediately after that game, Katcavage gained the starting berth at defensive end which he would not relinquish during his thirteen-year career with the Giants. Only Mel Hein (15 years) and Charlie Conerly, Joe Morrison, and George Martin (14 years) have played longer for the Giants than Katcavage.

During that tenure, Katcavage was credited with 3 safeties, which, at the time he retired, tied him for the NFL record. It still remains the Giants' standard.

According to the late Vince Lombardi, who had scouted Katcavage at Dayton and subsequently lobbied for drafting him, "Jim was a whiplash defensive end—fast, with good moves—the kind every quarterback hates to see lining up out there, knowing he's coming." Teammate Dick Lynch said, "Too bad they didn't record sacks when Katcavage was playing."

When his playing days ended after the 1968 season, Jim served as defensive line coach for the Giants under Alex Webster for five years. After that, he scouted for the Philadelphia Eagles and, in the last few years, has scouted for the NFL, evaluating would-be officials.

When he is not scouting around for the NFL, he works in automobile sales in the Philadelphia area, the same locale from which he commuted to New York during his thirteen years as a player and five as an assistant coach.

I'm a Philadelphia kid—born in Wilkes-Barre but moved to Philadelphia, where I've been ever since. I played football at Roman Catholic High School there. I also played on the basketball team. And that—the basketball—kind of changed where I ended up going to college.

In my senior year, I dislocated my shoulder playing basketball and had to have it operated on. A couple of the colleges who had expressed interest in giving me a football scholarship—and ones where I would have liked to have gone—weren't interested anymore. When they learned about the shoulder and the operation, they just faded away. My high school football coach managed to wangle a scholarship for me to Dayton University in Ohio. It was a one-year scholarship based on my making the team. I did, and after that they extended the scholarship for the following three years.

We played NCAA Division I then, but we did not play really big-time college football. In 1954, when I was a junior, though, we went down to play Tennessee; they had Johnny Majors as their tailback, and he was to become an All-American, and Tom "The Bomb" Tracy at fullback, who later played for a bunch of NFL teams. We were a big underdog, but we almost beat them—lost 14–7.

Dayton was a small school in terms of football. We didn't get much publicity outside of the city itself. I was lucky, though. After I finished there, I was invited to the College All-Star Game in Chicago, which was in 1956. There were an awful lot of good football players on our team: Earl Morrall of Michigan State, Hopalong Cassady of Ohio State, Ron Beagle from Navy, Lenny Moore of Penn State, Forrest Gregg of SMU, Bob Pellegrini from Maryland, Sam Huff from West Virginia—who, incidentally, played guard that game. Most of those guys went on to big careers in the NFL. But we were no match for the Cleveland Browns. [Lou] Groza kicked like four field goals and we lost [26–0]. But it was a real thrill coming from a smaller college and getting a chance to take part in it.

A couple of NFL teams had expressed some interest in me during my senior year and later out at the East-West Shrine Game, which I played in after the season. One of the more interested was the Giants. Vince Lombardi, who was on the coaching staff of the Giants then, scouted me my junior year. He watched me in spring practice before my senior year. I remember my coach, Hugh Devore, calling me in and saying there's this guy here to see you—Vince Lombardi. Hell, I didn't know who he was then. I sat down with him and he gave me all that rigamarole about someday you might be a good football player and crap like that. But I was pleased they were interested. Coincidentally, Hugh Devore had been the head coach of the Green Bay Packers in 1953 before coming to Dayton, and he would go on to coach the Philadelphia Eagles the same year I went into the NFL.

Well, the Giants did draft me. When I got there, I found out they had traded and got Andy Robustelli, who was not just a defensive end like I was but had already made All-Pro with the Rams a couple of times. And they had Walt Yowarsky, who had been with the Giants a couple of years. I was wondering how in hell I would ever make this team. But I did, and I had the starting job by the first regular-season game.

That rookie season, after I made the team and the preseason was over, Lombardi came up and said to me, "Jim, you did a real fine job. I'm glad I looked at you down at Dayton." Then he started to walk away but turned back. "You know, Jim," he said, "now that you're in the NFL you might need some life insurance." He was selling policies on the side in those days, and so I said, What the hell, and bought one from him. I think it was for $10,000.

I was actually coached by Tom Landry, who handled the defense. I think Tom idolized Paul Brown of Cleveland, had great respect for him as a coach who could win. But I'll tell you, when we went up against the Browns we were ready, and we really did a hell of a job defensing them. Their offense then was Jimmy Brown, and Landry knew how to get us to stop him. I think we were the only team that ever consistently stopped Brown. He was a great runner. But he was a lousy blocker. I always loved it when he tried to block me because that's when I could tee off on him.

Sam Huff was a rookie that year too. We [that is, the front four of Katcavage, Grier, Modzelewski, and Robustelli] used to tell him that we did all the work for him to set him up so he could make all those tackles and look good to the press and the fans. Without us, they wouldn't even know his name, we told him. We loved to kid him. But Sam was a hell of a ballplayer. He could really diagnose plays, and he was a big factor in why our defense was as good as it was in those days.

From the beginning, I used to commute to New York from Philadelphia. I'd take the train over to Penn Station and then the subway up to Yankee Stadium. I did that for eighteen years—thirteen as a player and five as a coach. Emlen Tunnell was from Philly too, and we used to ride over together until he retired, which was after the 1958 season. We were the best of friends. Emlen was truly a great ballplayer. He was a walk-on back in 1948. He had played at Iowa, but around that time there were very few blacks in the NFL. He asked for a tryout, made the team, and went on to the Hall of Fame. I played with him his last three years in New York. When Lombardi left in 1959, he took Emlen along with him to Green Bay. Tunnell was just an extraordinary athlete—a super defensive back, and no one could return punts and kickoffs like him. On top of that, he was just one hell of a nice guy who everybody on the team really liked to have around.

Our defensive line worked very well right from the start. We had different maneuvers we worked out. One thing was called "the twist" between me and Mo; others involved all four of us. The tricks—or schemes—were all geared to throw off the offensive line of the other team, surprise them. We just worked together very well as a unit.

You had to have different things going for you on the defensive line in those days. There were so many good offensive linemen when I came up in 1956, and they were all bigger than I was and a lot bigger than those guys I'd played against when I was with Dayton. There was Bob St. Clair of the 49ers—he was about 6'9" and 265 pounds, and he's in the Hall of Fame now. So is Forrest Gregg, who was with the Packers—he was about 6'4" and 240. And Lou Creekmur of the Lions and Mike McCormack of the Browns. The next year Jim Parker came on with the Colts, and there probably has never been a better offensive tackle in the NFL. He was over 260 and fast. Rosey Brown, who played for us, is the only offensive tackle who rates as high as Parker, in my opinion.

I was usually after quarterbacks on the other side, but

I played with a string of great ones on the Giants: Charlie Conerly, Y. A. Tittle, Earl Morrall, Fran Tarkenton. You see, we had everybody on the Giants in those years—great defensive players, great offensive players.

Conerly was a quiet, tough, down-home boy but a natural leader on the field. Tittle could throw every which way—from the pocket, on the run, sidearm. He always said he really liked playing in Yankee Stadium because when he got down to the infield he could kneel down and diagram the play for his receivers in the dirt. Those two, Conerly and Tittle, are the ones who contributed so much to our winning a lot of conference titles.

Besides the quarterbacks, we had Frank Gifford, Alex Webster, Kyle Rote, Del Shofner, Joe Walton, Joe Morrison, and Tucker Frederickson in our offense during the years I played. It was one fine group of runners and receivers.

The ones I played against? Well, the greatest quarterback had to be my old Lithuanian buddy Johnny Unitas at Baltimore. He was just a magnificent quarterback. But there was also Norm Van Brocklin when he was with the Rams and later with the Eagles. Norm had the quickest release of anybody I ever played against. We would blitz him, try all kinds of maneuvers, but we could almost never get to him before he got the ball away.

I got through the first four years pretty well. I don't think I missed more than a game or two. In 1960, however, I broke my collarbone. It was in the same game against the Eagles when Gifford got his concussion. Chuck Bednarik just turned him upside down and Frank hit his head on the ground; it was like Bednarik was wielding a sledgehammer. They gave Gifford the last rites in the locker room that day, it was that serious.

Earlier, on the third play of the game, I got my collarbone busted. I knew something was wrong, but I kept on playing and finished out the game. After the game, we all noticed my shoulder was a kind of huge lump. They agreed I better go to the hospital, so they put both Frank and me in the same ambulance and sent us over to St. Elizabeth's Hospital in New York. When we got there, they just whisked Frank away. Everyone was wondering about him, after the last rites and all that.

I knew I wasn't anywhere near that bad. They just sent me off for x-rays and then to wrap it up because it was pretty badly broken. About a year later, one of the doctors told me that when they x-rayed my shoulder, they found that the jagged part of my broken collarbone was right up next to my jugular vein. If I had hit somebody during the game in just the right way, they said, it would probably have jammed into it, and that would have been it for me. But, God bless, I got through three and a half quarters afterwards, and I'm still here. In those days they didn't have x-ray machines in the locker room. Today, they would know immediately what the situation was and would have sat my ass down.

The good thing was, both Frank and I made it back— me in 1961 and Frank in 1962.

With guys like Frank and Charlie Conerly and Y. A. Tittle and Alex Webster and, of course, our defense, we went to a lot of championship games during those years. We only won one, in 1956, my rookie year, then we lost the next five. The last was in 1963, and that was a big disappointment because we all thought we were a better team than the Bears that year, and we were confident going into the game. After that, we were never the team we had been.

Most of our team was traded away. Rosie Grier had been dealt to the Rams, Sam Huff went to the Redskins, and Mo [Dick Modzelewski] to the Cleveland Browns. The rest were about to retire shortly—guys like Frank Gifford, Andy Robustelli, Y. A. Tittle, Alex Webster, Jack Stroud. The only ones left by 1965 from the teams that won all those conference titles in the late 1950s and early 1960s were, besides me, Jimmy Patton and Dick Lynch from the defense, and Rosey Brown, Del Shofner, and Joe Morrison from the offense.

Two of the three years after our 1963 conference title

were disasters [1964, 2-10-2; and 1966, 1-12-1]. Then we got [Fran] Tarkenton in 1967 and, with his passing and great scrambling ability, it looked like things might turn around. He really teamed up well with [wide receiver] Homer Jones, who had been around since 1964. The two had a great year in 1967, when Jones gained more than 1,200 yards [1,209] on passes from Tarkenton and a couple from Earl Morrall [the 13 touchdown passes Jones caught and the average of 25 yards per catch were both NFL highs that year]. Tarkenton and Jones had another good one the following year, which was my last as a player.

A lot of the guys didn't like Tarkenton, but I did. He added a spark we hadn't had since Tittle retired. Still, both those years we couldn't get close to the Dallas Cowboys, who dominated our division. That was the period when they were really coming into their own under my old coach, Tom Landry. Dandy Don [Meredith] was at his best and, hell, they had guys like Bob Lilly and Bob Hayes and Lee Roy Jordan and Rayfield Wright. We were runner-up to the Cowboys each of the two years but we couldn't do any better than 7-7-0 either one.

After the 1968 season, I thought I had one more in me. I was thirty-four, but I still felt pretty good. We ended up with a new coach that year—1969. After we lost all our preseason games, Allie Sherman was canned and Alex Webster, who was an assistant then, was moved up to head coach. Right after the appointment, Alex came up to me and asked if I would be his defensive line coach. It was kind of like the handwriting on the wall: "We don't think you'll be playing much anymore. We want you to coach, but we don't want you to play."

The Giants had drafted Fred Dryer that year. He was a highly regarded defensive end out of San Diego State who

◀ A grand reunion. At Giants Stadium, the stars of the 1960s come back and take a plainclothes bow: from left, Ben Agajanian, Andy Robustelli, Rosie Grier, Herb Rich, Jim Katcavage, Kyle Rote, Charlie Conerly, Jack Stroud.

was their first-round draft pick. It was clear Alex wanted
him to start. Dryer was a big guy, tall, about 6'6", and he
was good. He went on to become much better known after
football when he starred in "Hunter" on television. So I got
to coach "Hunter" the three years he was with the Giants.
I don't think I had any effect on his acting abilities, though.

I coached in New York through the 1973 season; after
Webster resigned I moved to Philadelphia, where I became
a scout for the Eagles for the next thirteen years. After that,
Art McNally, the NFL's head coach of officials, hired me to
scout officials for the league, take a look at those guys
officiating in college games, and do some other things
related to officiating—something I'm still doing for the
league today.

◘

The Scrambler

The Giants' new quarterback in 1967, Fran Tarkenton, wrote a series of articles for *Sports Illustrated* when he first moved to New York. In the first piece (published July 17, 1967), he discussed his dislike for the moniker he had acquired while playing for the Vikings—"The Scrambler."

Sure, I scramble. When everything else breaks down, I don't hesitate to roam out of the pocket. . . . These wild sideline-to-sideline scrambles have become my trademark, and people have forgotten the simple truth of the matter, which is that I'm basically a pocket passer.

After we beat the Giants in 1964 there was a lot of stuff in the papers about my scrambling. It seems to me that the name stuck after that. I don't think there was a reporter covering the game who didn't tell about the time I popped out of the pocket, roamed forty yards behind the line of scrimmage, and finally completed a pass downfield for a ten-yard gain. And how many times do you think I scrambled in that ball game?

Once.

After the tag "The Scrambler" had become mine, all mine, the public misconceptions about me seemed to multiply. I'd play a game away from home and I'd scramble maybe two or three times, which is my average, and after the game all the reporters would come in and say, "Why didn't you play your usual style?" and "How come you threw so much from the pocket?" And I would try to say, "I threw from the pocket because that's my style."

"No, it isn't," they would say. "You're a scrambler."

"Okay," I would say, "I'm a scrambler." Anything to get to the shower.

Oh, c'mon, Fran, lighten up. You should have heard what the fans were calling some of the other quarterbacks just before you came and just after you left the Giants.

◘

Wellington Mara—
On Growing Up with
the Giants

Wellington Mara had a unique childhood—he grew up with the New York Giants football team. He was nine years old in 1925 when his father, Tim Mara, a New York bookmaker (a legal occupation in those days) and close friend of Governor Al Smith and Mayor Jimmy Walker, bought the franchise. He watched the team grow through the wide eyes of a youngster, then through the keen eyes of an expert on player personnel, and finally through the encompassing eyes of a club president.

Well, as his friends call him, was there on the bench with his father and older brother Jack at the Giants' very first home game at the Polo Grounds against the Frankford Yellow Jackets on October 18, 1925. He watched as a gimpy, thirty-seven-year-old Jim Thorpe tried to gain a few yards for the new franchise, and he saw a very talented Hinky Haines direct the team from his tailback position. He discovered other early greats such as Guy Chamberlin and Century Milstead on the field that day too. But he also saw the Giants blow their New York debut, losing by a score of 14–0.

From that moment on, however, professional football would be an integral part of his life. By the time he was sixteen, Well was his father's adviser on college football talent and would regularly present him with carefully researched lists of the college players who could aid the Giants' cause.

Among his first real coups was the snagging of running back Tuffy Leemans. It was autumn 1935, and Well, then a nineteen-year-old student at Fordham University, went to his father and told him that he needed to go to Washington, D.C., on business for the Giants. He explained that there was a fine running back there whom the Giants truly needed, a senior at George Washington University. His father agreed, so Well wired Tuffy Leemans to set up a meeting and then went to Washington.

When the young Mara approached Leemans in front of the gymnasium at George Washington, Leemans allegedly mistook him for some youngster wanting an autograph. After establishing his identity, Well then convinced Leemans of the efficacy of joining the New York Giants. Leemans would remain for eight seasons and become one of the Giants' all-time finest backs and eventually a Pro Football Hall of Fame enshrinee.

Wellington Mara pulled many great Giants names into the fold from the college talent pool. Two others he was responsible for were Charlie Conerly, whom he had to lure away from a lucrative contract offer by Branch Rickey, of the All-America Football Conference's Brooklyn franchise, and Emlen Tunnell, the Giants' first black player and a future Hall of Famer.

In this interview, Well offers a sharp insight into the world of professional football, his world since he was in the fourth grade, from a number of perspectives: fan, scout, player personnel director, unofficial team photographer, secretary of the club, and chief operating officer when he took over the duties of president in 1965 after the death of his brother, Jack.

My earliest recollection of the Giants was on a Sunday morning in the autumn of 1925; I was about nine years old. We were coming out of mass, and I remember my father saying to one of his friends, "I'm gonna try to put pro football over in New York today." Then I recall going to the game. I don't think my father had ever seen a football game before. I had seen one or two—

my brother, Jack, had taken me to a couple of Fordham games.

During the game—and I've told the story many times—we were sitting on the Giants' side of the field, and it was a little chilly. My mother complained to my father that we were sitting in the shade. Why couldn't we go over and sit in the sun where we'd be nice and warm? So, the next game, and from then on, the Giants' sideline in the Polo Grounds was in the sun.

Another thing I remember from those first days was that I wanted to sit on the bench, and I got to. I remember our coach, Bob Folwell, a former Navy coach, turning to one of the players on the bench—his name was Paul Jappe—and saying, "Jappe, get in there and give 'em hell!" I thought, boy, this is really a rough game.

My father came to own the Giants in a kind of round-about way. He was a bookmaker in New York, and he was very friendly with Billy Gibson, who was the manager of Gene Tunney, the boxer. My father had actually been instrumental in Tunney's early career. He also had been very friendly from boyhood with Al Smith, and through him with the political organization in New York City and New York state, and boxing at that time was very politically oriented. My father helped Tunney to get some fights that he otherwise might not have been able to get.

Anyway, Billy Gibson came into my father's office one day and brought with him a gentleman named Harry A. March, who was a retired army doctor. Dr. March had been interested in pro football and its origins out in Ohio—the Canton area. I don't think there was a pro football team in New York at that time, although I've heard that Jimmy Jemail, a columnist back then for the *New York Daily News*—he wrote "The Inquiring Reporter"—claimed that he had a team in New York in 1924 and that my father took over that franchise. [Actually, there had never been an NFL franchise in New York until Mara bought one in 1925.]

From what I heard later there was talk about buying an

NFL franchise. I heard that my father simply said, "How much will it cost?" and that was it. There are two versions of the answer to that: one was that it was $500, the other that it was $2,500. I know my father did say something to the effect that an empty store in New York City was worth that, whichever figure it was, and that's how he got into pro football.

In the beginning the football team, to put it mildly, was not a financial success. The first year we were bailed out, however, because Red Grange came to the Polo Grounds. I remember that very well. My father had gone out to the Midwest to try to sign Grange. Back then we didn't have a formal rule that said a player had to be drafted. And Red Grange, playing for Illinois, was the eighth wonder of the world in those days. My father went out to see him—around the time Red was playing his last collegiate game—with the intention of signing him to play for the Giants.

Jack, who was eight years older than I, was very excited, and so was I. We got a telegram from my father saying: "Partially successful. Will arrive on train and explain." We didn't really know what that meant because the day before we'd read in the paper that Red had signed with the Chicago Bears. As far as we were concerned, he was totally *un*successful. But what he meant was that he had booked an exhibition game in the Polo Grounds with the Bears and Red Grange.

The game sold out—more than seventy thousand paid to see that game—and my father made up what he had lost that year. Actually, it was my father and just two assistants who sold those seventy-odd-thousand tickets out of one small office in the Knickerbocker Building in New York.

One thing my father worried about in regard to that game was the weather. It had been very bad all week, and he was concerned about it. But about two in the morning on that Sunday a friend of his called and said, "Tim, look out the window. The stars are out."

Still, pro football in New York was very unsuccessful. My father's friends all told him that he was foolish to stay with it. I remember Governor Al Smith in our house one day after the team had just lost rather badly to Green Bay. Al Smith said to my father, "Your team will never amount to anything. Why don't you give it up?"

My father looked at Jack and me and said, "The boys would run me right out of the house if I did." I really think my father was talking more in terms of Jack than me, however, because Jack was of an age where he mingled with the players—as pals, more or less—and I was still in the hero-worshipping stage.

I didn't travel with the team at the start. I was too young. Jack did, though. I didn't really start traveling with the ball club until about the mid-1930s. Once in a while I was permitted to take a trip in the early '30s when I was still in school, if it wouldn't interfere with my Friday afternoon classes.

Money was very tight in the '30s. But at the same time, my father said that among the areas of the entertainment business, sports somewhat prospered during the Depression because they really offered the best entertainment for the money. A football game or a baseball game was great entertainment, and a man could get it for his whole family. Still, the Giants were just barely breaking even in the mid-1930s.

Of course, it was a very different game they played then. I remember a couple of things from it that give an idea of how it was different. I recall the days when you didn't have hash marks at all, and a little later when you did but to get the ball placed on one of them you actually had to go out of bounds. If you were tackled one yard from the sideline, that was where the ball was put in play. I remember teams having special plays for that. Along those lines, I remember Tony Plansky, a tailback from Georgetown, who had been a great decathlon athlete, drop-kicking a field goal for us from around the 40-yard line that

Longtime head coach Steve Owen (1931–53) accepts a silver service on his retirement. The Mara family looks on; from left, Wellington, Tim, and Jack.

won a game. The thing was, however, that he was way over to the left side of the field. He was ambidextrous and kicked it with his left foot, where ordinarily he did his kicking right-footed.

It was also a one-platoon game then. As Steve Owen used to say, men were men in those days. He was our great coach for so many years, and he saw a lot of truly sturdy, talented, sixty-minute men who played for and against us. Stamina played a great part of it in those days, and the players had to pace themselves. They couldn't go all out on every play—you just couldn't do that for sixty minutes of football-playing time. The player who played opposite you, however, was under the same handicap, but it still was grueling.

The individual skills were not as refined as they are today either. Some were, like those of Don Hutson. But he still had to play defense, even though his specialty was being a great pass receiver, probably as great as any receiver we have in the game today who only has to concentrate on catching footballs. Hutson wasn't able to hang up the statistics the receivers have today because he had to make tackles on defense as well. [Hutson's NFL record of 99 touchdown catches, however, lasted forty-four years until Steve Largent caught his 100th in 1989, just before retiring from the Seattle Seahawks.] Also, Arnie Herber, with the same Green Bay team, was a great passer, but he wasn't used all the time because he was a poor defensive player. And once a player was taken out of a game he couldn't go back in during the same period of play, which meant there were a lot of times Hutson was on the field and Herber wasn't.

Steve Owen was a true innovator. In 1937, he developed his version of the two-platoon system. We had a young team and a very deep bench at the time, and Steve used to change ten of the eleven men at the end of the first period and at the end of the third period. The only one who stayed on the field for the entire game was Mel Hein— he was too good both on offense and defense to take out. One time we were playing the Bears, in 1939, and the first period ended with them having third down and two yards to go on our 2-yard line. Steve changed ten of the eleven players, and they held.

Unlike today, the stars of those days were relatively anonymous. Mel Hein, as great a player as he was, a Hall of Famer, could walk down Broadway and I don't think anyone would have recognized him. I think players were a lot more closely knit at that time, however. The salaries weren't such that they could have their own homes or apartments. If you had a twenty-five man squad, probably twenty of them lived in the same hotel. Maybe two or three roomed together. We would travel by train. We'd go to Pittsburgh, for example, at noon on Friday and not get back until maybe noon on Monday. Being on the train so long is another example of how the players were thrown together a lot more back then.

The great majority of our players in those days came into New York during the season and then went back to where they were from after it was over. We used to try to get off-season jobs for as many as we could, but we weren't always successful. Most simply went back home. We had a great many boys from the farmlands, and they all went back when the season closed up. Steve Owen, in fact, came from Kansas. And, of course, we didn't have the far-flung scouting empires that we have today. A lot of Steve's talent-scouting was done through the eyes of people he had played with. They went to football games or coached football teams in Kansas and Oklahoma and Texas, and so we obtained a lot of players from those areas.

Steve Owen was an integral part of the Giants organization, and he was like a second father to me. He came in as a player, and he was one player who did stay in New York. He married a New York girl, and he worked in a coal company that my father owned and then later at the race track during the off-season. I admired him, was greatly attached to him, and respected him. He kind of brought me up in the football business. Starting in the early 1930s, I went to training camp and always felt like he was taking care of me.

Another Giant I remember well was Benny Friedman. He was really our first big star. Friedman had been with Cleveland and Detroit, but both those teams had folded. [They were the Cleveland Bulldogs and Detroit Wolverines, not to be confused with the Cleveland Browns and Detroit Lions of later vintage.] In fact, my father had bought out the remnants of the Detroit team and brought Benny Friedman in here with Roy Andrews, who was their head coach, Steve Owen's brother Bill, and several other players.

Benny Friedman made a great contribution to pro football in New York, off the field as well as on it. Several times a week he would go around to high school assemblies in the mornings and give tickets away to promote the game. He really did make an enormous contribution. He was also, of course, a fine player and a durable one. I don't think he ever missed a game because of an injury. Benny Friedman truly deserves to be in the Hall of Fame. The problem there, I think, is that I don't think enough people on the selection committee remember the guys who were the real pioneers of the game. Friedman was one of a kind and never got the proper recognition.

A Giant deservedly in the Hall of Fame is Mel Hein. I remember very well the first day he came into our camp. But the thing I remember most vividly is when he gave me a black eye. It was in the early '30s, and I was in my early teens. It was one of the first times I had been entrusted to stay overnight at training camp, which was a big thrill for me. I used to get out on the field with players. Mel Hein was centering to our punter, who was booting the ball downfield. There were players in two lines on each side of Hein, running down under the punts. Every once in a while Mel would run one down too. I was retrieving the balls as they were thrown back and putting them down in front of Mel. Well, he decided to run down under one just as I was bending over and putting the ball down. He ran right over me. It took my eye about thirty seconds to close tight.

Ray Flaherty was another of our favorites on the team. He was a tremendous competitor. We had two of the toughest players ever at our two ends in those days—Flaherty and Red Badgro—and at the same time they were two of the nicest guys you'd ever meet. Red Badgro was inducted into the Hall of Fame [1981], and Flaherty has been in for some time [since 1976].

Ray was also an assistant coach for us and later became a fine head coach for the Washington Redskins. I
recall one particular incident concerning Flaherty. He hurt
his hand in one game—really didn't hurt it badly, but the
doctor put a big bandage on it. Ray held it like it was
broken and in a sling, and he was pretending to be in great
pain. Everyone was very solicitous toward him. I don't
remember who the player was, but it was one of Ray's
friends and he was helping Ray over to the bench on the
sideline. "Are you all right, Ray?" he asked.

"Yeah, I'm all right," Flaherty said, and then punched
his friend in the stomach with his supposedly broken hand.

There was also Harry Newman. Harry was sort of a
Benny Friedman clone. We didn't have that term in our
vocabulary in those days, but Newman, who came from
Michigan, was short, stocky, and a very smart quarterback—just like Friedman. He had a couple of very successful years with us. I'll always remember one thing that Harry
did in those days. The rule is still in the book. When a
member of the punting team touches a punt but doesn't
actually down it—just touches it—the receiving team can
pick it up and advance it any time before the official blows
the whistle. And even if you fumble the ball and lose it, you
would still get the ball where the other guy touched it.
Harry Newman picked one up like that in Boston and ran it
back for a touchdown. I still remember the Boston player
coming off the field and saying, "I'll never do that again.
Never again!"

One of the greatest of them all was Ken Strong. He was
a fabulous all-around player, and he truly deserved to go
into the Hall of Fame. Ken Strong had been a great back at
New York University in the years when my brother Jack was
going to Fordham. That made him a hated rival, of course,
but we still thought he was the greatest. We wanted him for
the Giants very badly. My father had this employee who
was instructed to make every effort to sign Ken Strong. But
he failed, and we were very upset when Ken signed with

the Staten Island Stapletons, who were a key rival of ours. He then came over and beat us a couple of times.

Strong often played without a helmet. He was a great blocker, great punter, great runner, and could pass with the best of them until he broke his hand. When the Staten Island team disbanded, Strong came to us. My father said, "Well, Ken, you are three years too late. I never understood why you went over there for less money than we offered you."

Ken said, "What do you mean?"

"We offered you $10,000 a year."

"No, you didn't. You offered me $5,000."

Apparently, our employee was going to pocket the five-thousand-dollar difference or else he thought he was going to save the club some money and make some points for himself. I don't know which—all I know is that that's how we lost Ken Strong.

Shipwreck Kelly played for us in 1932. He was a fine player but an undisciplined one—always did the unexpected. I remember in one game he was back to receive a punt for us, caught it, and then punted the ball right back.

Then, of course, there was the famous "Sneakers Game" two years later [1934] against the Bears. It had been very, very cold that week in New York. There was a good amount of snow, and the field was frozen. Saturday night, Ray Flaherty, who was one of our assistant coaches and played end for us, called Steve Owen on the telephone and said, "One time when I played at Gonzaga in college we had a frozen field, and we borrowed sneakers from our basketball team and went out and beat a team that was much better than us."

It was an idea, Owen agreed, but it was Saturday night and there wasn't much that could be done about getting the shoes. And on Sunday all the sporting goods stores would still be closed in New York.

At the Polo Grounds on Sunday morning the field was completely frozen. We had a little fellow on the payroll

Wellington Mara. His father, Tim Mara, founded the team in 1925, and it has been an integral part of Wellington's life ever since. Acknowledged for his insight and expertise in recruiting and drafting football talent, he has run the team since the death of his brother Jack in 1965.

named Abe Cohen, a sort of jack of all trades. Abe was a tailor by profession, and he also worked for Chick Meehan, who was a famous coach at Manhattan College and was quite a showman in his own way. Meehan was the first coach to put what we call satin pants on a football team. He had done that first at NYU in the days of Ken Strong. Abe was his tailor and made the pants for the players. Steve Owen asked Abe to go up to Manhattan College, to which he had access—he had a key to their equipment room and the gym—and borrow the sneakers from the lockers of the basketball players and bring them over to the Polo Grounds for our players.

Abe got in a taxi and went to Manhattan. I think he had to break into the lockers. At any rate, he got back sometime in the second half with nine or ten pairs of sneakers.

Some of the players didn't want to put them on; but those who did had so much success that eventually most of our players put them on. Ken Strong, who kicked off for us, placekicked with the sneakers on and he lost a toenail on his big toe. One of the Bears players went over to the sideline and told George Halas, their coach, that we were wearing sneakers. "Step on their toes!" Halas shouted to his players.

With the sneakers on, we scored four touchdowns in the fourth quarter and won the game [30–13].

The following week after the championship game, the Bears were playing an exhibition game in Philadelphia—in those days you had barnstorming trips after the season was over—and Steve Owen and I went down to see the game. We went into the Bears' dressing room, I guess to crow a little bit, and the first thing we saw was about twenty-four pairs of sneakers on top of the lockers. Halas said to us, "I'll never get caught like that again."

The war came along and took the great majority of the athletes out of the NFL. It threatened to close pro football down altogether. George Halas was going back into the navy, and since he was going to be gone from football he kind of led a drive to cancel the season, call the whole thing off. George Marshall [Redskins owner], Bert Bell [Steelers owner], and my father crusaded to keep it going at any cost, even if we had to play 4-Fs and high school players, which we in fact did. I think that it very well may be that playing under those circumstances helped to save the NFL, because when the war was over Arch Ward started the All-America Football Conference. It started at a terrible disadvantage because we were already established. I think if we had suspended operations for three or four years and then tried to start it up again, the AAFC would have started on more equal terms with us, and the league might be a very different one from what it is today.

The game changed considerably after the war. The offenses became more sophisticated, there was a lot more passing, and the players were getting bigger and faster all the time.

We had some of our most noteworthy and memorable teams in the 1950s and early '60s. Jim Lee Howell, our head coach for much of that time, had the best pair of assistants ever under one roof: Vince Lombardi handling the offense and Tom Landry the defense. With Charlie Conerly and later Y. A. Tittle quarterbacking, backs like Frank Gifford and Alex Webster, and pass catchers of the caliber of Kyle Rote and Del Shofner, we provided a lot of exciting offense. And the defense! Well, it was simply one of the best ever: Andy Robustelli, Sam Huff, Rosie Grier, Em Tunnell, Dick Modzelewski, Jim Katcavage, Dick Lynch, Jimmy Patton, and others.

Certainly the game was less rewarding financially in those early days. Most of the players and coaches had to get other jobs to survive. Vince Lombardi, when he was with us in the late 1950s, I remember, had an off-season job with a bank. The game was still great fun, though, and the men who played it were very memorable.

Nothing, however, has been more gratifying to watch than the Giants of 1986 march through the season and the playoffs to the Super Bowl and triumph there in the Rose Bowl [Giants 39, Denver Broncos 20], and the Giants of 1990 to repeat down in Tampa [Giants 20, Buffalo Bills 19], giving us two world championships in five recent years.

◧

Super Bowl XXI
New York Giants 39, Denver Broncos 20

Rose Bowl, Pasadena, California, January 25, 1987
Attendance: 101,063

SCORING

Giants	7	2	17	13	39
Broncos	10	0	0	10	20

Denver—Rich Karlis, 48-yard field goal
New York—Zeke Mowatt, 6-yard TD pass from Phil Simms (PAT, Raul Allegre)
Denver—John Elway, 4-yard TD run (PAT, Rich Karlis)
New York—George Martin tackled John Elway in the end zone for a safety
New York—Mark Bavaro, 13-yard TD pass from Phil Simms (PAT, Raul Allegre)
New York—Raul Allegre, 21-yard field goal
New York—Joe Morris, 1-yard TD run (PAT, Raul Allegre)
New York—Phil McConkey, 6-yard TD pass from Phil Simms (PAT, Raul Allegre)
Denver—Rich Karlis, 28-yard field goal
New York—Ottis Anderson, 2-yard TD run (PAT by Raul Allegre failed)
Denver—Vance Johnson, 47-yard TD pass from John Elway (PAT, Rich Karlis)

INDIVIDUAL STATISTICS

Giants

Rushing:
Joe Morris—20 for 67 yards
Phil Simms—3 for 25 yards
Lee Rouson—3 for 22 yards
Tony Galbreath—4 for 17 yards
Maurice Carthon—3 for 4 yards
Ottis Anderson—2 for 1 yard
Jeff Rutledge—3 for 0 yards

Passing:
Phil Simms—22 of 25 for 268 yards

Receiving:
Mark Bavaro—4 for 51 yards
Joe Morris—4 for 20 yards
Maurice Carthon—4 for 13 yards
Stacy Robinson—3 for 62 yards
Lionel Manuel—3 for 43 yards
Phil McConkey—2 for 50 yards
Lee Rouson—1 for 23 yards
Zeke Mowatt—1 for 6 yards

Broncos

Rushing:
John Elway—6 for 27 yards
Gerald Willhite—4 for 19 yards
Steve Sewell—3 for 4 yards
Gene Lang—2 for 2 yards
Sammy Winder—4 for 0 yards

Passing:
John Elway—22 of 37 for 304 yards
Gary Kubiak—4 of 4 for 48 yards

Receiving:
Vance Johnson—5 for 121 yards
Gerald Willhite—5 for 39 yards
Sammy Winder—4 for 34 yards
Mark Jackson—3 for 51 yards
Steve Watson—2 for 54 yards
Clint Sampson—2 for 20 yards
Orson Mobley—2 for 17 yards
Steve Sewell—2 for 12 yards
Gene Lang—1 for 4 yards

▣

◫

Super Bowl XXV
Buffalo Bills 19, New York Giants 20

Tampa Stadium, Tampa, Florida, January 27, 1991
Attendance: 73,813

SCORING

Bills	3	9	0	7	19
Giants	3	7	7	3	20

New York—Matt Bahr, 28-yard field goal
Buffalo—Scott Norwood, 23-yard field goal
Buffalo—Don Smith, 1-yard TD run (PAT, Scott Norwood)
Buffalo—NY's quarterback Jeff Hostetler tackled by Bruce
  Smith in end zone for a safety
New York—Stephen Baker, 14-yard TD pass from Jeff Hostetler
  (PAT, Matt Bahr)
New York—Ottis Anderson, 1-yard TD run (PAT, Matt Bahr)
Buffalo—Thurman Thomas, 31-yard TD run (PAT, Scott
  Norwood)
New York—Matt Bahr, 21-yard field goal

INDIVIDUAL STATISTICS

Bills

Rushing:
Thurman Thomas—15 for 135 yards
Jim Kelly—6 for 23 yards
Kenneth Davis—2 for 4 yards
Jamie Mueller—1 for 3 yards
Don Smith—1 for 1 yard

Passing:
Jim Kelly—18 of 30 for 212 yards

Receiving:
Andre Reed—8 for 62 yards
Thurman Thomas—5 for 55 yards
Kenneth Davis—2 for 23 yards
Keith McKeller—2 for 11 yards
James Lofton—1 for 61 yards

Giants

Rushing:
Ottis Anderson—21 for 102 yards
Dave Meggett—9 for 48 yards
Maurice Carthon—3 for 12 yards
Jeff Hostetler—6 for 10 yards

Passing:
Jeff Hostetler—20 of 32 for 222 yards

Receiving:
Mark Ingram—5 for 74 yards
Mark Bavaro—5 for 50 yards
Howard Cross—4 for 39 yards
Stephen Baker—2 for 31 yards
Dave Meggett—2 for 18 yards
Ottis Anderson—1 for 7 yards
Maurice Carthon—1 for 3 yards

NFL Champion Giants

Year	Record	Championship Game	Coach
1927	11-1-1	(no championship game)	Earl Potteiger
1934	8-5-0	Giants 30, Chicago Bears 13	Steve Owen
1938	8-2-1	Giants 23, Green Bay Packers 17	Steve Owen
1956	8-3-1	Giants 47, Chicago Bears 7	Jim Lee Howell
1986	14-2-0	Giants 39, Denver Broncos 20	Bill Parcells
1990	13-3-0	Giants 20, Buffalo Bills 19	Bill Parcells

Runner-Up Giants

Year	Record	Championship Game	Coach
1929	13-1-1	(Green Bay Packers, 12-0-1, won title—no championship game)	LeRoy Andrews
1930	13-4-0	(Green Bay Packers, 10-3-1, won title—no championship game)	LeRoy Andrews
1933	11-3-0	Chicago Bears 23, Giants 21	Steve Owen
1935	9-3-0	Detroit Lions 26, Giants 7	Steve Owen
1939	9-1-0	Green Bay Packers 27, Giants 0	Steve Owen
1941	8-3-0	Chicago Bears 37, Giants 9	Steve Owen
1944	8-1-1	Green Bay Packers 14, Giants 7	Steve Owen
1946	7-3-1	Chicago Bears 24, Giants 14	Steve Owen
1958	9-3-0	Baltimore Colts 23, Giants 17	Jim Lee Howell
1959	10-2-0	Baltimore Colts 31, Giants 16	Jim Lee Howell
1961	10-3-1	Green Bay Packers 37, Giants 0	Allie Sherman
1962	12-2-0	Green Bay Packers 16, Giants 7	Allie Sherman
1963	11-3-0	Chicago Bears 14, Giants 10	Allie Sherman

Acknowledgments

The author wishes to extend grateful appreciation to the New York Giants football organization, especially Wellington Mara, president and co–chief executive officer. Without the cooperation and support of Well Mara and the various departments under his administration, this book would not have been possible.

Thanks are also extended to Joe Horrigan, curator and archivist at the Pro Football Hall of Fame in Canton, Ohio; and to David S. Neft and Richard M. Cohen, authors and compilers of the two-volume *Sports Encyclopedia, Pro Football* (New York: St. Martin's Press, 1988), which was an invaluable research source for determining the accuracy of both team and individual statistics.

And special thanks are offered to all the former Giants greats who generously gave their time and their wonderful story-telling talents in the interviews that resulted in the narratives appearing on the preceding pages.